MW00989871

Esther and Ruth

REFORMED EXPOSITORY COMMENTARY

A Series

Series Editors

Richard D. Phillips
Philip Graham Ryken

Testament Editors

Iain M. Duguid, Old Testament
Daniel M. Doriani, New Testament

Esther and Ruth

Iain M. Duguid

P&R
PUBLISHING
P.O. BOX 817 • PHILLIPSBURG • NEW JERSEY 08865-0817

Page design and typesetting by Lakeside Design Plus

Printed in the United States of America

Library of Congress Cataloging-in-Publication Data

Duguid, Iain M.
     Esther and Ruth / Iain M. Duguid.
        p. cm. — (Reformed expository commentary)
     Includes bibliographical references and indexes.
     ISBN-13: 978-0-87552-783-3 (cloth)
     ISBN-10: 0-87552-783-3 (cloth)
     1. Bible. O.T. Esther—Commentaries. 2. Bible. O.T. Ruth—Commentaries. I. Title. II. Series.

BS1375.53.D84 2005
222'.35077—dc22

2005047192

CONTENTS

Series Introduction

In every generation there is a fresh need for the faithful exposition of God's Word in the church. At the same time, the church must constantly do the work of theology: reflecting on the teaching of Scripture, confessing its doctrines of the Christian faith, and applying them to contemporary culture. We believe that these two tasks—the expositional and the theological—are interdependent. Our doctrine must derive from the biblical text, and our understanding of any particular passage of Scripture must arise from the doctrine taught in Scripture as a whole.

We further believe that these interdependent tasks of biblical exposition and theological reflection are best undertaken in the church, and most specifically in the pulpits of the church. This is all the more true since the study of Scripture properly results in doxology and praxis—that is, in praise to God and practical application in the lives of believers. In pursuit of these ends, we are pleased to present the Reformed Expository Commentary as a fresh exposition of Scripture for our generation in the church. We hope and pray that pastors, teachers, Bible study leaders, and many others will find this series to be a faithful, inspiring, and useful resource for the study of God's infallible, inerrant Word.

The Reformed Expository Commentary has four fundamental commitments. First, these commentaries aim to be *biblical*, presenting a comprehensive exposition characterized by careful attention to the details of the text. They are not exegetical commentaries—commenting word by word or even verse by verse—but integrated expositions of whole passages of Scripture. Each commentary will thus present a sequential, systematic treatment of an entire book of the Bible, passage by passage. Second, these commentaries are unashamedly *doctrinal*. We are committed to the Westminster Confession of Faith and Catechisms as containing the system of doctrine taught in the Scriptures of the Old and New Testaments. Each volume will teach, promote, and defend the doctrines of the Reformed faith as they are found in the Bible. Third, these commentaries are *redemptive-historical* in their orientation. We believe in the unity of the Bible and its central message of salvation in Christ. We are thus committed to a Christ-centered view of the Old Testament, in which its characters, events, regulations, and institutions are properly understood as pointing us to Christ and his gospel, as well as giving us examples to follow in living by faith. Fourth, these commentaries are *practical*, applying the text of Scripture to contemporary challenges of life—both public and private—with appropriate illustrations.

The contributors to the Reformed Expository Commentary are all pastor-scholars. As pastor, each author will first present his expositions in the pulpit ministry of his church. This means that these commentaries are rooted in the teaching of Scripture to real people in the church. While aiming to be scholarly, these expositions are not academic. Our intent is to be faithful, clear, and helpful to Christians who possess various levels of biblical and theological training—as should be true in any effective pulpit ministry. Inevitably this means that some issues of academic interest will not be covered. Nevertheless, we aim to achieve a responsible level of scholarship, seeking to promote and model this for pastors and other teachers in the church. Significant exegetical and theological difficulties, along with such historical and cultural background as is relevant to the text, will be treated with care.

We strive for a high standard of enduring excellence. This begins with the selection of the authors, all of whom have proven to be outstanding communicators of God's Word. But this pursuit of excellence is also reflected in a disciplined editorial process. Each volume is edited by both a series editor and a testament editor. The testament editors, Iain Duguid for the Old Testament and Daniel Doriani for the New Testament, are accomplished pastors and respected scholars who have taught at the seminary level. Their job is to ensure that each volume is sufficiently conversant with up-to-date scholarship and is faithful and accurate in its exposition of the text. As series editors, we oversee each volume to ensure its overall quality—including excellence of writing, soundness of teaching, and usefulness in application.

Working together as an editorial team, along with the publisher, we are devoted to ensuring that these are the best commentaries our gifted authors can provide, so that the church will be served with trustworthy and exemplary expositions of God's Word.

It is our goal and prayer that the Reformed Expository Commentary will serve the church by renewing confidence in the clarity and power of Scripture and by upholding the great doctrinal heritage of the Reformed faith. We hope that pastors who read these commentaries will be encouraged in their own expository preaching ministry, which we believe to be the best and most biblical pattern for teaching God's Word in the church. We hope that lay teachers will find these commentaries among the most useful resources they rely upon for understanding and presenting the text of the Bible. And we hope that the devotional quality of these studies of Scripture will instruct and inspire each Christian who reads them in joyful, obedient discipleship to Jesus Christ.

May the Lord bless all who read the Reformed Expository Commentary. We commit these volumes to the Lord Jesus Christ, praying that the Holy Spirit will use them for the instruction and edification of the church, with thanksgiving to God the Father for his unceasing faithfulness in building his church through the ministry of his Word.

Richard D. Phillips
Philip Graham Ryken
Series Editors

PREFACE

The Books of Esther and Ruth are not really stories about their respective "heroines." Rather, they are part of the Bible's larger story about God and his dealings with his people, and with the world. This is true even though the Book of Esther does not so much as mention the name of God. As in everyday life, God's intervention is everywhere visible in the Book of Esther, even though his presence is concealed. The essential conflict between the two kingdoms—the empire of Ahasuerus and the kingdom of God—plays itself out in the lives of flawed and unexpected individuals, as God delivers his people once again from the threat of extinction. Meanwhile, in the Book of Ruth, the Great Redeemer shows his love and compassion to the embittered Naomi as well as to her foreign daughter-in-law, Ruth. His grace brings home the disobedient prodigal daughter with empty hands, so that he can astonish her with unexpected fullness. In both stories, the grace of God to the undeserving and the outcasts is prominently on display. Both stories thus constantly point us forward to Christ as the one in whom that grace will fully and finally come to aliens and strangers, redeeming rebellious sinners and making them into God's new people.

Even though writing is a solitary task, no book is the product of a single individual. This is especially the case for a book that began as two series of sermons preached at Grace Presbyterian Church in Fallbrook, California. My thanks are due to the congregation there for the great encouragement and support we have experienced over the years we have served that community of God's people. It is a wonderful blessing for a preacher to serve a people with a hunger for God's Word and a never-failing enthusiasm to hear the gospel of grace over again. I also want to thank Rick Schaeffer and Ken Han, who served in ministry alongside me while these sermons were preached and revised. Your diligence and hard work freed me to be able to complete this work.

My thanks are also due to Westminster Seminary California, where I taught this material in a number of classes. Many students asked perceptive questions that helped me to refine my thinking and answer the question, "Now, how do you preach this?" A teacher always learns more from his students than they do from him.

I would like to thank my fellow editors for this series, Dan Doriani, Rick Phillips, and Phil Ryken, who were not slow to challenge my sloppy thinking or poor forms of expression. Their efforts have made this book much better; the remaining flaws, however, are all my own work. I would also like to express my gratitude to Al Fisher and the staff of P&R for encouraging this commentary series in the first place, and for producing it in such an excellent manner.

Finally, I would like to thank my family. My wife, Barbara, is both my best and most perceptive critic and, at the same time, the most enthusiastic encourager and supporter. You are truly a "helper corresponding to me" (Gen. 2:18). My children, Jamie, Sam, Hannah, Rob, and Rosie, sat regularly in the front row of the church, listening to me preach. They were always the first to say afterward, "Good job, Dad." Thank you for encouraging me in my labors; I pray that in the years to come you will continue to have the same enthusiasm for God's Word as you do now, and that as you go out in life, you may always find churches where grace is the dominant note in the chord.

Esther

THE HIDDEN KING DELIVERS

1

STANDING FIRM AGAINST THE EMPIRE

Esther 1:1—22

*If it please the king, let a royal order go out from him,
and let it be written among the laws of the Persians and
the Medes so that it may not be repealed, that Vashti is never
again to come before King Ahasuerus. And let the king give
her royal position to another who is better than she.*
(Esth. 1:19)

*I*magine living life teetering on an unstable perch in a hostile world, while trying to perform a difficult task. This is the metaphor that dominates the classic film, *The Fiddler on the Roof*. The main character, the Russian Jew Tevye, explains his life in these terms:

A fiddler on the roof—sounds crazy, no? But here in our little village of Ana - tevke you might say every one of us is a fiddler on the roof, trying to scratch out a pleasant, simple tune without breaking his neck. It isn't easy. You may ask why we stay up there, if it's so dangerous? Well, we stay because Anatevke is our home. And how do we keep our balance? That I can tell you in one word: Tradition!

Fiddling on the Roof

The image of the fiddler on the roof applies to the Jews in Persia in Esther's time just as much as it does to early-twentieth-century Russian Jews. They were not like those who lived around them, and they knew that their over-lords could not be trusted. The Persians held all the power in their hands and the Jews had none. Even though these Jews had been born in Persia, they were exiles far from their homeland, surrounded by strangers. Their property could be seized or their life ended in a moment on the whim of some petty bureaucrat. On the other hand, if fortune smiled on them, they might yet survive to a good old age and make a reasonable living. As Tevye put it, "It isn't easy . . . but it is home." In such a difficult situation, why should the Jews take the risk of living a distinctive lifestyle? Why not just give in to the empire's demands and allow themselves to be assimilated and become invisible? To reverse the old Japanese proverb, "The nail that doesn't stick out is much less likely to get hammered."

But is that the right way of putting it: "If fortune smiled on them . . . ?" Wasn't there a God in heaven, a God who had committed himself to the Jewish people in an ancient covenant? Didn't he take care of their forefathers when they were strangers and aliens in a land not their own? Didn't he bring them out of Egypt with a strong hand and a mighty arm? Wouldn't he look after his own people even in the midst of this present darkness? Or would he? After all, it had been a long while since that wonderful story of the crossing of the Red Sea, and why would he deign to look down on ordinary folk eking out very ordinary lives in distant Persia? They couldn't see this God, they hadn't heard from him lately, and in any case, they were living miles from the land he called his own. Did this invisible God still have what it takes—in terms of power and interest—to reach out and touch their lives?

When we think about it in these terms, it becomes clear that the situation of Tevye and that of Esther are not so far distant from ours as we might first have thought. We may not personally face direct persecution based on our nationality or our faith, although many of God's people today in different parts of the world are confronted with exactly such a reality. However, we too are strangers in the land in which we live, called to be *in* the world but not *of* it. We may be citizens of the country in which we live, yet we are in a profound sense the subjects of a different king, with loyalties and

4

allegiances different from those of our neighbors. Sometimes that difference doesn't seem particularly important; we are all part of the same community. Yet at other times it becomes painfully clear that we are not operating under the same management as those who live all around us. In a pluralistic society, we too face the struggle to stand for our primary allegiance, and in a culture where those who stand for truth regularly find themselves getting hammered. It isn't easy—but it is home.

What is more, we too struggle with the invisibility of God. The God who can part the Red Sea and raise Jesus from the dead does not choose to exercise that same power very often in our experience. We struggle when the goals and dreams we had for our lives are trampled underfoot by circumstances, even though perhaps they were good and godly dreams that God could easily have brought to fruition. Tevye dreamed of being a rich man and wondered what cosmic scheme of God's would have been ruined if he had been given a better life. Perhaps all we ever wanted, though, was to be happily married, or to have children, or to raise those children, but God didn't bring that dream to fruition. Perhaps our heart's desire was to serve God in a full-time ministry, or to see our dearest friend come to faith in Christ, but it never happened. We cried out to God, asking what cosmic scheme would be disrupted by answering our prayers, but there was no response. God remained hidden, his will inscrutable. Like the Jews of Esther's time and the Russian diaspora, we too may find ourselves "fiddlers on the roof," struggling desperately to keep our balance in a confusing world.

The Twin Temptations: Assimilation and Despair

We can relate, then, to the two primary temptations that the Jews faced in Esther's day. On the one hand, the power of the pagan empire was intensely visible and tangible. They heard it daily in the footsteps of the marching soldiers and the rumble of chariot wheels. They saw its opulent wealth and absolute control of the details of life. They smelled its power in the incense offered in a hundred state-sponsored pagan temples all around them. Why not just give up the distinctive motto, "We are God's covenant people," and be assimilated into the crowd? That was the goal of the Persian Empire. In the science fiction series *Star Trek: The Next Generation*, there was a particularly nasty opponent of the Federation called "The Borg," who operated by

5

incorporating their enemies into their collective and extracting from them whatever was of value. Their slogan was "Resistance is futile, you must be assimilated." In just the same way, the Persian Empire sought to assimilate the various peoples that inhabited their territory into a single entity.

What made the temptation to assimilation particularly pressing was the fact that most of the really enthusiastic "As for me and my house, we will serve the LORD" (Josh. 24:15) people among the exiles had left and returned to Jerusalem at the time of Cyrus's decree in 538 B.C., or during the generation that followed. Now, more than fifty years after that event, those who remained in Susa, the Persian capital, were strongly tempted to settle into a comfortable (perhaps too comfortable) coexistence with the generally benign autocracy that surrounded them. Exile had been kind to them. They had come to terms with the powers of the day and had forgotten that the pagan environment in which they lived was always at least potentially hostile and could never be trusted. They had forgotten that "the powers that be" were fickle masters who could easily turn against them.

If assimilation was one temptation that faced the people of Esther's day, then despair was surely another. They were surrounded by a fickle, all-powerful empire that might well turn out to be antagonistic, and they followed a God whose ways were often inscrutable, invisible, and mysterious. What, then, could keep them from despair? As the Borg realized, despair and assimilation are closely related. The reason they constantly repeated the "Resistance is futile" slogan is that those who have given up hope are easily assimilated. How then could the Jewish exiles hold on to hope and faithfulness in the midst of a hostile pagan environment? How can we hold firm in the face of the trials and disappointments of our lives? As Tevye discovered as the movie *Fiddler on the Roof* unfolded, something more than the answer "Tradition" would be necessary to maintain a distinctive community.

To the twofold temptation to assimilation and despair, the Book of Esther offers a twofold answer. In the first place, it satirizes the empire, mocking its claims to power and authority. Satire takes the object of fear, the authority, and makes fun of it, showing its ridiculous side. The book is meant to make us laugh. For oppressed and powerless people, satire is a key weapon, cutting the vaunted splendor of the empire down to size. Dictatorships and totalitarian states have never had much of a sense of humor when it comes to their sense of self-importance. Books like *Animal Farm*, in which George

Orwell depicted and parodied the Soviet system of government, swiftly find themselves being banned by the empire, because it fears the power of satire. If the people once perceive that the emperor indeed has no clothes, then the empire's power to command obedience and instill fear is broken. The one who is able to laugh in the face of the Borg will never be successfully assimilated. Satire is thus a powerful antidote to despair. The Book of Esther shows us that the great empire is not run by fearsome giants after all, but by petty bureaucrats. The ruling class of Persia is depicted not so much as "The Magnificent Seven" but more like "Ahasuerus and the Seven Dwarfs."[1]

The second approach the Book of Esther takes is to show us that God is often at work in this world in an entirely different mode from, say, the events of the exodus. In the Book of Exodus, God's work is all thunder and lightning, full of dramatic interventions that expose the emptiness of the Egyptian gods. There are great heroes like Moses and Aaron to lead the people and a trail of miracles to attest to God's presence with them. In the Book of Esther, however, we see God working invisibly and behind the scenes.[2] Here there are neither dramatic miracles nor great heroes, just apparently ordinary providence moving flawed and otherwise undistinguished people into exactly the right place at the right time to bring the empire into line and to establish God's purposes for his people. God is not mentioned by name anywhere in the book. However, when it comes to a conflict between the empire of Ahasuerus and his dwarfs on one side and the kingdom of the almighty, invisible God on the other, there is only one possible outcome.

LIFESTYLES OF THE RICH AND FATUOUS

The Book of Esther begins by introducing us to the great empire of Ahasuerus:

1. The same satirical motif is visible in the stories of Daniel 1–6, for example, in the repeated lengthy list of different classes of government officials who turn up to worship Nebuchadnezzar's golden statue, and the similar long and repeated list of instruments that are played to give the command for worship. The empire cannot resist the temptation to put on a great show! Yet its vaunted power is thwarted by the simple refusal of Daniel's friends to give in to its agenda.

2. Sandra Berg comments, "The Book of Esther, then, does not ignore the presence of divine activity; rather, it points to the hiddenness of Yahweh's presence in the world" (*The Book of Esther: Motifs, Themes and Structure* [Society of Biblical Literature Dissertation Series 44; Missoula, MT: Scholars Press, 1979], 178).

Now in the days of Ahasuerus, the Ahasuerus who reigned from India to Ethiopia over 127 provinces, in those days when King Ahasuerus sat on his royal throne in Susa, the capital, in the third year of his reign he gave a feast for all his officials and servants. The army of Persia and Media and the nobles and governors of the provinces were before him, while he showed the riches of his royal glory and the splendor and pomp of his greatness for many days, 180 days. And when these days were completed, the king gave for all the people present in Susa, the citadel, both great and small, a feast lasting for seven days in the court of the garden of the king's palace. There were white cotton curtains and violet hangings fastened with cords of fine linen and purple to silver rods and marble pillars, and also couches of gold and silver on a mosaic pavement of porphyry, marble, mother-of-pearl and precious stones. Drinks were served in golden vessels, vessels of different kinds, and the royal wine was lavished according to the bounty of the king. And drinking was according to this edict: "There is no compulsion." For the king had given orders to all the staff of his palace to do as each man desired. Queen Vashti also gave a feast for the women in the palace that belonged to King Ahasuerus. (Esth. 1:1–9)

This Ahasuerus was no teacup tyrant: he ruled 127 provinces from India to Ethiopia, from sea to shining sea. What is more, Ahasuerus knew how to throw a party, a six-month-long event, for his military leaders, his princes, and his nobles—all of the power brokers of the kingdom. Anyone who was anyone was there. There were marble pillars and hangings of white and violet linen in the gardens, couches of gold and silver—even mosaic pavements made of costly materials. The very ground on which the guests walked and the seats on which they sat were made of things that other hosts would have kept safely locked away as precious treasures. No two of the wine cups were identical and the wine flowed freely, matching the king's generosity.

This lengthy description serves an important purpose in the narration. We are meant to be impressed and awed by this display of excess—and a little revolted by its wastefulness. Just as we are both impressed and revolted when we read reports of the weddings of Hollywood stars—the flowers, the bands, the choirs, the fireworks, the outrageously expensive dress—so too here we should be both impressed and revolted. Ahasuerus is the very picture of power and wealth, both of which are squandered on his own appetites. And remember, these would have been our tax dollars at work!

But a key detail begins the process of deconstructing the empire in front of our very eyes, setting us up for the revelation that the emperor who has such a beautiful closet actually has no clothes. That detail comes in verse 8: "And drinking was according to this edict: 'There is no compulsion.' For the king had given orders to all the staff of his palace to do as each man desired." This continues the theme of Ahasuerus's power: even the very drinking at his party must conform to his law. No detail escaped the empire's notice and regulation: an edict was required to ensure that no one was under compulsion! But power that must regulate conformity at this level inevitably invites a petty bureaucracy. Real power does not consist in regulating such detailed minutiae. In fact, the tendency to regulate such details is actually a sign of weakness not power. The stories that circulate of government regulations requiring bananas to conform to certain criteria of straightness and size do not impress us as shining examples of government efficiency but rather of bureaucrats run amok, compensating for lack of real significance by inordinate attention to minuscule details.[3] Such was the empire of Ahasuerus, and as we read its description, it is hard to resist a chuckle.

Deconstructing the Empire

The process of deconstructing the empire continues in the next scene. The king—Great King Ahasuerus—had been drinking for seven straight days and was predictably in high spirits. With a characteristic touch of overkill, he sent no fewer than seven of the royal eunuchs who served him to summon his queen, Vashti, wearing her royal crown, so that the people and the nobles could admire her beauty: "On the seventh day, when the heart of the king was merry with wine, he commanded Mehuman, Biztha, Harbona, Bigtha and Abagtha, Zethar and Carkas, the seven eunuchs who served in the presence of King Ahasuerus, to bring Queen Vashti before the king with her royal crown, in order to show the peoples and the princes her beauty, for she was lovely to look at" (Esth. 1:10–11). The Rabbis may have been

---

3. The government in question is the European Commission, whose regulation No 2257/94, concerning banana standards, requires that bananas must be "free from malformation or abnormal curvature of the fingers" and lays down a minimum length of 14 cms. and minimum grade of 27 mms. Although often dismissed as a myth, this regulation is apparently real, although in practice unenforced. See Blake Morrison, "Adventures in Euroland," *The Guardian*, December 17, 2001.

going beyond the text when they interpreted the command to Vashti to appear wearing her royal crown as requiring her to wear nothing else apart from the crown, yet they were not too far off the mark in discerning the offensiveness of Ahasuerus's intentions. To command his wife to appear dressed up in her royal finery for the enjoyment of a crowd of drunken men was to treat her as a doll, a mere object who existed for the king's pleasure, and to show off his power—a "trophy wife," in the contemporary jargon.[4] Not for her the decree "There is no compulsion" (1:8). Here we see the dark side of placing so much power in the hands of a man whose only thought is for himself.

But here the raw power of the empire encountered a snag: "But Queen Vashti refused to come at the king's command delivered by the eunuchs. At this the king became enraged, and his anger burned within him" (Esth. 1:12). The law of the Medes and the Persians, which could not be revoked, could nonetheless be refused. Queen Vashti, who in accordance with Persian custom had been holding a separate feast for the women (Esth. 1:9), refused to comply with Ahasuerus's unreasonable demands. The law might be able to compel people to drink as they wished, but it could not ultimately compel the king's wife to be treated as a sex object. A mere woman stood up and said "No!" and the empire was powerless to enforce its will. The mouse had roared and the glorious empire was shaken to its foundations by her refusal.

What was to be done? A royal conference of the wise men of the empire was required to work out how to deal with this dangerous threat to authority: "Then the king said to the wise men who knew the times (for this was the king's procedure toward all who were versed in law and judgment, the men next to him being Carshena, Shethar, Admatha, Tarshish, Meres, Marsena, and Memucan, the seven princes of Persia and Media, who saw the king's face, and sat first in the kingdom): 'According to the law, what is to be done to Queen Vashti, because she has not performed the command of King Ahasuerus delivered by the eunuchs?' " (Esth. 1:13–15). For their part, Ahasuerus's advisors were terrified that the queen's "just say no" policy would spread to every home in the empire:

4. On this scene, see Adele Berlin, *Esther* (JPS Bible Commentary; Philadelphia: Jewish Publication Society, 2001), 11.

Then Memucan said in the presence of the king and the officials, "Not only against the king has Queen Vashti done wrong, but also against all the officials and all the peoples who are in all the provinces of King Ahasuerus. For the queen's behavior will be made known to all women, causing them to look at their husbands with contempt, since they will say, 'King Ahasuerus commanded Queen Vashti to be brought before him, and she did not come.' This very day the noble women of Persia and Media who have heard of the queen's behavior will say the same to all the king's officials, and there will be contempt and wrath in plenty." (Esth. 1:16–18)

Horrors! What would happen to a man's position in his own home once it became known that Queen Vashti had refused the command of the king?

The Empire Strikes Back

Yet what did Vashti's resistance really achieve? She personally lost her position of power and prestige as the queen, for the imperial advisors said, "If it please the king, let a royal order go out from him, and let it be written among the laws of the Persians and the Medes so that it may not be repealed, that Vashti is never again to come before King Ahasuerus. And let the king give her royal position to another who is better than she. So when the decree made by the king is proclaimed throughout all his kingdom, for it is vast, all women will give honor to their husbands, high and low alike" (Esth. 1:19–20).

Thus Vashti was stripped of her title. The law, it appears, triumphed, for the regulation that she resisted also set her punishment (Esth. 1:15), though it is clear already that "the law" merely serves as a fig leaf to cover the whim of the king and his advisors. Since she chose not to appear before the king when she was summoned, she would never again appear before him. Instead, her place would be given to someone "better than she." Her suffering freed no one, not even herself, and was ultimately a foolish gesture. Pragmatically, Vashti is a model of how *not* to get things done within the empire: the nail that dared to raise its head was indeed hammered for it. Esther would have to be much more circumspect and subtle in dealing with the empire if she was to defuse its danger. Yet Vashti's refusal nonetheless serves to reveal the weakness of the law to command behavior. Resistance is possible. Assimilation to the will of the empire is not inevitable.

11

That lesson appears to have been lost on the empire, which busily set about making another law that it was powerless to enforce: "This advice pleased the king and the princes, and the king did as Memucan proposed. He sent letters to all the royal provinces, to every province in its own script and to every people in its own language, that every man be master in his own household and speak according to the language of his people" (Esth. 1:21–22). Consider the futility of this regulation: "that every man be master in his own household" (Esth. 1:22). The entire weight of imperial authority was placed behind this edict: it was a royal decree, a law that could never be repealed (see Esth. 1:19). The entire resources of the empire went into disseminating this edict through the royal mails, the intricate system of horses and dispatch riders which carried the emperor's wishes speedily to the most distant provinces. But what was actually achieved by all this huffing and puffing? Was the social order of Persia really threatened by this one woman's resistance? Even if it were, can such a principle of male authority in the household really be imposed by governmental decree? Are all men to exercise power in such a self-centered way as Ahasuerus did, and then expect instant obedience? Is every man supposed to banish his wife if she fails to submit to his will?

In fact, the edict deconstructs itself, serving merely to publicize throughout the vast empire and in the language of every people group Ahasuerus's lack of authority in his own household. If it was meant to inspire respect for husbands and respect for Ahasuerus, its actual effect was surely the exact opposite. If he was afraid that the story of his impotence would spread through gossip, now his own edict has done its best to ensure that everyone would hear the story. Once again, at the same time as we are impressed by Ahasuerus's power, we find it hard to restrain a chuckle as he slams his sledgehammer down on a nut, and misses.

The fact that the emperor has no clothes is hardly a comforting reality for his subjects. As the Book of Esther unfolds, we shall see that Ahasuerus has little political acumen or capacity for personal thought.[5] His decree concerning Vashti is symptomatic of a more general weakness in his character. At the same time, he is surrounded and manipulated by advisors who like-

---

5. See Michael V. Fox, *Character and Ideology in the Book of Esther*, 2nd ed. (Grand Rapids: Eerdmans, 2001), 171–77.

wise wield their power with more enthusiasm than skill. It is as if we were to see the surgeons about to operate on us practice by cutting logs with chainsaws and repeatedly miss the target. This is the world in which God's people found themselves then, and often still find themselves: a world in which the reins of power are in the hands of the incompetent, and in which we are guided at best by the amoral and at worst by the immoral. It is that way for some in the workplace or even in the home. Many Christians throughout the world live in countries that are practical dictatorships, or where the real power seems to lie in the hands of the local mafia or a drug cartel, not in the elected government officials. This world is a dangerous place, where power and wisdom are frequently unconnected. The reality of living with such people holding the power of life and death may seem to be no laughing matter, but sometimes laughter is the best way to begin to respond.

Living under the Empire

What do we learn from the opening chapter of Esther for our own walk in the world?

First, Esther 1 reminds us not to take the power and the glory of this world too seriously. Sometimes we just have to laugh. The world takes itself all too seriously, and it wants us to take it seriously too. We live in a society that routinely elevates the trivial. Whole magazines are devoted to the antics of soap opera stars, while our culture pays incredible amounts of money to grown men whose only talent is hitting or throwing a little ball. And we think Ahasuerus was wasteful? We live in a world that considers the car we drive an extension of who we are and is more impressed by where someone went to school than by what one learned there. And we think Ahasuerus's bureaucrats were focused on trivialities?

The empire of materialism in which we live takes stuff desperately seriously. It wants us to study the empire's laws and learn how to get ahead by the empire's standards. It wants us to dream of six-month-long banquets in beautifully decorated gardens, and then to devote our lives to pursuing the dream. It is easy for us to be dazzled by the empire's ostentatious show, but it is empty of real power at the center. The empire of this world is a glittering hologram that has no real substance. To defend ourselves against the danger of being assimilated, we must learn to laugh at the empire. We must

13

learn to laugh at those around us whose lives are wasted in pursuit of so many worthless goals, and to laugh at ourselves when we see our own hearts getting weighed on the empire's scale of values. What shall it profit a man if he can throw six-month-long parties with gold couches on mother-of-pearl pavements? How much more ridiculous are we, then, when we spend so much time and energy desiring a new sports car, or a great pair of shoes at the mall, or the latest home improvement in the mail-order catalog? Ultimately, it is all empty. The emperor's costly clothes are transparent, and what may be seen through them by the discerning eye is ridiculous. True value lies in the values of an altogether different empire.

Second, Esther 1 shows us that sometimes we have to wait to see what God is doing. God is nowhere to be seen in this chapter. That is no surprise, since he is hardly visible anywhere in the whole Book of Esther. However, that we cannot see God working doesn't mean he isn't at work. He is busily occupied throughout the Book of Esther as the unseen director of history, arranging all things for the good of his people. Esther and Mordecai have not yet even made an appearance on stage, but events are still moving according to God's good pleasure. Why did Vashti throw away her position and privilege for a noble but predictably futile gesture? Why did Ahasuerus make his foolish demand in the first place? Who came up with the idea of replacing Vashti with a better woman, instead of quietly resolving the offense Ahasuerus had caused? All of these events are on one level entirely explicable as normal human events, with no miraculous component. Yet all of them are necessary to make way for the process by which Esther will rise to the position where she can use her power and influence to protect God's people against a powerful enemy. Coincidences? By no means. Rather, they are the hand of God at work in a different mode from that seen elsewhere in the Bible.

Notice, however, that none of these events would have seemed significant to the Jewish community in Susa at the time. A change in queen? Who cares what those pagans are doing? What has that got to do with the price of fish in the market? Only with the benefit of hindsight is it possible to see all the intricate details of God's plan working together for the good of his people. So also in our own lives, we may well have no idea what God is doing. He may seem hidden and remote, refusing to answer our prayers and to give us what we so earnestly ask of him. Wait! The end of our story has not yet been told, and who knows how the pieces of the jigsaw that at present seem to have no logical connection with one another will ultimately come together? Even though we cannot see God acting, it does not follow that he is not doing anything. God's work is not all slam-bang action; sometimes it is a quiet faithfulness to his promises in the seemingly ordinary providences of life, bringing about in the hearts of his people what he has purposed.

Third, this passage shows that God's kingdom is not like the empire of Ahasuerus. The Book of Esther repeatedly invites us to compare and contrast the kingdom of God and the empire of Ahasuerus. There are superficial similarities between the two kingdoms, but in each case they hide deeper differences. The Lord too is a great king whose decrees cannot be challenged or repealed. His sovereignty governs all things, great and small. He must be obeyed, or we will certainly suffer the consequences. Yet his law is beneficial for men and women, unlike the drunken meanderings of a man at the mercy of his shrewd counselors. God doesn't use people for his own purposes as if they were disposable commodities. Rather, he graciously invites them into a loving relationship with himself. His kingdom grows and does its work not through the outwardly powerful and attractive, but rather in hidden but effective ways. For that reason, Jesus compares the kingdom of God to the growth of a mustard seed, or to the work of leaven. It starts small and hidden, but it achieves its goals nonetheless (Matt. 13:31–33). Big is not necessarily beautiful in God's service.

The theme of the messianic banquet provides another point of comparison and contrast between the kingdom of God and the empire of Ahasuerus. The Lord too has prepared a sumptuous banquet for his people on the last day. But when God summons his bride (the church) to his banquet, he does so not to expose her to shame but to lavish his grace and mercy upon her. He doesn't force sinners to come unwillingly to his feast, but gently woos them and draws them to himself. We can see why Queen Vashti was reluctant to appear before Ahasuerus, but who would refuse such a wonderful invitation from God to experience life in all its fullness? There is nothing noble about refusing to appear in the presence of such a good and gracious God. On the contrary, it is the height of folly and ingratitude. Have you heard and responded to his call to come? If not, then you too, like Vashti, are doomed to be banished from his presence forever. Why would you choose to die? Why not lay down all your resistance and come to the feast?

15

This is all the more the case when we consider what Christ has done for his bride. Far from regarding her as a beautiful object existing solely to feed his pride and pleasure, he took one who was by nature completely unattractive and gave himself for her, laying down his own life for his people. It was while we were still dead in our transgressions and sins that Christ gave himself for us, his life as a ransom for the ungodly. Everything we have, even the very righteousness in which we are clothed to appear before God, comes from his good hand. How can our hearts not be touched again with fresh love for a King who has loved us so freely, and so graciously? With such a husband calling us, why would we not be delighted and overjoyed to come at his bidding? A King who has done so much for us can surely ask any level of obedience from us in response.

Indeed, this is how the Lord establishes male headship in the home. Like King Ahasuerus, God too decrees that men should lead their homes, but the differences are far more pronounced than the similarities. His decree is not an empty and futile gesture. For men who follow Jesus, headship can never be merely the exercise of raw power, as it was for Ahasuerus. Such so-called headship, which simply uses that term as an excuse for domineering control, is a far cry from the biblical model. On the contrary, Christian male leadership in the home and in the church is established and rooted in Christ's own self-sacrificing love for his bride. The obverse of the coin inscribed "Wives, submit to your own husbands . . . as the church submits to Christ" is the motto "Husbands, love your wives, as Christ loved the church and gave himself up for her" (Eph. 5:22–25). This is what true love is: not husbands using their wives as objects to meet their needs and satisfy their desires, but rather giving themselves up for their wives, gently leading them to fulfill their gifts and godly aspirations. The gospel truth of Christ's love for us is the foundation for new minds that delight to submit to his ordering of creation. If Christian husbands were more like Christ and less like Ahasuerus, then perhaps we would find our wives more ready to submit to our leadership.

Who then is your real king and to whom is your heart committed? The empire wants to make us its slave. It wants to assimilate us into its ways of thinking. It offers us glittering prizes for compliance to its ways—a "successful" life, according to its own definitions. Have you been enticed and trapped? Flee from these things to the kingdom that is solid and substantial, the kingdom that Jesus Christ came to establish. Learn to laugh at the emptiness of the empire's priorities and edicts. Come to Christ by faith and rest in his provision of forgiveness and life, thanking him for his gift of himself for us on the cross. Live according to his edicts, in which true wisdom resides. Trust that he is at work as he promised, working through even the evil impulses of the empire for good in our lives and the lives of all of his people. Finally, remember that this world is not our home: one day, when Jesus returns, our balancing act on the roof will be over and the true banquet will begin.

2

Beauty and the Beast

Esther 2:1–23

*When the turn came for Esther the daughter of Abihail the
uncle of Mordecai, who had taken her as his own daughter,
to go in to the king, she asked for nothing except what Hegai the
king's eunuch, who had charge of the women, advised. Now
Esther was winning favor in the eyes of all who saw her. And
when Esther was taken to King Ahasuerus into his royal palace
in the tenth month, which is the month of Tebeth, in the seventh
year of his reign, the king loved Esther more than all the women,
and she won grace and favor in his sight more than all
the virgins, so that he set the royal crown on her head
and made her queen instead of Vashti.* (Esth. 2:15–17)

There are some competitions that it is no great privilege to win.
Each year, for example, the Golden Raspberry Award Foundation bestows a "Razzie" on what it considers to be the worst
movie put out by Hollywood that year—a kind of negative counterpart to
the Oscars. Needless to say, this is one award for which few actors would be
thrilled to be nominated.

The search for Queen Vashti's replacement was in some ways a competition like the Golden Raspberry Award. The original idea when Vashti was

deposed and sent away from the king's presence was to find a better woman to fill her royal position (Esth. 1:19). By "better," the king's advisors presumably meant someone more compliant than Vashti, someone who would toe the royal line and obey her husband. Yet strangely enough, in their search for a replacement it never seems to have occurred to those in charge to include a character assessment. Instead, only three virtues were necessary in this "better" woman: she had to be young, she had to be unmarried, and she had to be extraordinarily good-looking:

> After these things, when the anger of King Ahasuerus had abated, he remembered Vashti and what she had done and what had been decreed against her. Then the king's young men who attended him said, "Let beautiful young virgins be sought out for the king. And let the king appoint officers in all the provinces of his kingdom to gather all the beautiful young virgins to the harem in Susa the capital, under custody of Hegai, the king's eunuch, who is in charge of the women. Let their cosmetics be given them. And let the young woman who pleases the king be queen instead of Vashti." This pleased the king, and he did so. (Esth. 2:1–4)

Notice that this was not a competition that someone had to apply to enter. Everyone's hat was in the ring simply by virtue of living within the empire. Since the whole purpose for existence in Persia was to serve the empire, no permission was needed for the empire to draft a young woman into this particular branch of the civil service. The empire didn't care whether parents had other plans for their daughter. Remember, "Resistance is futile; you must be assimilated." There was nothing sexist about this perspective, either: the empire would also happily draft people's sons to serve as the king's eunuchs, if it felt there was a need and if they were qualified. The modern slogan "My body, my choice" wouldn't translate well in ancient culture. In the world of the Persians, everything anyone possessed, including one's body, could be and was claimed by the empire if the empire wanted it.

In fact, even to call the process of collecting the women a competition is a little misleading, since none of the contestants would be going home afterward. The king wished to add to his collection of living dolls; those chosen would live in secluded splendor for the rest of their lives, even if they were only rarely taken out and played with. Indeed, it wasn't a bad life on the scale of existence within the empire. The women would receive regular meals.

19

Probably very few would have resisted the royal summons, and many would have regarded it as a wonderful opportunity to have a comfortable, if pointless, existence. For many, it would seem almost like winning the lottery. If that seems a bizarre notion in our culture, where personal freedom is so idolized, think of the many people around us who pour their entire working careers into jobs they dislike, or even despise, in return for a comfortable salary and relative job security. The empire may have changed its shape and the kinds of demands it makes of us and of our children, but our world is not so very different after all.

Mordecai and Esther

In the midst of this all-consuming empire, two relatively insignificant people, Mordecai and Esther, step onto the stage:

> Now there was a Jew in Susa the citadel whose name was Mordecai, the son of Jair, son of Shimei, son of Kish, a Benjaminite, who had been carried away from Jerusalem among the captives carried away with Jeconiah king of Judah, whom Nebuchadnezzar king of Babylon had carried away. He was bringing up Hadassah, that is Esther, the daughter of his uncle, for she had neither father nor mother. The young woman had a beautiful figure and was lovely to look at, and when her father and her mother died, Mordecai took her as his own daughter. (Esth. 2:5–7)

Mordecai was a descendant of Kish, from the tribe of Benjamin. He was therefore related to King Saul, a fact that will become significant later on in the story. One of his ancestors was carried off into exile in the time of Jehoiachin (Jeconiah) in 597 B.C. (see 2 Kings 24:14–15). In fact, exile was the defining feature of Mordecai's position, as Esther 2:6 makes clear: literally it says that his ancestors "had been exiled from Jerusalem with the exiles who had been exiled with Jehoiachin, king of Judah, whom Nebuchadnezzar exiled." As a second- or third-generation exile, he would thus have known nothing other than life in Persia under the empire. Exile defined his existence.

The clash of cultures that exiles like Mordecai experienced is evident already in the way he is introduced. On the one hand, he is identified as "a Jew," with a kosher genealogy that stretches back to the golden days of Israel.

More than one hundred years of exile had passed since the destruction of his homeland in 586 B.C., but he had still not been assimilated. Susa was his address, but it was not his home. On the other hand, however, his name is Mordecai, a Hebraized form of the Babylonian name *marduka*, which includes within it the name of the Babylonian god Marduk. That is not to say that Mordecai was a worshipper of Marduk; many faithful exiles had both Hebrew and Babylonian names. Daniel and his three friends were also renamed by their captors. However, Mordecai's introduction expresses the ambivalence of his position as the citizen of two kingdoms. At home, he was Mordecai *the Jew*, faithful servant of the living God. At work, he was just plain *Mordecai*, faithful servant of the empire.

Mordecai lived in the citadel of Susa, along with the imperial employees, rather than out in the city of Susa itself.[1] The other member of his household was his cousin, whom he had taken into his care because she was an orphan. She too had dual names and a dual identity. She had a Hebrew name, "Hadassah," which means "myrtle." She had a kosher heritage; she was the daughter of Abihail (see Esth. 2:15). The empire, however, knew her by her Persian name Esther, or "Star" (perhaps also with an allusion to the pagan goddess Ishtar). She too, like all the exiles, had to live in two worlds. As her life unfolded, though, there would come a day when she would have to decide which of those two worlds defined her.

GOING WITH THE FLOW

Those two worlds collided one fateful morning in the citadel of Susa. Ahasuerus's officials were collecting his new flock of young women, according to the edict that his advisors had framed for him. It is not clear whether they had to use jackboots and rifle butts to ensure the compliance of the chosen, or whether it was those who were left behind who were the disappointed ones ("What do you mean, I'm not pretty enough and young enough for the king?"). Most likely, the majority accepted it simply as a matter of course. This was just the way the empire worked. Some were chosen; some would be left behind. Esther was one of those who were taken: "So when the king's

1. Susa had a distinct acropolis, or royal area, separate from the city. On the layout of Susa, see Carey A. Moore, "Archaeology and the Book of Esther," *Biblical Archaeologist* 38 (1975): 71–73.

order and his edict were proclaimed, and when many young women were gathered in Susa the citadel in custody of Hegai, Esther also was taken into the king's palace and put in custody of Hegai, who had charge of the women" (Esth. 2:8). We had anticipated this fate as soon as Esther was introduced to us as a woman who had a beautiful figure and was lovely to look at. In fact, the text makes the point that she is actually more than qualified: the officials are searching for one who is "good to look at" (*tovot mar'eh*), but Esther is both "fair of form" (*yefat-to'ar*) and "good to look at" (*tovot mar'eh*; Esth. 2:7). Visually speaking (which is all that the empire—then and now—cares about), she is doubly blessed. There seemed to be no point arguing with the empire about it, any more than she could have argued with God when he took her parents away and left her an orphan, or Mordecai's ancestors could have resisted being exiled from Jerusalem. Some things simply cannot be changed; resistance was futile.

Esther quickly learned not simply how to survive, but how to thrive in her new situation: "And the young woman pleased him and won his favor. And he quickly provided her with her cosmetics and her portion of food, and with seven chosen young women from the king's palace, and advanced her and her young women to the best place in the harem" (Esth. 2:9). Esther learned that the harem was simply life in the empire in miniature: a relatively pointless existence, where life was regulated in all its details, and promotion depended not on talent or character, but on pleasing those in charge. Thus Esther learned to be a pleaser, first of all charming Hegai—the "keeper of the women," to give him his official title.

Of course, Esther had some natural assets in this pursuit. She was, to use the Hebrew idiom, "good in his sight," meaning physically attractive (Esth. 2:9). This idiom underlines the fact that the whole empire runs on the superficialities of what may be seen, not the substance of who people are at the core of their being. It is the opposite of God's scale of values, which begins with the heart (1 Sam. 16:7). But Esther's competitors were good-looking as well; otherwise, they wouldn't have been drafted in the first place. Esther didn't merely "find favor" (*matsa' hen*) in Hegai's sight, a more passive idiom; still less was favor in Hegai's sight given to her as an unsought gift by God, as was the case with Daniel and his three friends (see Dan. 1:9). Rather, the writer uses an unusual idiom to tell us that Esther "won favor" (*nasa' hen*) in Hegai's sight: she worked for her promotion in the house of women, by fitting into the agenda that the empire set for her.[2] She was willing to let the empire define her reality. Resistance was not high on her program at this point; on the contrary, she seemed content, even eager, to be assimilated.

In return for this compliance, Hegai rewarded Esther with special food and an early start to her beauty treatments: "The turn came for each young woman to go in to King Ahasuerus, after being twelve months under the regulations for the women, since this was the regular period of their beautifying, six months with oil of myrrh and six months with spices and ointments for women" (Esth. 2:12). These special beauty treatments included six months in oil of myrrh and six months in spices and ointments. It has been suggested that the women may literally have spent their time "in" these elements, with ointments being applied by means of a chemical bath or fumigation![3] The food they were given was likewise more than mere sustenance: it was intended to enhance their beauty, perhaps by fattening up these scrawny commoners (see Dan. 1:15). The modern Western cult of "thin is beautiful" would undoubtedly have been regarded as a bizarre preference in the ancient world, as it is in many parts of the world to this day.

ESTHER AND DANIEL

The similarity of Esther's position to that of Daniel and his three friends, exiled and incorporated into the imperial system, highlights also what is different about them. Daniel and his three friends stood up to the empire, quietly but firmly requesting permission to be faithful to their own beliefs by not eating the royal food (Dan. 1:8–16). They received permission to do so and God in turn blessed them, against all the odds. They remained unassimilated, and yet were nonetheless respected by the empire because of God's direct intervention. Unlike Daniel and his three friends, however, Esther had apparently no ethical qualms about eating the empire's food and being used as the emperor's plaything. And following Mordecai's advice, her Jewishness remained perfectly concealed: "Esther had not made known her people or kindred, for Mordecai had commanded her not to make it known. And every

---

2. See H. Bardtke, *Das Buch Esther* (Kommentar zum Alten Testament; Gütersloh: Gerd Mohn, 1963), 303.

3. Michael V. Fox, *Character and Ideology in the Book of Esther*, 2nd ed. (Grand Rapids: Eerdmans, 2001), 35.

day Mordecai walked in front of the court of the harem to learn how Esther was and what was happening to her" (Esth. 2:10–11).

When, after a year of preparation, Esther's turn finally came to go in to the king for her one-night audition, she was careful to follow Hegai's instructions:

> When the young woman went in to the king in this way, she was given whatever she desired to take with her from the harem to the king's palace. In the evening she would go in, and in the morning she would return to the second harem in custody of Shaashgaz, the king's eunuch, who was in charge of the concubines. She would not go in to the king again, unless the king delighted in her and she was summoned by name. When the turn came for Esther the daughter of Abihail the uncle of Mordecai, who had taken her as his own daughter, to go in to the king, she asked for nothing except what Hegai the king's eunuch, who had charge of the women, advised. Now Esther was winning favor in the eyes of all who saw her. (Esth. 2:13–15)

At this point in the story, Esther was the perfectly compliant child of the empire, the ultimate anti-Vashti, and her tactics appeared to be succeeding. Wherever she went, she won with her compliant ways the favor of all who saw her.[4]

We are therefore not surprised to find out that sweet little Esther also charmed the heart of King Ahasuerus: "And when Esther was taken to King Ahasuerus into his royal palace in the tenth month, which is the month of Tebeth, in the seventh year of his reign, the king loved Esther more than all the women, and she won grace and favor in his sight more than all the virgins, so that he set the royal crown on her head and made her queen instead of Vashti" (Esth. 2:16–17). Here surely was the "better woman" than Vashti that he had been seeking: as beautiful as the former queen, but much more compliant. What could be more perfect? The king "loved" Esther more than all the women; he had found what he was looking for. Ahasuerus made Esther queen in Vashti's place, a substitution that is underlined by the reference to the royal crown (the one Vashti refused to appear in) and to a feast given in her honor: "Then the king gave a great feast for all his officials and servants; it was Esther's feast. He also granted a remission of taxes to the provinces

4. Don't miss the visual idiom here, "she won favor with all who saw her," which underlines the externality and superficiality of the empire's mode of judging people.

and gave gifts with royal generosity" (Esth. 2:18). "Sense," in the shape of Esther, has apparently triumphed over "Sensibility" (Vashti), to use the model of Jane Austen's book.

The result of Esther's promotion was happiness and blessing all around. When King Ahasuerus was happy, so was everyone else in Susa: there was a trickle-down effect of that happiness to his subjects as taxes were remitted and gifts handed out with royal liberality (Esth. 2:18), the same phrase that described the distribution of the wine at the first feast (cf. Esth. 1:7).

Through all of this lengthy procedure Mordecai had been keeping a watchful eye on his cousin, advising her along the way. He daily visited the court of the harem to find out, doubtless through intermediaries and messengers, news of what she was doing and what was being done to her (Esth. 2:11). He was the one who advised her to keep secret her Jewish identity—not because the empire was inherently anti-Semitic, but because, in his opinion, one could never be too careful in a place like Susa. He knew the way the empire operated. Walls have ears and information is power. Even after she became queen, it was because of Mordecai's command that Esther kept her ancestry quiet: "Now when the virgins were gathered together the second time, Mordecai was sitting at the king's gate. Esther had not made known her kindred or her people, as Mordecai had commanded her, for Esther obeyed Mordecai just as when she was brought up by him" (Esth. 2:19–20). Here, indeed, was a woman who knew her place, perhaps because Mordecai's command fitted perfectly her natural temperament. Her motto was "Blend in like a chameleon, don't stand out in any way, and we can survive and even thrive, in spite of the empire."

A PLOT UNCOVERED

Mordecai himself proved the power of the right information used in the right way, when he uncovered a plot to harm Ahasuerus:

> In those days, as Mordecai was sitting at the king's gate, Bigthan and Teresh, two of the king's eunuchs, who guarded the threshold, became angry and sought to lay hands on King Ahasuerus. And this came to the knowledge of Mordecai, and he told it to Queen Esther, and Esther told the king in the name of Mordecai. When the affair was investigated and found to be so, the men

were both hanged on the gallows. And it was recorded in the book of the chronicles in the presence of the king. (Esth. 2:21–23)

Two of the king's eunuchs, Bigthan and Teresh, conspired to kill the king. Mordecai became aware of their plot while he was sitting at the king's gate.[5] He passed the information on to the king through Esther, who herself was careful to give credit to Mordecai. In that way, both of their positions were made a little more secure by putting the empire in their debt. The result was that the conspirators were hanged (or impaled on stakes),[6] while Mordecai's name was inscribed in the royal annals.

The result also *ought* to have been recognition for Mordecai. In general, the Persian kings were extremely diligent and generous in rewarding those who had served well. They kept careful lists of "the king's benefactors," those who had done them a favor, in order that no good deed (from the empire's perspective) might go unrewarded. Yet strangely, this particular good deed *did* go unrewarded at the time. Mordecai probably spent weeks and months waiting in vain for some token of appreciation. Unlike God, who is never negligent in rewarding his faithful servants, the Persians sometimes failed to reward faithful service. Yet, as we shall see, that uncommon forgetfulness on the part of Ahasuerus was absolutely necessary in God's plans. Timing is everything in the work of providence, and even though his hand is still invisible, God is nonetheless at work accomplishing his own ends.

DISOBEDIENCE AND ITS CONSEQUENCES

The first lesson that this chapter of Esther teaches us is that disobedience and sin—even the disobedience and sin of others—have far-reaching consequences. Why was Esther caught up and condemned to this apparently

5. This location identifies him as an official of the king, although whether he held such a position already before Esther's rise to the throne or received it through Esther's influence is not clear. Joyce Baldwin argues for the latter (*Esther* [Tyndale Old Testament Commentaries; Downers Grove, IL: Inter-Varsity, 1984], 70), although the fact that Mordecai already lived in the citadel of Susa rather than in the city (2:5) before Esther was taken may point in the opposite direction.
6. Both practices existed in the Persian period. The interest in the height of the gallows, at least in Haman's case (Esth. 5:14), may point toward hanging rather than impaling (Carey A. Moore, *Esther* [Anchor Bible; Garden City, NY: Doubleday, 1971], 31). For the Persians, impaling was not generally the means of execution, but a subsequent step, designed to expose the body to public shame.

meaningless life in a gilded cage? In part, at least, because she lived in Susa. The edict to gather all of the good-looking unmarried women in the empire was presumably carried out with more thoroughness in Susa, under the nose of the emperor, than in the more distant provinces. Why was she living in Susa? She was there because of the sin and disobedience of her forebears. It was disobedience that had brought the family of Mordecai and Esther into exile at the time of Jehoiachin. The destruction of Jerusalem was not simply an accident of fate: it was the culmination of the judgment of God upon his own people who had abandoned him. Disobedience brought God's people into exile in the first place.

What is more, it was disobedience that kept Mordecai and Esther's family in exile. In 538 B.C., Cyrus issued a decree permitting the Jews to return home. Some went back with Zerubbabel at that time (Ezra 1–2), but many stayed, comfortably settled where they were, outside the land of promise. Compared to a backwater like Jerusalem, Susa seemed a much better place to make progress and advance in the service of the empire, as Mordecai discovered. But those who play the empire's game are likely sooner or later to find themselves playing by the empire's rules. Had Mordecai and Esther (or their parents) returned to Jerusalem at some time in the previous fifty years, would Esther still have been taken by the harem recruiters? Perhaps, but she certainly wouldn't have been such an easy target. The result of the family's history of disobedient compromise was that Mordecai and especially Esther found themselves in a position that, for all its worldly advantages, was potentially disastrous spiritually. Esther ended up married to an uncircumcised pagan and virtually cut off from the community of faith, successfully pretending *not* to be a child of the true and living God. Was it possible completely to privatize one's faith as an exile, to be a faithful believer in private but never let it show in any outward way during five years of life in the king's harem? Surely not. Her enviable progress in one world, the world of the empire of Ahasuerus, came at the cost of completely suppressing her identity as a citizen of the kingdom of God.

This is surely a temptation with which we can identify, and all the more because the pressure was so subtle. Esther wasn't instructed to deny her faith, only to conceal it in order to avoid potential problems. And the pressure to conform came from within her own family, not just from the pagan empire. Was it really such a big deal for her to hide her Jewishness? Is it really such a big deal for us to hide our faith in order to gain tenure at a public university, or to fit in with the business environment, or to earn the friendship of our peer group? Caving in to pressure and concealing our faith may lead to progress in the world, but at what cost to our souls?

Yet we see in this chapter more than just the bitter fruit of disobedience. We also see God's ability to turn our disobedience—and the sour fruits of our parents' sins—to his own glory and his people's good. Ahasuerus and his cronies meant their edict purely for the satisfaction of the king's selfish pleasures. Mordecai and Esther found themselves impaled on the horns of a dilemma because of their earlier compromises with the empire. They found it much easier to comply with the empire's wishes than to resist assimilation—and which of us can be sure that we would have charted a different course? Yet God's hand hovers over every detail, moving the pieces into the place he has determined—even through their sin and compromise—in order to achieve his own good purposes.

Learning from Esther

We would hardly coin the slogan "Dare to be an Esther" at this point in the story. All that she has shown us so far is a sweet and compliant spirit toward those around her. Is that good or bad? In some ways, it is good insofar as she is respecting the family and civil authorities God has set over her. Children should, in general, obey their parents, and citizens should, in general, obey the empire's laws. Yet there are times for throwing a "sanctified fit" over the unsanctified demands of one's family, as Sarah did in Genesis 21:10, and the unsanctified demands of the empire, as Daniel and his friends did in Daniel 1–6. In both instances, God specifically endorsed his people's refusal to submit to authority. There are times in each of our lives when we should refuse to conceal whom we serve. We are all too often motivated to conceal our faith, or to refuse to confront someone who needs to hear the truth, because we want to please people and avoid conflict.

When we stand up for our faith, though, we need to be ready for the consequences of our actions. Sometimes the empire may surprise us by backing down, as in Daniel 1, when the four young Jews were allowed to dictate their own diet. More often, however, it will throw us into the fiery furnace or the den of lions, as in Daniel 3 and 6. If God chooses miraculously to rescue us, well and good. But if not, our God is worthy of such sacrifice, and we should offer it joyfully, rather than bow down to the idols that the empire presents to us for worship (see Dan. 3:18).

At this point in the story, Esther is certainly no Daniel. She is both in the world *and* of the world, fully complying with the empire's outrageous demands with the goal of winning the "love" of an unworthy royal husband. She would perhaps have objected that she had little choice, but if someone is willing to suffer the consequences, full obedience to God's law is always an option. Vashti, the pagan, had already shown in the previous chapter that the empire cannot ultimately compel our obedience. Esther is certainly not a model for us in her compromise—yet we should not miss the fact that her history of compromise and sin will not disqualify her from the opportunity for later obedience, an obedience that will bring blessing for her people. Gaining generous tax-relief from the government of Ahasuerus (Esth. 2:18) will not go down in history as Esther's crowning achievement!

Here is hope for all those who find themselves in difficult circumstances in the present because of their past sin and compromise. Here is hope for people who married a non-Christian husband or wife, even though they knew it was wrong. The person who chose a career based on all the wrong motivations, or who has wasted a lifetime in pursuit of the wrong goals can discover that God is sovereign even over those sinful choices and wasted opportunities. Perhaps he has brought us to where we are today so that we can serve him in a unique way. If so, that doesn't make those wrong decisions and sinful actions right. But it should cause us to give thanks to God that he is able to form beautiful pictures out of our smudged and stained efforts. Past failures do not write us out of a significant part in God's script for the future.

THE PREPARED BRIDE

Finally, consider what Esther was willing to put up with for the sake of the empire. She was willing to be poked and prodded, fattened and fumigated, perfumed and prepared over a period of twelve months for her one-night stand in the royal bedroom. This is actually no worse than the preparation that many endure for the sake of a potential career in Hollywood, or as a high flyer in business. Many are willing to endure almost anything in order to achieve the glittering prizes that this world has to offer. Pain often seems to be the necessary prerequisite for beauty and success. Yet how little are we willing to endure God's beauty treatments that prepare us for Christ?

This observation presses us to see both the similarities and differences between the empire of Ahasuerus and the kingdom of God. Like the empire of Ahasuerus, God's claims on our lives are absolute. He owns our bodies, our sexuality, our career plans, our hopes, our dreams, our children . . . everything we have and are is his to do with as he wills. When we were baptized into his community, we were marked out with his name—the name Christian—and he will not share our loyalty with others. God demands and will exercise complete sovereignty over our beings. Of course, this is relatively easy to confess in the abstract. What is much harder is to continue to confess that sovereignty joyfully when God takes our lives and the lives of those around us in directions different from those we had hoped and prayed for, and of which we had dreamed. When God brings trials into our lives and calls us to submit willingly to the loss of the very things that this world calls most precious—money, friends, reputation, health, strength, dreams, and aspirations—how do we respond? With Esther's sweet and compliant spirit? On the contrary, our hearts swiftly revolt against God whenever things do not go our way, whenever *our* will is not done.

Yet God is not a tyrant like Ahasuerus, for whom dreams were disposable and people a mere commodity that the empire produced for his consumption. Not at all! When God exercises his claims on our lives, he does so to bring us good. He wants to move us on in our spiritual walk, to develop and deepen and display our faith before a watching world (1 Peter 1:6–7). As we suffer loss, and as he pries our fingers off the idols to which they are so desperately attached, then our hearts are prepared more and more to be with Christ, and to see in him our only good in this world.

What a husband we are being prepared for! Christ is no despot in the mold of Ahasuerus, eager to use us and dispose of us, like so many discarded toys. Such a man would not be worthy of our eager submission. But our husband is Jesus Christ, who has loved his bride, the church, with an everlasting love. For our sake, he took on a form utterly without beauty, was despised and rejected by those he came to save, was cut off from the land of the living (Isa. 53:2–3). In contrast to Esther's twelve-month-long course of beauty treatments, our divine husband undertook a thirty-three-year pilgrimage, stripped of his eternal radiance. No comfortable beds and fattening food for him, nowhere to lay his head and nothing to call his own. His pain was the prerequisite for our beauty.

This self-sacrifice is what gives him the right to call us to follow him through the worst of trials. Does the course he has laid out seem unbearably painful? Whatever path he leads us down is a path he himself has trodden ahead of us, and he promises to walk it alongside us. Even though we walk through the valley of the shadow of death, his presence will remain with us, and we have the assurance that he is already familiar with the twists and turns of that road.

What motivated Jesus in his pursuit of us? Certainly not our radiant beauty and sweet spirit! We had all gone astray like rebellious sheep, piling up the mound of transgressions and iniquities that he would have to pay for (Isa. 53:5–6). Nevertheless, he loved us and gave himself for us. He has prepared a glorious banquet for our honor, a crown of splendor to beautify us in the sight of everyone, and a place of honor by his side! What wondrous love is this! Yet we are all too reluctant to give ourselves to him and to submit to whatever beautifying sufferings and disciplines he would have us undergo. Our hearts are quick to grumble about the course his providence has charted for us. We are so slow to prepare to meet with him day by day and spend time in his presence along the way. We are so reluctant to fix our eyes on the heavenly banquet he has prepared. Yet what on earth could be sweeter than that heavenly meal?

That feast is the antidote to the twin temptations to assimilation and despair. When our eyes are set on our heavenly bridegroom, we will see through the empty charade of the empire. When our hearts are comforted by the certain knowledge of God's love for us in the gospel, we will be insulated from the temptation to despair. If this God has loved us enough to send his Son to the cross for us, what in all creation can separate us from that love? The answer must be "Nothing and no one." When our eyes are fixed on Christ, we can laugh at the best and not fear the worst that the empire has to offer. We will be strengthened to stand firm by faith, waiting for our sure salvation.

3

MORDECAI MAKES A STAND

Esther 3:1—15

*And all the king's servants who were at the king's gate bowed
down and paid homage to Haman, for the king had so
commanded concerning him. But Mordecai did not bow down or
pay homage. . . . And when Haman saw that Mordecai did not
bow down or pay homage to him, Haman was filled with fury.
But he disdained to lay hands on Mordecai alone. So, as they had
made known to him the people of Mordecai, Haman sought to
destroy all the Jews, the people of Mordecai, throughout
the whole kingdom of Ahasuerus.* (Esth. 3:2, 5–6)

*T*here comes a point in every good Western when it is time for
the hero to make a stand. A lady's honor has been insulted, perhaps, or the peace-loving townspeople have been threatened by
some villain. At which point the hero puts down his glass, pulls up his belt,
tips back his hat, and faces up to the man in black. "A man's gotta do what
a man's gotta do," he says in a slow drawl—and proceeds to do just that, making Main Street safe once again for civilized folk.

HAMAN THE AGAGITE

Is that what we see in Esther 3: Mordecai the hero facing down Haman
the bad guy, so that the world is once again a safe place for decent people?

It is certainly a showdown of sorts, but not exactly the sort of showdown we find in the old Westerns: "After these things King Ahasuerus promoted Haman the Agagite, the son of Hammedatha, and advanced him and set his throne above all the officials who were with him. And all the king's servants who were at the king's gate bowed down and paid homage to Haman, for the king had so commanded concerning him. But Mordecai did not bow down or pay homage" (Esth. 3:1–2).

Mordecai refused to pay homage to the newly appointed vizier, Haman. Opinions vary as to why exactly Mordecai refused to bow. The king had commanded it, and everyone else was doing it—but not Mordecai. He alone was refusing to bow. Why? Some scholars have thought that Mordecai didn't want to bow down before any human being, giving worship to man that is due to God alone. Yet Mordecai apparently had no qualms about bowing down before Ahasuerus, the king. In chapter 8, Esther likewise would throw herself down at the king's feet to beg for her people to be spared. It was only bowing to Haman that Mordecai found problematic. Other scholars have argued that Mordecai was being obstinately arrogant in his refusal to bow, or that he was jealous of Haman for having been promoted to the office of vizier. But there is no hint of either of those attitudes in the text.

Actually, the text itself suggests the reason why Mordecai didn't bow, if we look closely enough. Haman was an Agagite.[1] He was thus a descendant of Agag the Amalekite, the ancient tribal enemy of the Jews. When Israel came out of Egypt, the Amalekites attacked them in the wilderness, for which God cursed them and condemned them to extinction (Ex. 17:8–16). Because of that assault, God declared that there would be a lasting enmity between the two peoples, and he committed himself to blot out all remembrance of Amalek from the face of heaven. In the time of King Saul, God sent Israel to carry out that sentence on Amalek, destroying man and beast (1 Sam. 15). But Saul failed to carry out the terms of holy war, as God had commanded him to do. Instead, he spared the best of the animals and King Agag himself, the best of the people. Saul claimed that he had the best of motives, of course. He said that he simply wanted to offer the animals as sacrifices before the Lord (which, of course, left unanswered the question of what he intended

---

1. Karen Jobes, *Esther* (New International Version Application Commentary; Grand Rapids: Zondervan, 1999), 119–20.

to do with King Agag; a king's ransom is perhaps the most obvious goal in leaving him alive). In God's sight, however, obedience is better than sacrifice. Doing what God says is better than creatively attempting to produce our own plan to serve him. For this act of disobedience, Saul was abandoned by God and rejected (1 Sam. 15:28).

So for Mordecai, whose genealogy links him to King Saul's family (see Esth. 2:5), to bow to Haman, a descendant of King Agag's family, was just too much to swallow. It would have seemed to be giving in to a hated enemy, whom God had cursed. Bowing to King Ahasuerus, the pagan authority set over God's people by God on account of their sin, was one thing; bowing to Haman was another thing altogether.

Further evidence for this interpretation comes in the ensuing events: "Then the king's servants who were at the king's gate said to Mordecai, 'Why do you transgress the king's command?' And when they spoke to him day after day and he would not listen to them, they told Haman, in order to see whether Mordecai's words would stand, for he had told them that he was a Jew" (Esth. 3:3–4). Mordecai presumably recounted the history of his people to the other servants of the king when they challenged him over his repeated refusal to bow to Haman. This rationale explains why, when they finally reported him to Haman for his insubordination, Mordecai's Jewishness was a key element of their report.

MORDECAI AND DANIEL'S FRIENDS

Not for the first time, the text of Esther invites us to compare the characters in its story with those in the Book of Daniel. Earlier we saw how Daniel and Esther were both offered the king's food and how very different their responses were from one another. Daniel's three friends also refused to bow the knee at the king's command, though in their case it was not a matter of bowing to an official of the king, but to a huge golden idol (Dan. 3). In their case, obedience to God left them no choice: whether God delivered them or not, they could not in good conscience bow before this idol (Dan. 3:17–18). The issue was black and white; they would burn before they would turn.

In comparison to Daniel's grand act of defiance, Mordecai's stand, while at one level justifiable enough in its motivation, seems to latch onto a relatively secondary issue. It was an issue involving shades of gray, rather than black and white, the kind of question over which faithful believers might come to different conclusions. It is not that Mordecai was being totally unreasonable in his reluctance to bow to Haman, but we wonder whether *this* was the right issue for making a stand. Think how many other compromises Mordecai has made in order to remain alive and employed in the Persian court!

Indeed, Mordecai worked so hard to fit in as a good citizen of the empire that when we hear the Jewish exiles described as those whose laws are different from those of every other people and who do not obey the king (Esth. 3:8), we feel that Mordecai, at least, was being grossly misrepresented. Even though the charge *should* have been true of all of God's people, Mordecai was far from being an obstinate standout. He showed little enough concern over the ethical issues involved in his cousin Esther being taken into the harem of the Gentile king, with its defiling food and corrupting practices. In fact, he was the one who insisted that far from being in the least bit different from other peoples, Esther should entirely conceal her Jewishness. He was no Shadrach, Meshach, or Abednego; he had been a good servant of the empire, quietly obeying all of the other laws of the king, committed to fitting in. Yet now bowing to Haman was a bridge too far. Here he stood and could do no other, his conscience captive to a higher call. Is it better that he had discovered some convictions late than never to have found any at all? Perhaps, but Mordecai's line in the sand was still drawn over what seems to have been a relatively secondary issue.[2]

All too often that is true of us as well. Jesus complained about the Pharisees of his day that they swallowed camels but strained out gnats (Matt. 23:24). What a vivid picture of many of our churches! We are expert gnat-strainers, sieving out with precision the wrong movies, the inappropriate clothes and hairstyles, the sinful styles of music, any minor deviancies from traditional church practice, wherever and whenever we encounter them. Yet at the same time we may easily tolerate in ourselves and those around us camel-sized sins, such as gossip about others, or pride in our own accomplishments, or prayerlessness. We won't bow the knee to Haman, come what may, but we will easily fall for many greater sins.

2. Compare Michael Fox's nuanced assessment of Mordecai's character, which evidences a similar unease (*Character and Ideology in the Book of Esther*, 2nd ed. [Grand Rapids: Eerdmans, 2001], 192–93).

35

This is not to say that we should let the gnats slide down our throats unchallenged. Jesus did not mean that we should become careless about what we watch, or about how we conduct ourselves before a watching world. Mordecai was not necessarily wrong to refuse to bow before Haman. But let's major on the majors. There were perhaps other places where Mordecai should have first started to exercise his newfound convictions. We might say to Mordecai, "Get a sense of priorities. Don't shoot flies with cannonballs!"

The Complications of Sin

Bowing to Haman was only a secondary issue. Furthermore, it was an issue only because of past failure on the part of God's people. If King Saul had carried out his commission properly in the first place, there wouldn't have been any Agagites left to threaten his descendants. This is a perennial problem. Past sins have a way of coming back repeatedly to haunt us, and sometimes our children after us. How many difficult ethical decisions, over which we agonize for hours, wouldn't even be confronting us were it not for our past sins? People's lives can become horribly complicated to the point where the wisdom of Solomon is needed to know how to proceed. Yet in many cases, the most substantial complications come as the direct byproducts of past sins.

Once the complications begin, they tend to proliferate. So it was for Mordecai. It didn't take long before Mordecai's behavior was brought to Haman's attention. Mordecai's associates were interested to see what their mutual boss would think of his behavior (Esth. 3:4). They don't seem to have had a particular grudge against Mordecai, or to have been looking for an excuse to get him in trouble. On the contrary, they first tried to talk to Mordecai personally, and only when that approach failed did they go to Haman (3:4). Whatever their intentions, though, the result of their report was a quick change for the worse in Mordecai's prospects: "And when Haman saw that Mordecai did not bow down or pay homage to him, Haman was filled with fury. But he disdained to lay hands on Mordecai alone. So, as they had made known to him the people of Mordecai, Haman sought to destroy all the Jews, the people of Mordecai, throughout the whole kingdom of Ahasuerus" (Esth. 3:5–6).

The Persian Empire was normally relatively tolerant of ethnic minorities and their sensibilities—this was one of the reasons why it was attractive to many of the Jews to stay there rather than return to Jerusalem. However, that famed tolerance was not in evidence in this case. Mordecai soon discovered that although the empire may seem superficially benign and tolerant, it can turn nasty in short order. If we stand out from the crowd and stand up against the empire, we had better be ready for consequences when the empire strikes back, as Vashti had discovered.

Haman scorned a simple revenge upon Mordecai as a personal enemy. Eliminating a single individual was far too small a payback for his wounded vanity. Instead, he planned an end to all of Mordecai's people throughout the empire. Mordecai's stand for truth would have repercussions not just in his own life but also in those of his family, his friends, and his community (Esth. 3:6). The whole people group would have to pay for the actions of a single individual.

This remains a reality in many parts of the world. There are powerful enemies who wish to harm Christians, and we can't always count on the empire bailing us out. Christians who stand up for their faith may suffer not merely the loss of their own goods, but in some cases, they are forced to watch as their loved ones suffer for their commitment to the cause of the gospel. Does that mean that we should not make a stand for the gospel? By no means. There are times when we all need to stand up and be counted. However, it does mean that we need to count the cost carefully and pick our battles wisely.

The reason that this conflict is so often part of our earthly experience as Christians is that there is a hidden spiritual conflict that has been going on since the beginning of the world. Haman's enmity toward God's people was merely the latest manifestation of Satan's ongoing warfare against the people of God. The struggle for the hearts and minds of mankind that began in the garden continues on throughout time and space, and those who belong to the people of God will frequently feel the assaults of the Evil One. Our expectation of life ought to be of a constant spiritual battle in which unseen spiritual adversaries are constantly ranged against us, against whom we need to be on our guard, protected by the whole armor of God (see Eph. 6:10–20).

HAMAN'S PLAN

Having decided on a plan to eliminate the Jewish people, Haman needed to put it into action. The first thing to do was to consult the fates to find the most suitable date for this massacre. So Haman held a lottery to determine when the ugly deed would take place: "In the first month, which is the month of Nisan, in the twelfth year of King Ahasuerus, they cast Pur (that is, they cast lots) before Haman day after day; and they cast it month after month till the twelfth month, which is the month of Adar" (Esth. 3:7). Haman's plan to destroy an entire people group could not be carried out on his own authority, either. In order to make it work, he needed the compliance of King Ahasuerus. Not that such permission was hard to come by. The empire could be manipulated by a skilled political operator, its laws used to oppress and destroy. All that was needed was for those who should have been in charge to stand by and let it happen:

> Then Haman said to King Ahasuerus, "There is a certain people scattered abroad and dispersed among the peoples in all the provinces of your kingdom. Their laws are different from those of every other people, and they do not keep the king's laws, so that it is not to the king's profit to tolerate them. If it please the king, let it be decreed that they be destroyed, and I will pay 10,000 talents of silver into the hands of those who have charge of the king's business, that they may put it into the king's treasuries." So the king took his signet ring from his hand and gave it to Haman the Agagite, the son of Hammedatha, the enemy of the Jews. And the king said to Haman, "The money is given to you, the people also, to do with them as it seems good to you." (Esth. 3:8–11)

So why did Ahasuerus allow Haman to pass his decree? In the first place, he didn't care enough to find out what was really going on. Haman's description of the problem was remarkably vague: there is a certain group of people who keep to themselves, have their own laws, and do not obey the laws of the king. The quality that was attractive in the imperial drinking cups—that every one should be different—was apparently a drawback for ethnic groups. The Israelites had committed the ultimate sin against the empire: the sin of not being assimilated. So, as Haman went on to add, "It is not to the king's profit to tolerate them" (Esth. 3:8).[3] Apparently, Ahasuerus never even inquired who the people were or what exactly it was costing him to leave them alone. As in chapter 1, where he asked what

---

3. The English "tolerate them," that, is "leave them alone," barely captures the theological overtones of the Hebrew hiphil of *nuah*, which can also mean "to give them rest." God, the Great King, is the one who really gives his people rest, as key texts such as Deut. 12:10, Josh. 11:23, and 2 Sam. 7:11 affirm.

should be done according to the law when he had no real interest in legal argument, so too here Ahasuerus cared little for the truth. All he needed was enough reason to do what seemed in his best interest. He was the victim of flimsy logic, the kind of superficial argument that can easily persuade the lazy mind.[4]

Indeed, that point is even clearer when we see the connection between this chapter and chapter 2. Chapter 2 ended with Mordecai saving the king's life by uncovering a plot to kill him, and with this deed being recorded "in the presence of the king" (Esth. 2:23). Then, continuing on into chapter 3, the king promoted . . . *Haman*! How thoughtless of the king not simply to pass over rewarding the one who has saved his life and to promote another, but also carelessly to pass an edict that is designed to result in his death! Ahasuerus didn't think clearly about what was happening, because he didn't really care.

Second, however, Ahasuerus was motivated by simple greed. To put it in the language of contemporary political discourse, "It's the economy, stupid." Haman offered him a vast sum of money, ten thousand talents of silver— more than half of the annual tax revenue of the entire empire. Where Haman proposed to come up with such a vast sum is not clear. It is clear, however, that his motivation was not financial, for even if he personally appropriated all the plunder of the Jews, he would still have been out of pocket a considerable amount. Yet Ahasuerus seemed as unconcerned by that question as he was by any others. When he weighed the potential financial benefit against the cost of signing off to destruction an obscure, unidentified people, there was no contest. The result was that he handed his power over to an evil man, who used it to plot genocide. Meanwhile, the king and his trusted advisor gave the ramifications of the whole matter so little thought that they went off to celebrate the deal with a drink or two (see Esth. 3:15).

WE THE PEOPLE

It is easy to condemn Ahasuerus, but perhaps we should be careful that we don't condemn ourselves in the process. In a democratic political sys-

---

4. Fox, *Character and Ideology*, 173–74. Compare the description of Ahasuerus in C. F. Keil, *Esther*, trans. S. Taylor (Grand Rapids: Baker, 1988 reprint), 306–7.

tem, "we the people" are the ones who possess the signet ring. When we vote, we assign that power to others to exercise for us. How often do we take seriously our responsibility to examine carefully the arguments presented to us by the different political parties? We too may be guilty of being easily deceived by flimsy logic, because we are too lazy to engage in serious thought. We may simply vote our pocketbook, supporting whichever party seems more likely to benefit us personally. Some may not even vote, simply standing by while others assign the power for which we are accountable. We often fail actively to petition those who represent us, making sure that they know our views and the reasons that support them. Insofar as this is true, we can hardly be surprised or shocked if our government passes laws that are repressive toward religion or genocidal toward the unborn. We gave the politicians the signet ring and went off to celebrate, while others paid the price.

Nor is the comparison between ourselves and Ahasuerus apt only on the political front. It also applies in our personal lives. What drives us to do the things that we do? Do we think carefully before we act? Are we driven by gospel-directed logic in all of our decision making? Or have we handed over the signet ring of our lives to the enemy of our souls, who has deceived us through his shallow logic, making us the slave of our appetites? Many have sold their integrity for far less than Ahasuerus's ten thousand talents. We value our honesty less than a few dollars, so we cheat on our income taxes or fail to point it out when the shop assistant gives us the wrong change. We value our morality less than satisfying our appetites, and so we give in to the temptation to lust or gluttony. We are often proud of ourselves because we have not committed any great sins, yet does not the very smallness of our sins sometimes condemn us? How little we have received in return for our integrity! How cheaply we have allowed ourselves to be bought!

GOD AND THE EMPIRE

So the edict for the destruction of God's people was signed, sealed, and delivered to the furthest corners of the empire, in the various languages of the peoples:

Then the king's scribes were summoned on the thirteenth day of the first month, and an edict, according to all that Haman commanded, was written to the king's satraps and to the governors over all the provinces and to the officials of all the peoples, to every province in its own script and every people in its own language. It was written in the name of King Ahasuerus and sealed with the king's signet ring. Letters were sent by couriers to all the king's provinces with instruction to destroy, to kill, and to annihilate all Jews, young and old, women and children, in one day, the thirteenth day of the twelfth month, which is the month of Adar, and to plunder their goods. A copy of the document was to be issued as a decree in every province by proclamation to all the peoples to be ready for that day. The couriers went out hurriedly by order of the king, and the decree was issued in Susa the citadel. And the king and Haman sat down to drink, but the city of Susa was thrown into confusion. (Esth. 3:12–15)

The mail delivery system that had carried the king's fatuous decree declaring men heads in their own households now carried this darker decree with the same haste. The city of Susa was thrown into confusion, showing that not everyone in the empire was against the Jews. But what could be done, now that an edict for their destruction had been sent out, a law of the Medes and Persians, which could not be changed? It was just one of those things. In the same way during World War II, many people in occupied Europe felt helpless to do anything to avert the fate of Jewish friends and neighbors. It was simply the way the empire operated. The lot had been cast, the edict issued. It seemed that nothing could now prevent the impending tragedy.

However, the Persian populace had reckoned without God. Haman was wrong when he thought that the future lay in the stars, to be discerned by the casting of lots. As Proverbs 16:33 puts it: "The lot is cast into the lap, but its every decision is from the LORD." So it transpired. The date selected by lot was far enough away that God's rescue plan had plenty of time to unfold. Similarly, Ahasuerus was wrong when he said to Haman, "The people also [are given to you], to do with them as it seems good to you" (Esth. 3:11). The people were ultimately not his to give into Haman's power. They were God's people, and he would not allow them to be destroyed at the whim of the empire. Proverbs 16 addresses this fundamental reality too:

41

"In his heart a man plans his course, but the LORD determines his steps" (Prov. 16:9 NIV).

THE KING OF LOVE

Ironically, God himself has far more reason to act against us and our families than Ahasuerus did against the Jews. We have not kept God's law. We have refused to bow down before him and submit to him as we ought, giving him the honor that is his by rights as our creator. It is actually true in our case that it is not to God's profit to tolerate us, since we are born cosmic rebels against his goodness and grace. What is more, we have a cosmic enemy, Satan, who would happily present plenty of valid reasons why we should not be allowed to live. The edict for our destruction could legitimately have been signed against us by our Great King. But that is not how God, the true sovereign King, has chosen to deal with us.

Look at what our King has done instead. He has not listened to the case that Satan brings against us. Instead, he has taken his own dear Son, the one who is as precious to him as a signet ring, and has handed him over to his enemies to buffet. God said, in effect, "Satan, do with my Son as seems good to you. Let him be punished for sin—but let his people go! Destroy, kill, annihilate Jesus, for sin must be paid for. Plunder his few goods and distribute them among those who are putting him to death; torture and mock him, execute him on a cross. But as for my people, you shall not touch them."

Here is no shallow logic and lightly considered reasoning. Here is the deepest logic of all, a logic that predates time itself in the eternal counsels of God, whereby the actions of one man—the man Christ Jesus—now have redemptive consequences for his whole people as they place their trust in him. Instead of letters of death winging their way speedily to all corners of the empire in every language, now the gospel of life goes to every tribe and nation in their own tongues. Indeed, as the gospel penetrates our hearts, we ourselves become living letters from God (2 Cor. 3:2–3). We are God's mail delivery system to bring his message of life to our neighbors and to the furthest nations. We carry the aroma of Christ everywhere we go (2 Cor. 2:15).

Who would not gladly bow down before such a King? Who would not prostrate themselves in his presence and go at his command to declare his praises among the nations? We can all gossip the good news to our neighbors and friends; God will call some of us to take that news to the ends of the earth. Sadly, however, Paul reminds us that there are some who remain enemies of the gospel, who will not come and submit to Christ. To them, our message is not the scent of life, but the stench of death (2 Cor. 2:16). To them, this supreme wisdom of God seems like foolishness. How awful it would be to be found amongst those who have scorned Christ!

Ultimately, there are only two classes of people in this world: those who bow to Christ and submit to him with joyful, thankful hearts, and those who refuse to bow and will one day pay the price for their stubborn attachment to their sins. The edict has been signed and sealed by the sovereign Lord of heaven and earth and cannot be changed, for it is based on the fundamental logic that our sins must be paid for, either by ourselves or by Christ in our place.

This means that our silver and gold cannot save us, even if we were to offer as great a sum as Haman offered. Our righteous acts and our best efforts cannot deliver us from the edict's threat. Turning over a new leaf cannot atone for our past sins. Nothing and no one can evade the reality of God's law. We all deserve to die on account of our transgressions. We have all earned the wages of our sin. Death is God's verdict on all who are outside of Christ, whether male or female, young or old, adult or child. But by God's grace, those in Christ have that awful sentence lifted because he has taken their place. To us comes the glorious good news of the free gift of God, which is eternal life in his Son. The law's voice is stilled, its claims met for us by Christ. There is grace that extends as widely as our sins and promises us mercy and acceptance for Christ's sake. What a God we serve! What a gospel we have to declare! What a Christ we follow! As John Newton put it so eloquently:

Let us love and sing and wonder,
  let us praise the Savior's name!
He has hushed the law's loud thunder,
  he has quenched Mount Sinai's flame:

> He has washed us with his blood,
>> he has brought us nigh to God.

If this is so, there are two great surprises in the world: that God has loved us so much, and that we in return continue to love him and trust him so little. May God increasingly press into our hearts the reality of the gospel, until our whole beings burn with passionate love for him!

4

The Dog That Didn't Bark

Esther 4:1—17

*Then Mordecai told them to reply to Esther, "Do not think to
yourself that in the king's palace you will escape any more than
all the other Jews. For if you keep silent at this time, relief and
deliverance will rise for the Jews from another place, but you and
your father's house will perish. And who knows whether you have
not come to the kingdom for such a time as this?" (Esth. 4:13–14)*

*I*n the conclusion to "The Adventure of the Silver Blaze," the
famous detective Sherlock Holmes explained how he had solved
that case by drawing the police inspector's attention to "the curious incident of the dog in the nighttime." Holmes's reference to the dog puz-
zled the inspector since, as he observed, the dog did nothing in the nighttime. But this was precisely the curious incident that Holmes had noticed.
The case was solved by observing that the dog *didn't* bark, even though one
would have expected him to do so.[1]

In a sense, the whole Book of Esther is similarly about the one character
who never appears on stage, never speaks, and is never actually spoken to:
God. Nowhere is that more true than in chapter 4, where Esther must place

---

1. Arthur Conan Doyle, "The Adventure of the Silver Blaze," in *The Complete Adventures of and
Memoirs of Sherlock Holmes* (New York: Bramhall House, 1975), 172–87.

her life in the hands of the unseen, unheard, and unrecognized God. The fate of the whole community lies in the balance. Here is how they responded—but notice what is missing: "And in every province, wherever the king's command and his decree reached, there was great mourning among the Jews, with fasting and weeping and lamenting, and many of them lay in sackcloth and ashes" (Esth. 4:3).

The previous chapter ended with the city of Susa thrown into confusion by Haman's plot. Bad news traveled fast, especially when it was disseminated by the official Persian postal service, and it wasn't long before the Jewish community throughout the empire knew the whole story. They responded by putting on sackcloth and ashes as a sign of mourning, with loud cries, fasting, and weeping. Once again, though, we must be on the lookout for the dog that didn't bark—for what the narrator doesn't tell us, as well as what he does. What normally accompanies such fasting, mourning, sackcloth, and ashes? It is prayer. Even the pagans of Nineveh knew how to repent properly: when Jonah preached to them, they immediately put on sackcloth and ashes, started fasting and calling out mightily to God (see Jonah 3:5–8). In this case, however, the dog didn't bark. For all the sackcloth and ashes and weeping, there is no mention here of prayer.

MORDECAI'S PLAN

Mordecai too mourned the decree: "When Mordecai learned all that had been done, Mordecai tore his clothes and put on sackcloth and ashes, and went out into the midst of the city, and he cried out with a loud and bitter cry. He went up to the entrance of the king's gate, for no one was allowed to enter the king's gate clothed in sackcloth" (Esth. 4:1–2). Even though the empire had turned against him, Mordecai was still carefully law-abiding in everything (except bowing to Haman). He didn't enter the king's gate dressed in sackcloth because that was forbidden under Persian law. Yet instead of crying out to God, Mordecai's first thought was to appeal to the king through Esther. He couldn't go and speak to her directly, sequestered as she was, so he went to the entrance of the king's gate in his sackcloth and ashes, knowing that word would get back to Esther of his condition.

And so it did: "When Esther's young women and her eunuchs came and told her, the queen was deeply distressed. She sent garments to clothe Mordecai, so that he might take off his sackcloth, but he would not accept them. Then Esther called for Hathach, one of the king's eunuchs, who had been appointed to attend her, and ordered him to go to Mordecai to learn what this was and why it was" (Esth. 4:4–5). Esther's maids and eunuchs brought her the news that Mordecai was in mourning, and Esther was greatly troubled. Yet she didn't catch on to the seriousness of the situation immediately. Her first response was to send clothes to Mordecai to take the place of his sackcloth, as if her only concern was to stop her relative making an exhibition of himself, not to deal with whatever issues were causing his distress. Only after Mordecai had refused her clothes did she send her servants to find out why he was mourning.

Notice how isolated Esther had become from the rest of the covenant community. Every Jew from India to Ethiopia was mourning and lamenting Haman's edict, but Esther had no clue. She was apparently the only person in the whole Persian Empire who had not heard the news. Perhaps she didn't have time between her manicures, pedicures, and other beauty treatments to keep up with the local coffee klatch about the fortunes of her own people. Perhaps bad news, like sackcloth, was not permitted inside the king's palace. In addition, since she had done such a good job of concealing her identity, why would anyone think to inform her of the threat to this particular people? In just the same way, when we compromise with the world, we easily find ourselves becoming isolated and distant from God's people and out of touch with God's concerns in the world, just as Esther did.

Esther was not allowed to remain comfortably in the dark for long. Through her messenger,[2] Mordecai informed her of the details of the plot:

> Hathach went out to Mordecai in the open square of the city in front of the king's gate, and Mordecai told him all that had happened to him, and the exact sum of money that Haman had promised to pay into the king's treasuries for the destruction of the Jews. Mordecai also gave him a copy of the written decree issued in Susa for their destruction, that he might show it to Esther and explain it to her and command her to go to the king to beg his favor and plead with him on behalf of her people. (Esth. 4:6–8)

---

2. The narrator's repeated references to the intermediaries who carry the conversation back and forth highlight Esther's isolation (Michael V. Fox, *Character and Ideology in the Book of Esther* [Grand Rapids: Eerdmans, 2001], 59).

47

As in chapter 2, Mordecai's information sources were impeccable: he could both tell Esther everything that went on, down to the exact size of the bribe Haman offered for permission to destroy the Jews, and provide her with a copy of the written text of the edict. But unlike in chapter 2, Mordecai was now powerless to intervene to foil the plot. His purpose in passing the information to Esther was so that she might go to the king to seek his mercy and plead with him for her people. The language he adopts of "begging his favor" and "pleading" is precisely the language of the prayer that would normally accompany fasting and sackcloth (compare Dan. 9:3). Is this, perhaps, why the dog didn't bark? Instead of seeking God's favor and pleading with him for deliverance, by means of prayer, it seems that Mordecai was placing his hopes on an intervention at the human level, with King Ahasuerus.

POINT AND COUNTERPOINT

Esther's response to Mordecai's first request was neutral. She didn't say whether she would or wouldn't go to the king. However, she underlined the risk that such a strategy would involve for her personally:

> And Hathach went and told Esther what Mordecai had said. Then Esther spoke to Hathach and commanded him to go to Mordecai and say, "All the king's servants and the people of the king's provinces know that if any man or woman goes to the king inside the inner court without being called, there is but one law—to be put to death, except the one to whom the king holds out the golden scepter so that he may live. But as for me, I have not been called to come in to the king these thirty days." (Esth. 4:9–11)

According to custom, visitors had to be summoned into the presence of King Ahasuerus; no one could appear unannounced. The penalty for violating this law was death, unless the king extended his scepter in welcome. Everyone knew this, even people from the outlying provinces (see Esth. 4:11). The implication of Esther's reference to these outsiders was, "How much more should you, Mordecai, as a civil servant, know the seriousness of what you are asking!" What is more, Esther hadn't been summoned into the royal presence for thirty days—not a good sign, since doubtless the king had not been sleeping alone. So Esther didn't actually refuse to go, but by reminding

Mordecai of the likely consequences, she implicitly asked him to reconsider his request.

Mordecai was not so easily deterred. His second request to Esther was even stronger: "And they told Mordecai what Esther had said. Then Mordecai told them to reply to Esther, 'Do not think to yourself that in the king's palace you will escape any more than all the other Jews. For if you keep silent at this time, relief and deliverance will rise for the Jews from another place, but you and your father's house will perish. And who knows whether you have not come to the kingdom for such a time as this?' " (Esth. 4:12–14). In other words, Esther should not count on her comfortably isolated position in the royal palace. She too was part of the Jewish community, and her fate was intertwined with theirs. If they were to die, she would likely die too. But the Jewish community would not, in fact, die. Even if Esther were to keep silent, help and deliverance would come from somewhere else. If she didn't act to help her community, though, she would be judged for failing to do her part and would suffer the consequences. But if she did intervene, things might perhaps turn out well after all. As Mordecai said, "Who knows whether you have not come to the kingdom for such a time as this?"[3]

Because we are familiar with the end of the story, we are apt to see the answer to this question as obvious. Would Esther be in such a position of royalty if God had not raised her up? But given the nature of Esther's rise to prominence through an ethically doubtful marriage to a pagan and the concealing of everything distinctly Jewish about her lifestyle for the past five or six years, the question is real. It is as if someone who has risen up the corporate ladder by shady manipulation of the books, along with neglecting his family and any connection with the church, were to be asked to stand up at a board meeting for his faith over a crucial issue. His response might well be, "Could God really use someone like me after everything I've done—or failed to do?" The surprising answer in Esther's case is yes! God's providence works through all kinds of sinners (which, after all, is the only material he has available).

In his speech, though, Mordecai performed a remarkable feat: he made a request to Esther that was everywhere grounded in the reality and neces-

3. The New International Version reads, "Who knows but that you have come to royal position for such a time as this?" The English Standard Version gives a more optimistic ring to this statement by adding a negative "Who knows whether you have not come to the kingdom for such a time as this?" implying a positive outcome, but the Hebrew is entirely neutral.

sity of God's intervention, but in the process he completely avoided mentioning that fact. Consider: from where else would help arise if Esther didn't step forward? Mordecai had no plan B, nor did anyone else. There were no other highly placed Jews who could intervene, and a secular universe would have no interest in or infallible commitment to the preservation of the Jewish people. If there were no God, why should the Amalekites not win in the end through the agency of Haman the Agagite? A meaningless world would have no guarantee of a happy ending. The future of Mordecai's people was assured only if the God who had inextricably linked his name to his people in the ancient covenants would provide deliverance for them for the sake of his name. But instead of stating that fact as the ground of confidence, Mordecai said vaguely, "Help will arise from some other place."

In addition, if Esther were to remain silent and the Jews were nonetheless delivered, who would bring the lethal consequences upon Esther of which verse 14 warned? Was Mordecai threatening reprisals from the Jewish community? It is possible that this was his intention, as Josephus thought, but surely it is more likely that the judgment he envisaged would have come directly from God.[4] Once again, though, the divine name remained uninvoked.

Third, when Mordecai said, "Who knows whether you have not come to the kingdom for such a time as this?" he was arguing that there is a meaningful course of history. But who can provide such meaning, except for God himself? Mordecai was saying essentially what Joseph said to his brothers in Genesis 45:5: "God sent me before you to preserve life"—but once again Mordecai does not mention God. God is the unexpressed presupposition of every one of Mordecai's thoughts—but don't miss the significance of the canine failing to give voice. The theological presupposition remains constantly unexpressed, a rhetorical strategy that might make sense if Mordecai had been addressing a pagan audience who didn't share his religious perspectives. However, he was speaking to Esther, a child of the covenant people, who ought to share these presuppositions. He was asking her to put her life on the line in response to his case. If ever there was a time to mention God's

---

4. D. J. A. Clines, *Ezra, Nehemiah, Esther* (New Century Bible Commentary; Grand Rapids: Eerdmans, 1984), 302.

name, surely it was now. Yet the dog still didn't bark, for reasons we will explore in a moment.

ESTHER'S CHOICE

Esther now had a clear and life-changing choice to make. She could no longer live in the blurred shadows of two worlds. Up until now, she had been living as an undercover believer. Inwardly she still regarded herself as part of the covenant community, but outwardly she had become entirely separated from it.[5] To continue to do so was no longer possible. One option would have been to take her privatized faith a step further and deny her connection to the Jewish people completely, trusting the empire to protect her against itself. The only other alternative was to identify herself publicly with the covenant community in its hour of need and risk her life in an attempt to save her people. Neither option held out much hope. If she appeared uninvited before the king, she stood a good chance of finding herself hanging (like Bigthan and Teresh, the two eunuchs who had plotted against Ahasuerus). On the other hand, if she trusted in the empire and survived alone, it would mean complete and final separation from her community and from any source of meaning in her life, a slow and lingering death of a different kind.

Faced with these unpalatable alternatives, Esther made her choice: "Then Esther told them to reply to Mordecai, 'Go, gather all the Jews to be found in Susa, and hold a fast on my behalf, and do not eat or drink for three days, night or day. I and my young women will also fast as you do. Then I will go to the king, though it is against the law, and if I perish, I perish.' Mordecai then went away and did everything as Esther had ordered him" (Esth. 4:15–17). So Esther agreed to show solidarity with the Jewish community. A mark of this new connection was that she asked Mordecai to gather the Jews in Susa together to fast for her for three days (Esth. 4:16). She and her maids would do likewise, and then she would go in to see the king. From the viewpoint of human policy, this was counter-intuitive, to say the least. The king liked his women well-fed (see 2:9) and looking their best, and three

---

5. This is stressed in the Hebrew of Esther 4:13, where the prospect of her escaping alone "out of" the Jews is expressed with *min*, a preposition that "expresses primarily separation and distance" (Paul Joüon, *A Grammar of Biblical Hebrew* [Rome: Editrice Pontificio Istituto Biblio, 1991], 133e).

days of fasting would hardly enhance that side of Esther's appeal. Since she was not allowed to speak to the king unless he first chose to receive her, all she had to offer him was her appearance. However, now at least the whole community would be involved in this appeal, silently rooting for Esther to succeed.

Esther's fast makes sense only as a community appeal to God to do the miraculous and enable her to find favor with King Ahasuerus. Fasting in the Bible is a means of expressing sorrow over sin and dependence upon God. Community solidarity would do Esther no good without divine intervention on her side. Under the circumstances, therefore, one might have anticipated her to utter a prayer of the kind Nehemiah offered along with his fasting and mourning, seeking success and favor in the sight of the king (Neh. 1:4–11). If ever there was a time to pray such a prayer, this was it. But once again, the dog remained silent.

Esther's only recorded words were "I will go to the king, though it is against the law, and if I perish, I perish" (Esth. 4:16). However, the Hebrew construction makes it clear that she is not talking about death simply as one possible outcome of her obedience to Mordecai, but as an almost inevitable outcome of choosing that course.[6] As the commentator Lewis Paton put it, this is the "despairing expression of submission to the inevitable . . . she goes as one would submit to an operation, because there is a chance of escaping death that way."[7] The same attitude of despairing resignation is evident in Jacob's similar cry—"If I am bereaved of my children, I am bereaved"—in Genesis 43:14. In that instance, Jacob was sending Benjamin down to Egypt in the tender (?) care of his brothers, not expecting ever to see him again but knowing that he had no alternative but to let him go. If Benjamin went with his brothers, there was little chance of his returning, but if they all stayed in Canaan, they would all certainly die. So too Esther's speech is a statement of resignation to the inevitable, rather than one of robust faith, a whimper rather than a bark.

---

6. For the Hebrew conjunction *ka'asher* as an expression of resignation, see F. Brown, S. R. Driver, and C. A. Briggs, *A Hebrew and English Lexicon of the Old Testament* (London: Oxford University Press, 1907), 455b. See also the comprehensive discussion in Charles D. Harvey, *Finding Morality in the Diaspora? Moral Ambiguity and Transformed Morality in the Books of Esther* (Berlin and New York: de Gruyter, 2003), 34–35.

7. Lewis Paton, *A Critical and Exegetical Commentary on the Book of Esther* (International Critical Commentary; New York: Scribner, 1908), 226.

(RE-)LEARNING HOW TO BARK

This portrayal of Mordecai and Esther and the Jewish community with them as dogs who have forgotten how to bark—people whose entire lives are built around theological presuppositions whose existence and implications they studiously ignore—is at odds with the way many have read the book. In their desire to rescue Esther from herself, some fill in the "woof" for Esther, drawing out the implicit theology of the chapter that God is working in history and turning her into a bold heroine, eager to seize the moment for God. Others neuter the dog altogether, making the book an entirely secular tale in which the Jews survive through their inner strength and potential for self-help.[8]

Neither approach does justice to the author's literary artistry, which in fact highlights a very real conundrum that pastors wrestle with on a weekly basis. Simply put, it is this: "How can people who confess an orthodox creed week after week so easily and completely lose track of the implications of that theology whenever problems emerge in daily life?" Mordecai's worldview may have been based on a solid theology, but he had difficulty connecting that theology to the issues of everyday life. If we know people, and the motions of our own hearts, we will not have to travel back to ancient Susa for examples of this phenomenon. In times of crisis, for all our orthodox theology, our own first response is frequently the whimper of resignation or human strategy rather than the bark of robust faith in God. We believe in God, but in practice react to life's crises as if we were virtual atheists.

The point of contact between Mordecai's world and ours comes at the moment when the hostile nature of this world becomes clear. This is a world at enmity with God and at enmity with his people, as Jesus reminded us:

> If the world hates you, know that it has hated me before it hated you. If you were of the world, the world would love you as its own; but because you are not of the world, but I chose you out of the world, therefore the world hates you. Remember the word that I said to you: "A servant is not greater than his master." If they persecuted me, they will also persecute you. If they kept my word, they will also keep yours. But all these things they will do to you on

8. See Fox, *Character and Ideology*, 241.

account of my name, because they do not know him who sent me. (John 15:18–21)

Our experience of this opposition will sometimes take the form of personal attack, verbally or physically, as it did for the Jewish community in the Persian Empire. In a fallen world, though, it also includes the assaults of disease and disaster, in all their monstrous shapes. It includes unemployment and cancer, hurricane and miscarriage, divorce, unfaithfulness, and death. This world is not a safe home, but hostile terrain.

At times like these, the reassuring shades of gray around us resolve into disconcertingly sharp black and white contours. When life-threatening illness strikes, or when we are faced with the choice between compromise and losing our job, or when someone we love abandons us, do we live out the theology we proclaim? Do we remind ourselves that God is in control of all things and has promised to work all things together for his glory and our good?

At times like these we can no longer pretend to serve God *and* our idols. Now we must choose which refuge we will take in the midst of the storm. These are the defining moments that both uncover and shape who we are at our deepest levels. Without them, we might have been able to persist in our comfortably compromised ways, just as Esther may have hoped to live out her life comfortably concealing her true identity. In the harsh light of hard problems, however, we need to choose whose we are and whom we serve—and the nature of those choices cannot but be public. In the midst of the storm, everyone will see where we are seeking refuge. So how do we respond when reality presses itself in upon us? Like Mordecai and the Jewish community of Susa, we need to fall to our knees in fasting, come together, and identify ourselves as part of the community of God's people. And we need to add the missing "bark" of prayer. We need to call directly on God to bring the presence of his Spirit into our situation of need.

FASTING AND PRAYER

In biblical times, fasting was a normal means of expressing contrition for sin and dependence upon God in the face of difficulty, whether personal or national. It was also a statement that there is more to this life than mere physical existence, a public disavowal of the philosophy "Eat, drink, and be merry, for tomorrow we die." Fasting continues to be an appropriate response for God's people to personal or corporate problems. When we face overwhelming difficulties in our lives, or in our churches, it is appropriate for us to fast and seek the Lord's face (Deut. 9:18; Ezra 10:6; Neh. 1:4). Sometimes it is good for us to fast as individuals (2 Sam. 12:16–23; Ps. 35:13), and sometimes as a community of God's people (Acts 13:2), reminding ourselves that our normal state of life in this world is not fullness but hunger, and appealing for God to grant us what we so desperately need.

We should not just appeal to God implicitly, however, through abstaining from food, as if fasting were simply another technique to accomplish our desires. Rather, we should appeal to the Great King explicitly through humble and persistent prayer, seeking his favor more fervently than a merely human solution to life's problems. Again, fasting can be an aid to this. If we find that we are forgetful to pray for a particular need, fasting will remind us to pray over and over through the alarm clock of our hunger pangs! If we find ourselves short of time for prayer, fasting creates space to pray in the time we would otherwise have spent eating.

So why do we not fast? Perhaps it is because we have comfortably isolated ourselves from the grim realities of the world around us. The Jewish community was not fasting either until the beginning of chapter 4. They didn't see the need to fast while life was going well for most of them. Being assimilated into the empire, to a greater or lesser degree, was a successful strategy. But in an instant, their world was turned upside down. Or, more accurately, their perception of the world was suddenly re-oriented in line with reality. The empire didn't suddenly become a hostile place at that point. Rather, the latent hostility that was always lurking just below the surface broke out against them, and so they fasted.

Even when most of her compatriots had begun to fast, though, Esther herself was still oblivious of their danger and need. Living in the king's palace, she was comfortably isolated from her community and either didn't know or didn't care what was happening to her people. It was only when Mordecai brought the reality of the threat home to her own boudoir that she finally put aside the fattening portions that the empire had provided and joined her sisters and brothers in a communal fast.

Esther's actions raise serious questions for each of us to answer. Am I still blind to the true nature of the world and the plight of many of God's people around me? Do I know enough about what is going on in the world to mourn and lament the situation of God's persecuted people? Often we do not know the burdens of our brothers and sisters in the church well enough or care about them deeply enough to fast and pray. We do not even know enough about what is going on in our own hearts to mourn and lament our sin. We are so blinded by our own good lives that we neither hear nor heed the cries of God's people. If our eyes are opened to the true nature of our world, then surely we will find plenty of reasons to fast and cry out to God.

In fact, our actions will reveal whom we regard as our true community. When those around us in school or at work mock Christianity and we remain silent, we deny that we are part of God's people by our silence, effectively declaring instead that the world is our true community. When we judge ourselves and others according to the world's values of what is fashionable and desirable, we declare that the world and not the people of God is our true community. What do our speech and our silence say about who our people are?

FASTING AND ACTING

By itself, however, all the fasting in the world would accomplish nothing for God's covenant people in Persia. What they needed was a mediator. They needed someone who was willing and able to go and plead their case where they could not go, into the presence of the king. They could not appear in the king's presence to seek mercy for themselves; someone else had to do it for them.

Esther therefore had to act as well as to fast. She needed to take her life in her hands, risking everything for her people. She did so without any explicit promises from God to protect her, or to bring about a successful conclusion to her mission. The question, "Who knows if you have risen to royal position for just such a time as this?" could just as well have been answered in the negative as the positive. There was no voice from heaven commanding Esther to act, no burning bush to convince her of God's call, no miraculous signs that she could perform to persuade the king to let her people go. Perhaps God would remain hidden and allow many of his people to die, including Esther herself, as he has on other occasions in history. There are no guarantees of success when we stand up for God, if success means getting what we want.

Yet at another level, Esther's success was guaranteed. God had committed himself to maintain a people for himself, not so that they could be comfortable, but so that they could bring him glory. No matter what sinful paths had led Esther to where she was, she was undeniably now in a position to give God glory by publicly identifying with her people and, if necessary, laying down her life through that identification. She could glorify God by perishing as well as by convincing the king. It was up to God how to glorify himself through Esther's obedience, whether by delivering the people through her or allowing her to be martyred in his service, but he would be glorified one way or another.

It is the same for us, when we step out in faith, however weak and trembling. We cannot know ahead of time how God will choose to use us. He may heal our diseases, transform our breaking marriages, and plant thriving ministries through us. Or he may sustain us in obedient submission to him as our earthly hopes are dashed and our lives poured out for apparently little purpose. Either way, though, we have the guarantee that he will use even our faint faith as the means of bringing glory to himself. With this assurance we can add to Esther's cry: "If I perish, I perish—simply let me perish in a way that brings glory to God."

A BETTER MEDIATOR

If it is true that a mediator was needed to intercede with King Ahasuerus, how much more do we need a mediator to intercede for us with God, the Great King. The Lord is utterly different from Ahasuerus in nearly every respect, for he is a wise, kind, just, and faithful ruler. Nonetheless, he is the great King of kings, the sovereign ruler of the universe, against whom we have rebelled. Fallen, sinful people cannot therefore simply saunter into his presence, unannounced and uninvited. On the contrary, his edict has gone forth against us, declaring us worthy of death because of our sin. The truth has been disseminated throughout his empire that "the soul who sins shall die" (Ezek. 18:4). His decree is settled and determined, all the more so because it was not formulated in ignorance and haste, but by perfect wisdom before the foundation of the world. Who then will argue our case? Who will come to bring relief and deliverance for us?

The answer is Jesus Christ. The true mediator between God and man, in the fullness of time he took flesh and appeared in this world. Far from being comfortably isolated from his community, as Esther was, Jesus identified with us fully. He took on the form of a servant and lived as one of us in this fallen and sin-sick world. Then, after he had completed his life of perfect obedience, he went in before the Father, knowing that he was not just risking his life but laying it down. For him, "If I perish, I perish" meant not just the potential probability of death, but the absolute certainty of the cross. It was not just a swift blow from an ax that he faced, but the full torment of hell. It was no light burden. The sweat fell like drops of rain from his brow in Gethsemane as he faced up to his great encounter with death. In agony, he sought some other way: "My Father, if it be possible, let this cup pass from me!" (Matt. 26:39). But there was no other way in which our sin could be judged and we could be saved. So he drank the cup of God's wrath down to its last drops for you and for me. Through his death, we have received life.

Raised from the dead, Jesus Christ once again appears before the Father, where he continues to intercede for us. "Father," he says, "sustain this one through her battle with cancer. Give this one strength to stand up for what he believes and endure the cost." Now, though, he is no longer alone but accompanied around the throne by a host of glorified saints. These are his people whom he has brought safely through all the trials of this hostile world. Some bear the marks of torture for Christ, others the inner scars of countless spiritual struggles, but all are now triumphant in him, redeemed by his blood.

Nor is this Jesus suffering any longer. His time of deprivation and abstinence is over. Now in heaven Jesus is already beginning the glorious feast prepared for all those written in the Lamb's book of life. We, however, are still called to fast, for Jesus is not physically present with us right now. Our time of suffering continues. Remember what Jesus said to John's disciples when they asked him why his disciples weren't fasting. He said, "Can the wedding guests mourn as long as the bridegroom is with them? The days will come when the bridegroom is taken away from them, and then they will fast" (Matt. 9:15). So we fast at present, since Jesus is no longer with us in his physical presence. Now we experience the pain and fallenness of this world in full measure and cry out to God in the midst of our pain and doubt. But this world is not the ultimate measure of reality. A day is coming when we will no longer fast. When Jesus comes back, there will be no more fasting, as well as no more tears, no more crying, and no more pain. There will be feasting forever in the presence of the King for all of the King's redeemed people. And then, at last, we shall share in his glory and taste the fullness of his goodness.

5

MEEKNESS AND SUBTLETY

Esther 5:1—14

*And as they were drinking wine after the feast, the king said to
Esther, "What is your wish? It shall be granted you. And what is
your request? Even to the half of my kingdom, it shall be fulfilled."
Then Esther answered, "My wish and my request is: If I have
found favor in the sight of the king, and if it please the king to
grant my wish and fulfill my request, let the king and Haman
come to the feast that I will prepare for them, and tomorrow
I will do as the king has said." (Esth. 5:6–8)*

In the British science fiction series of the same name, Dr. Who
battled a series of terrifying alien menaces. At the conclusion of
each weekly episode, there was always a cliffhanger ending, with
the Doctor or one of his assistants finding themselves in deadly peril just as
the picture faded from view and the theme music sounded out. A whole
week would pass by before viewers could find out how the Doctor would
evade seemingly certain destruction.

The end of Esther 4 provided a similar cliffhanging moment. Esther
declared her commitment to put her life on the line by appearing unsummoned before King Ahasuerus. Humanly speaking, such an act was playing
Russian roulette, for those who appeared before the king without invitation

were liable to immediate execution. This was no empty threat. Contemporary depictions of the Persian king excavated at Persepolis show him seated on his throne holding his scepter, flanked by various officials, including a soldier with an ax.[1] The Jewish community fasted, along with Esther, and we hold our breath. . . .

A CLIFFHANGER RESOLVED

Chapter 5 quickly takes us to the resolution of that tension:

On the third day Esther put on her royal robes and stood in the inner court of the king's palace, in front of the king's quarters, while the king was sitting on his royal throne inside the throne room opposite the entrance to the palace. And when the king saw Queen Esther standing in the court, she won favor in his sight, and he held out to Esther the golden scepter that was in his hand. Then Esther approached and touched the tip of the scepter. (Esth. 5:1–2)

After her three-day fast, Esther dressed in her royal best and presented herself before the king. Against all expectations, she won favor in his sight and he extended the scepter to her in a gesture of recognition and welcome. At this point, we breathe a corporate sigh of relief. The threat of death is now removed: Esther will not die, but live.

Actually, though, in some respects we have breathed too soon. Just as in the *Dr. Who* series, the resolution of the immediate cliffhanger does not mean the complete end of danger. The direct threat to Esther's life from King Ahasuerus may have been defused, but behind that threat was the far greater danger to Esther and her whole community posed by the edict to destroy the Jews. This decree was issued by Haman in the king's name. It had now become a law of the Medes and Persians, which according to custom could not be changed. It would take all of Esther's skill and subtlety to unpick this Gordian knot. In antiquity, the famous knot of Gordius was held to be impossible to untie. According to legend, the man who untied it was destined to become lord of Asia. Alexander the Great was shown the knot and, being

1. See Edwin Yamauchi, *Persia and the Bible* (Grand Rapids: Baker, 1990), 360. The king is either Darius or Xerxes (Ahasuerus).

unable to untie it, proceeded to cut it with his sword. The rest is, as they say, history. But Esther could not and did not adopt nearly such a direct approach.

HOOKING AND PLAYING THE FISH

The difficulty of the task facing her seems to be the reason why Esther did not respond directly to the king's invitation to unburden her heart. The king was doubtless aware of the enormity of the risk Esther had taken in appearing unbidden in his presence. Something important was clearly troubling her, so he invited her to name her request: "What is it, Queen Esther? What is your request? It shall be given you, even to the half of my kingdom" (Esth. 5:3).

Anything Esther asked would be given to her, up to half a kingdom. It might have seemed tempting at first for Esther to lay out her request immediately, while the opportunity was there, but consider the numerous challenges that faced her. First, she was asking for the reversal of an irreversible law, which had been sponsored by the most powerful man in the empire and signed with the king's own signet ring. Granting her request would cost the king ten thousand talents—less than half his empire, to be sure, but as much as half the annual tax revenue of his empire, and so no small sum. Perhaps even worse, though, it would be hard for the king to accede to her request without losing face, since the edict had been officially authorized by his own royal person. Finally, in order to make her request she would have to reveal her hidden Jewish identity, risking a potential backlash from the husband she had been deceiving for the past five years.

Nothing short of a miracle would enable Esther's request to be favorably received, and even though she had spent three days fasting and (implicitly) requesting divine assistance, she was in no position to presume on extraordinary assistance from on high. Unlike Moses and Elijah, she had no dramatic signs and wonders that she could call upon to convince a skeptical audience. Instead, she would have to follow the best strategy she could come up with and rely on God to make it effective in changing the king's heart.

In response to Ahasuerus's invitation to unburden her soul, therefore, Esther merely invited her husband to come to a feast that she was arranging that day, bringing Haman in tow: "And Esther said, 'If it please the king, let the king and Haman come today to a feast that I have prepared for the king'" (Esth. 5:4). Ahasuerus kindly accepted Esther's invitation: "Then the king said, 'Bring Haman quickly, so that we may do as Esther has asked.' So the king and Haman came to the feast that Esther had prepared" (Esth. 5:5). More literally, the king acted "according to the word of Esther." So much for his earlier decree that each man should be master in his own house (see Esth. 1:22)!

At the feast, the king once again invited Esther to reveal her request: "And as they were drinking wine after the feast, the king said to Esther, 'What is your wish? It shall be granted you. And what is your request? Even to the half of my kingdom, it shall be fulfilled'" (Esth. 5:6). Ahasuerus must have recognized that she hadn't risked her life earlier in appearing before him simply in order to get a date for the evening! Once again, it seemed to be a prime opportunity: the wine had been served, the king was in a mood of expansive generosity, again offering Esther anything she desired, up to half his kingdom. Esther seemed almost about to comply, starting to say, "My wish and my request is . . ." (Esth. 5:7). But then she broke off and merely asked the king and Haman to come to another feast the next day, at which all supposedly would be revealed: "If I have found favor in the sight of the king, and if it please the king to grant my wish and fulfill my request, let the king and Haman come to the feast that I will prepare for them, and tomorrow I will do as the king has said" (Esth. 5:8).

Why didn't Esther strike while the iron was hot? Did she simply lose her nerve and so fail to make the request when the opportunity was there? Perhaps, but there is a more likely explanation. Esther was playing the king like a trophy fish, taking her time and not rushing to reel him into her net. She was carefully maneuvering him into a position where he would be virtually obligated to do whatever she asked, without his even being aware that he had been hooked. He had now twice publicly offered to grant Esther whatever she desired, up to half his kingdom. Her response was a study in meekness, an attribute she knew the king valued in women. She began, "If I have found favor in the sight of the king, and if it please the king . . ." (Esth. 5:8),[2] making the king feel as if he were in full control of his fate. Since all she was

2. In her speech, Esther deliberately adopts the more passive idiom "find favor" (*matsa' hen*) rather than the active idiom "win favor" (*nasa' hen*) used by the narrator in verse 2 (Michael V. Fox, *Character and Ideology in the Book of Esther*, 2nd ed. [Grand Rapids: Eerdmans, 2001], 68).

overtly requesting the king to do was to come to another feast the next day, it is hard to see how the king could reasonably have refused her invitation. This is all the more true, since the purpose of the feast was to "do as the king has said"—that is, to reveal her petition. Curiosity alone would have made it hard for the king to stay away.

Yet if the king came to her second feast, he was implicitly agreeing in advance to grant her wish and fulfill her request, whatever it was (Esth. 5:8). If he tried to back out at that point, there would have been three public strikes against him. He would lose a great deal of face if he went back on such a public and repeated promise.[3] It seemed that Esther had laid her plans well and executed them with patience, care, and cunning. All that now remained in this desperate game of chess was to wait until the pieces were in exactly the right position before making the decisive move that would (hopefully) checkmate Haman. It might still be a long shot, but she had done everything in her power to give it the best chance of success.

HAMAN'S HIGHS AND LOWS

Haman, meanwhile, was as unaware as the king that he was being played. He went out from the feast in high spirits, not just from the effects of the alcohol but also from the intoxicating effects of prestige. What Haman craved above all things was not simply significance, but rather being *seen* to be significant. It was quite an accolade, he thought, that he alone was summoned to this unprecedented and intimate party with the king and queen. Surely his star was now rising to unparalleled heights.

It didn't take much to spoil his happy mood, however, because on the way out of the banquet Haman saw Mordecai sitting calmly at his desk: "And Haman went out that day joyful and glad of heart. But when Haman saw Mordecai in the king's gate, that he neither rose nor trembled before him, he was filled with wrath against Mordecai" (Esth. 5:9). Once again Mordecai failed to show Haman proper respect by rising before him or trembling with fear in view of the recent edict. Haman's failure to instill either fear or respect in his enemy pricked his bubble and turned his joy into wrath.

3. D. J. A. Clines, *Ezra, Nehemiah, Esther* (New Century Bible Commentary; Grand Rapids: Eerdmans, 1984), 305.

Haman's whole world revolved around his fragile ego. When it was stroked (as when the invitation came to Esther's party), he felt blessed, even though nothing in the real world had actually changed. His power had not actually increased, yet Haman rejoiced. Likewise, his power was not really diminished by Mordecai's refusal to bow, yet Haman was incensed by it. His emotional strings were being pulled by his idol, which was public respect. When that idol was fed, he felt good; but when his idol was challenged, it led him to malice and anger, the same malice that caused his earlier decree to eliminate the Jewish people. His joy and his anger were simply the outward expressions of his heart's idolatry. For now, however, he simply bided his time: "Nevertheless, Haman restrained himself and went home, and he sent and brought his friends and his wife Zeresh" (Esth. 5:10).

Once home, Haman set about the task of boosting his dented ego. He summoned his friends and his wife and required them to listen to a lengthy recitation of his exploits: "And Haman recounted to them the splendor of his riches, the number of his sons, all the promotions with which the king had honored him, and how he had advanced him above the officials and the servants of the king" (Esth. 5:11). His wealth, his sons, his promotions—all of these were listed in detail, even though this was all old news for the audience (presumably his wife, for one, had not forgotten how many sons they had!). Then he announced the plum piece of news: "Even Queen Esther let no one but me come with the king to the feast she prepared. And tomorrow also I am invited by her together with the king" (Esth. 5:12). Haman alone, in company of the king, had been summoned to Esther's banquet that day and was invited to another of the same tomorrow. But as far as Haman was concerned, even this was of no consolation as long as Mordecai refused to worship him. "Yet all this is worth nothing to me," Haman said, "so long as I see Mordecai the Jew sitting at the king's gate" (Esth. 5:13).

COUNSELING HAMAN

Haman is a case study in what happens in our hearts when our idols are challenged.[4] He had made public recognition his idol, and the result was

4. For a stimulating study of the impact that idolatries have on our hearts, see Edward T. Welch, *When People Are Big and God Is Small: Overcoming Peer Pressure, Codependency, and the Fear of Man* (Phillipsburg, NJ: P&R, 1997).

that as long as he was receiving adulation he felt great. However, when the achievement of his goal was challenged, he responded by lashing out in rage and seeking to feed his idol through boasting. Even though he still possessed unparalleled power in the kingdom, that wasn't enough. There was a void at the center of his life that no amount of success could fill.

Haman is an unsympathetic character in the story with little to make us feel sorry for him, so we are unlikely to feel his pain. Yet at this moment in the story he was crying out for someone to guide him and direct him as to how he should handle his overpowering negative emotions. What he needed was wise biblical counsel. This is a situation with which we can all identify, whether in dealing with our own hearts or seeking to help others work through anger issues in their lives. It may be salutary, therefore, to use this case study to advance our own counseling skills. What would we have said to Haman, had we been his wife, or one of his friends? What words might have led his life in a different, more positive direction?

A skilled counselor would have advised Haman to trace back his negative and positive emotions and discover what was driving his life. His rage was an opportunity to discern the condition of his heart, to uncover what was filling the God-shaped hole in the center of his life. What was it in life that made him feel overwhelmingly joyful? What were the events that triggered such inordinate anger in his heart? If Haman had been as little in touch with his emotions as many men, then on most days he might not have been able to give an answer. Looking back over that particular day, however, Haman wouldn't have had far to search to discern his need for public recognition.

Once he had recognized his idolatry, Haman might have been shown how the reign of his idol was being challenged by the day's events. He could have been directed to repent of that idolatry by seeing how the gospel answered his need for true significance, the kind of value in life that is not challenged by what people think of us. He could have been introduced to the God who loves his people unconditionally, in spite of their sin. He could have been shown that he needed to abandon seeing the world revolving around him and his successes and instead see a world revolving around God, in which his achievements had value as a means of bringing God the glory he deserved.

Such counsel might have saved Haman's soul, and perhaps even his life, if he had indeed been willing to turn from his idol to the true and living God. Unfortunately, Haman did not seek biblical counseling, but rather was

66

content to receive the wisdom of his wife and his friends. Their counsel was simply to "go with the feeling" and give full vent to his rage: "Then his wife Zeresh and all his friends said to him, 'Let a gallows fifty cubits high be made, and in the morning tell the king to have Mordecai hanged upon it. Then go joyfully with the king to the feast'" (Esth. 5:14). This idea pleased Haman, and he had the gallows made. But the problem with this advice was that it sought to eliminate the negative emotion of anger by feeding Haman's idolatry rather than by mortifying it. It sought to bolster Haman's need to feel important by going for a "giant size" vengeance.

Even superficial thought should have shown that this solution would never deal with Haman's underlying problems. Indeed, the very size of the gallows would have unintentionally elevated Mordecai to a position of significance: his very death would have drawn all eyes to him (and away from Haman) in a way that a smaller gallows would not have done. Inevitably that is what happens when we seek to deal with our idolatries by feeding them rather than by starving them. We end up emptier than ever, in even greater bondage than before, and it is only a matter of time before something else reignites our negative emotions. The counsel Haman received led him nowhere.

The idea of counseling Haman is an exercise in historical imagination. Haman is beyond our help, and would probably never have received such counsel, even had it been available in a city in which God's own people had forgotten many basic biblical truths. But our purpose in pursuing this idea is essentially practical. Our hearts face the same temptation to bow to idols, whose identities are likewise most easily exposed by analyzing our strongest emotions, both good and bad. What is it that causes us to be angry out of all proportion to the offense? There is a clue that one of our idols is being threatened. What is it that makes us feel an unusually strong sense of achievement? It may be one of our idols being stroked. Our strong emotions are clues enabling us to read our own hearts better. Though we cannot counsel Haman, certainly we can counsel ourselves and others who find themselves in similar turmoil.

ESTHER'S SUBTLETY AND GOD'S SOVEREIGNTY

This chapter also shows us that dealing with the empire sometimes demands great subtlety. Some portions of the Bible might seem to suggest that a simple, straightforward, direct approach is always the best. "Dare to be a Daniel" and let the chips fall where they may. And often that *is* the best approach. However, there are times in the providence of God when a more indirect approach will yield greater results. A direct confrontation isn't always the wisest response to conflict with the world. Sometimes subtlety and meekness are more effective in the long run.

In the light of Esther's dilemma, it is instructive to consider Peter's counsel to the wives of unbelievers: "Likewise, wives, be subject to your own husbands, so that even if some do not obey the word, they may be won without a word by the conduct of their wives—when they see your respectful and pure conduct" (1 Peter 3:1–2). Peter here counsels these women not to go in with verbal pyrotechnics or outward adornment (royal robes?) but rather to win their husbands over with holiness, gentleness, and meekness. There are times to be direct and times to be indirect.

That having been said, however, it was not Esther's subtlety alone that ultimately transformed the situation. God used Esther's subtlety, to be sure, but he also used Mordecai's stubborn refusal to bow and Haman's self-centeredness to bring each protagonist to the exact place where he wanted them. Regardless of her intent, Esther's invitation to Haman puffed up his pride. Mordecai's presence at the gate when Haman went home, and his continued refusal to bow the knee, pricked Haman's happy mood. The counsel of Haman's wife and his friends in response to his inner turmoil led him to build the massive gallows and seek an audience with the king early the next morning. All of these events were necessary for the unfolding of God's plan. If Esther jumped the gun, as it were, and presented her request too soon, the king's memory of Mordecai's act in saving him would not yet have been stirred. Nor would the gallows yet have been constructed on which to hang Haman with such perfect poetic justice. It was undoubtedly God's plan for the whole scenario to play out the way it did, so that he could bring the individual conflict between Haman and Mordecai to its perfect denouement before the wider conflict was also resolved.

Notice that God's plan in this case was worked out without thunder and lightning, or a parting of the sea in order to save his people. No one was delivered from a fiery furnace or miraculously preserved in a den of lions. God's work here is every bit as subtle as Esther's. It proceeds by unobtrusively nudging each of the characters in the story to behave exactly in accord with their own wishes and temperaments, while at the same time they do exactly what he has decreed.

So God's plan proceeds in the world around us. It goes forward, not in spite of our desires and inclinations, whether sinful or righteous, but precisely through shaping us to be the people we are. A little girl once asked: "If God is in control of everything, does that mean that he plays with us, like we play with the dolls in the dolls' house?" The answer is yes and no. Yes, God is in control of all things and he works all things according to his holy will for his glory and our good (Rom. 8:28). However, we are not passive and helpless in this process, like the dolls in the dolls' house. On the contrary, we do exactly according to our own desires and temperaments. God's sovereignty operates in such a way that our freedom and responsibility to act are not compromised, yet the end result is still exactly what God has purposed from the beginning. Just as Esther, Mordecai, Haman, and Ahasuerus were not compelled to act contrary to their wills, but still did exactly what God had planned, so too we are never mere robots, yet we see God accomplishing his purposes in and through us. It was this truth that led the apostle Paul to write: "work out your own salvation with fear and trembling, for it is God who works in you, both to will and to work for his good pleasure" (Phil. 2:12–13). What is more, God achieves his perfect goals not just through our best intentions and most self-sacrificing acts, but even through our greatest sins and compromises.

THE WELCOMING KING

Once again, when we consider the empire of Ahasuerus and the kingdom of God side by side, we cannot but be struck at the contrast. Praise God that we serve an altogether different king than the one that Esther knew. Approaching God is not like approaching Ahasuerus, with our knees trembling and hearts wondering whether we will survive the encounter. Who can predict how such a capricious ruler will respond? One day suppliants might find favor in his eyes, and he would welcome them in; the next day it would be "off with their heads"—literally!

Our God, however, invites us to come into his presence regularly, indeed frequently, so that we may make known to him our petitions and requests. No special subtlety is required in framing our desires. We don't need flowery court language or crafty psychological maneuvers to trick God into giving us what we need. On the contrary, he is a Father to us, and if even earthly fathers provide good things for their children, how much more will our heavenly Father give us the things we need to grow and prosper? What a contrast in tone there is between Mordecai's admonition to Esther to put her life on the line in order to seek favor with Ahasuerus and Paul's command to the Philippians: "Do not be anxious about anything, but in everything by prayer and supplication with thanksgiving let your requests be made known to God" (Phil. 4:6). Or the exhortation in Hebrews: "Let us then with confidence draw near to the throne of grace, that we may receive mercy and find grace to help in time of need" (Heb. 4:16). Our King has an open-door policy.

This contrast is not because there is no cost to gain access to the King, however. Our entry to the heavenly court is free, but it was not cheaply bought. As sinners, a death is required before we can enter the presence of the all-holy One. God can hold out the golden scepter of favor to us only because the fierce rod of his judgment has fallen upon Christ. Our peace with God is paid for in Christ's blood. However, having been paid at such a high price, our peace has thereby been purchased once and for all. No one and nothing can now separate us from God's favor and the right to bring all of our concerns directly to the throne of grace. Neither death nor life, neither heavenly forces nor earthly trials, neither adversity nor prosperity—in short, nothing in all creation can separate us from the love of God in Christ Jesus (Rom. 8:38–39).

What have we done with this privilege? We have an entry card, signed in blood, which gives us access to the throne of grace. We can bring our prayers and petitions to the Lord of the universe, whose word accomplishes all his holy will. What have we done with that glorious invitation? If we are honest, most of us have to admit that we have done precious little with it. It may not even have had the impact on our hearts that Esther's invitation had on Haman's, filling us with abundant joy. We ought to be constantly on our knees before God, rejoicing with overflowing hearts for all of his undeserved favor. Yet all too often we live as practical atheists, as if the future of our lives depended entirely on our ability to extract the right response from the empire through our personal subtlety and skill. Often it is only when the situation is absolutely desperate that we will be found crying out to God.

The truth is that our emotions are not lastingly shaped as they should be by the unexpected and undeserved invitation we have received to the royal banquet. Haman's elevation by the king and the honors that continued to be poured out upon him should have insulated his heart from the impact of minor difficulties. Instead, his thoughts were rapidly transformed from joy to despair by the perceived slight to his honor and status that Mordecai represented. What a ridiculous overreaction! Yet are not we equally fickle? Shouldn't our joy in our salvation be far more impregnable than Haman's, because it is based on the unparalleled glory of God's incredible goodness to us? In reality, though, how often have we said to ourselves, "Yes, I know that God has made me his child, and a coheir of Christ's glorious inheritance, yet all this is worth nothing to me as long as I do not have _____ [fill in the relevant comfort, security]"? Perhaps our joy is lost because of lack of love at home, or lack of respect from our peers, or lack of acknowledgement at work. We are cast down by minor earthly setbacks because we have lost sight of the incredible glories of our heavenly inheritance.

Perhaps the first petition we need to make to the Lord, then, is to transform our hearts. It is not coincidental that when Jesus compares his heavenly Father to earthly fathers, the good gift he promises to those who ask is the Holy Spirit (Luke 11:13). Above all else, this is what we need from God. We need for him to grant us his Spirit that we may have our hearts and lives increasingly reoriented in a God-centered direction. It is the work of the Holy Spirit to lift up Christ in our hearts, to fill us with a desire to worship and to pray, and to bring to fruition the slow work of sanctification in our souls. If we receive this gift from God, then our hearts will gradually become more and more filled with gratitude for the privilege that we have in Christ. Then any worldly slights or setbacks that face us when we leave the throne room to go back into the world will make but little impression on us. If we have the King's favor, who cares what those around us think of us?

We have the promise of God himself that he will answer our prayers when we ask him for the Holy Spirit. We are to ask, then, with boldness and confidence, so as to receive freely from the King.

Yet for now we receive God's precious gift only in part. He has promised his presence with us, and he will not leave us or forsake us. Nevertheless, we are still left longing for the fullness of that presence that is yet to come. Here we may experience God's presence with us in part, but only in part. The gift of the Spirit is itself only the down payment on our great inheritance (see Rom. 8:23). Knowing God is still the richest treasure that this world affords, even when only partially experienced. But the fullness of knowledge awaits us beyond the veil of death, when we shall know even as we have been fully known (see 1 Cor. 13:12). This is the hope for which we wait and long; then we shall indeed know Christ fully, and the power of his resurrection (see Phil. 3:10–11).

In the meantime, while we wait for Christ's return, we continually wrestle with our hearts as unmortified idolatries constantly rise up to challenge our peace and joy. And in the meantime we also wrestle with the empire, exercising all of our subtlety and strength, while still recognizing that God is the only one who can bend the empire to do his will. But we do not wrestle alone: God gives his Holy Spirit to begin his work in us, producing his fruits in and through us. What is more, we do not wrestle forever: one day, our wrestling work will be done and we will be ushered into God's immediate presence forever. For those who are in Christ, there will be no fear on that day, for Christ himself has opened the door to us, and no one and nothing can shut it in our face. What unconquerable joy and peace will be ours then! What unconquerable joy and peace should be ours now!

6

THE MAN THE KING DELIGHTS TO HONOR

Esther 6:1—14

So Haman came in, and the king said to him, "What should be
done to the man whom the king delights to honor?" And
Haman said to himself, "Whom would the king delight to
honor more than me?" . . . Then the king said to Haman,
"Hurry; take the robes and the horse, as you have said, and do
so to Mordecai the Jew who sits at the king's gate. Leave out
nothing that you have mentioned." (Esth. 6:6, 10)

here's an old slogan that runs like this: "They said to me, 'Smile! Things could be worse!'—so I did smile, and things *did* get worse!"

We said at the outset of our journey through Esther that there would be a lot to laugh about in this book, and so there was in chapter 1. However, for the past several chapters, things have steadily been getting worse for God's people, and there hasn't been much to induce a smile. In chapter 3 Haman's edict for the destruction of the Jewish people was published throughout the empire as a law of the Medes and Persians which could not be changed. Moreover, even though at the end of chapter 4 Esther agreed to step forward to seek deliverance from the king for her people, so far she hasn't made much progress toward that goal. To be sure, she won the king's favor when she appeared in his presence unsummoned, thereby avoiding immediate disaster and her own death (Esth. 5:2). And now she is in the midst of putting into effect a subtle plan, which involves inviting the king and Haman to a series of feasts. But it is still far from clear at this point in the story whether she will actually be able to pull deliverance out of the jaws of disaster. She is like an emergency room doctor operating on a critically ill patient: she seems confident of what she is doing and the patient is still alive, but time is running out and it is by no means certain that the operation will be a success.

To make matters worse, the clock was not counting down to zero hour for God's people alone. That was the problem of which Esther was aware, and which she was seeking to counter. However, in chapter 5 we discovered that a separate clock was ticking for Mordecai's own fate, a danger of which Esther was as yet totally oblivious. The edict against the Jews still had several months to run, but Haman's determination to execute Mordecai required only hours to run its course. The pole on which Mordecai's body was to be impaled had been erected (all seventy-five feet of it), and Haman was set to ask the king to hang Mordecai on it as soon as morning rolled around. It seems that even if Esther's subtlety saved the Jews, that salvation would come too late to save Mordecai. Things were getting worse every minute and the darkness was deepening! From where would deliverance come to rescue Mordecai? Humanly speaking, there seemed no hope left, no way out.

But in the Bible, we are never simply speaking humanly. Even in a book like Esther, where God's name is never mentioned and the characters in the story (including his own people) do their best to ignore his existence, he refuses to be written out of the script. Between the lines and behind the scenes, out of focus and incognito, the Lord continued to work to accomplish all his holy will. Esther 6 is a perfect case study in God's way of working all things together for the good of his people, those whom he has called according to his purpose (see Rom. 8:28).

Sleepless in Susa

It all started with the king being unable to sleep: "On that night the king could not sleep" (Esth. 6:1). Kings, like the rest of us, occasionally have sleepless nights. Their beds may have been above the average comfort level in the ancient world, but they were well short of current standards for luxury. But notice what it was that kept this king awake: precisely nothing! Unlike Nebuchadnezzar, who was kept awake at a key moment by a dream from God (Dan. 2:1), or Darius, who was so troubled by Daniel's likely fate in the lions' den that he found no rest (Dan. 6:18),[1] Ahasuerus simply couldn't sleep. There were no dreams, nor was he apparently troubled—as he surely ought to have been—by his genocidal edict. Perhaps the noise from the construction of Haman's spike was what kept him awake. That would certainly have been a fitting irony for a chapter filled with fitting ironies, but the text itself gives no reason for Ahasuerus's insomnia. There was no apparent reason for it, except God's sovereign purpose to deliver his people.

God's sovereignty didn't end with keeping the king awake. He also directed his choice of alternative activities for the night. In the absence of late-night television, an insomniac like Ahasuerus had no lack of potential entertainments: food, drink, dancing girls . . . not to mention an enormous harem; all kinds of pleasures waited at his disposal. Yet he chose instead to listen to a reading from the government records, the chronicles of his reign: "And he gave orders to bring the book of memorable deeds, the chronicles, and they were read before the king" (Esth. 6:1). Those who have read the annals of ancient Near Eastern kings will know that these are not exactly riveting reading: they tend to be a stock catalog of victories won, lands conquered, and tribute imposed. It was about as compelling as reading income tax regulations. Perhaps that was the point. If anything would send Ahasuerus back to sleep, it was surely a monotone reading of his own life story!

In the midst of the reading, however, Ahasuerus found himself jolted wide awake. The scribe had come to the part where Mordecai had saved his life by revealing a plot against his life: "And it was found written how Mordecai had told about Bigthana and Teresh, two of the king's eunuchs, who guarded the threshold, and who had sought to lay hands on King Ahasuerus" (Esth. 6:2). It made the king wonder: "What honor or distinction has been bestowed on Mordecai for this?" (Esth. 6:3). Persian kings were famous for their diligence in rewarding those who assisted them; it was good for public relations, to say nothing of personal safety. The reply he received from his young atten-

---

1. The phrase is exactly parallel to Esther 6:1, only in Aramaic.

dants was shocking: "Nothing has been done for him" (Esth. 6:3). Nothing? Who would save the king's life next time, if there were no certainty of a reward?

We can almost picture the king leaping out of bed impulsively— everything Ahasuerus did was impulsive—and striding out of the royal bed- chamber in the dawn's early light, trailing servants behind him. This omis- sion must be rectified and it must be rectified now! But how? For all his impulsiveness, the king is helpless without his advisors. He counts on them constantly to tell him what to do.[2] So he asks his servants, "Who is in the court?" (Esth. 6:4). In other words, which of my counselors is around to tell me what to do?

POETIC JUSTICE

Normally at this time of the morning there might well have been no one in the courtyard. But divine providence had been moving the other pieces into place as well, and Haman was in the courtyard, early though it was: "Haman had just entered the outer court of the king's palace to speak to the king about having Mordecai hanged on the gallows that he had prepared for him. And the king's young men told him, 'Haman is there, standing in the court.' And the king said, 'Let him come in'" (Esth. 6:4–5). Haman had come for an entirely different purpose, intending to speak to the king about hang- ing Mordecai on his spike so that he could enjoy the rest of his day. Thus he probably thought it a lucky moment when he was called in to see the king so early, for unlike Esther, he wasn't about to risk his life by appearing unsum- moned before Ahasuerus. As events would prove, it wasn't a lucky moment at all, but rather a providential moment, and Providence had something far different in mind for him than Haman expected. In a delicious irony, Haman himself was asked what should be done: "So Haman came in, and the king said to him, 'What should be done to the man whom the king delights to honor?'" (6:6).

In making his request for advice, the king left out the crucial piece of infor- mation about who was to be honored, just as Haman himself had left out the

---

2. On this aspect of the character of Ahasuerus, see Michael V. Fox, *Character and Ideology in the Book of Esther*, 2nd ed. (Grand Rapids: Eerdmans, 2001), 174.

crucial piece of information about the identity of the people to be destroyed in chapter 3. Haman was not slow mentally to fill in the blank, however, and with his own name. He said to himself, "Whom would the king delight to honor more than me?" (Esth. 6:6). Given Haman's past trajectory, this was not an unreasonable assumption. He had been elevated above all the other princes and nobles, to become second only to the king. Why shouldn't the king ask him to name his own reward, while tactfully omitting his name so that he wouldn't have to be embarrassed about asking for what he really wanted?

Haman imagined that this was his opportunity to ask whatever he wished of Ahasuerus, up to half his kingdom. Yet he showed none of Esther's subtlety and circumspectness in responding to the king. Far from delaying the moment of request until he was sure the iron was hot, as she did, Haman plunged right in with his request, not even pausing to frame it with the usual oriental phrases of courtly courtesy: "If it seems good to the king"; "If I have found favor in the king's sight"; and so forth. Haman cut right to the chase, rolling the delicious words around on his tongue, savoring their sweetness: "For the man whom the king delights to honor . . ." (Esth. 6:7).[3] His request was exactly what we would have expected, given the idolatry of public recognition that we saw in the last chapter. Haman wanted neither wealth nor power, for he had those in abundance already. All he wanted was to be treated like the king in public:

> Let royal robes be brought, which the king has worn, and the horse that the king has ridden, and on whose head a royal crown is set. And let the robes and the horse be handed over to one of the king's most noble officials. Let them dress the man whom the king delights to honor, and let them lead him on the horse through the square of the city, proclaiming before him: "Thus shall it be done to the man whom the king delights to honor." (Esth. 6:8–9)[4]

Haman's parade would process through the populous plaza of the city, so that everyone would see the extent of his honor. This was his dream day.

---

3. Jon D. Levenson, *Esther* (Old Testament Library; Louisville: Westminster John Knox, 1997), 97.

4. For the supposedly magical associations of robes worn by royalty, see Fox, *Character and Ideology*, 77. Ancient reliefs show horses with headgear in a Persian context (see Carey A. Moore, *Esther* [Anchor Bible; Garden City, NY: Doubleday, 1971], plate 4). It is humorous to note that the Persian king liked his horses the same way he liked his queens, wearing a royal turban!

HAMAN'S TERRIBLE, HORRIBLE, NO GOOD, VERY BAD DAY

Then reality rained on Haman's parade: "The king said to Haman, 'Hurry; take the robes and the horse, as you have said, and do so to Mordecai the Jew who sits at the king's gate. Leave out nothing that you have mentioned'" (Esth. 6:10). Imagine Haman's face when he discovered for whom these honors were actually intended! The honors that he coveted above all else were actually to be bestowed on Mordecai the Jew, his prime enemy, and, worst of all, he personally would be the one to proclaim Mordecai's elevation: "Haman took the robes and the horse, and he dressed Mordecai and led him through the square of the city, proclaiming before him, 'Thus shall it be done to the man whom the king delights to honor'" (Esth. 6:11). Haman's own words had come back to haunt him, and the phrase he had so delighted to pronounce must have tasted like ashes in his mouth by the end of a long day of shouting it in front of Mordecai. His dream day turned into his worst nightmare.

At the end of the day, the two men went their separate ways. For his part, Mordecai "returned to the king's gate" (Esth. 6:12). He seems to have been virtually unaffected by the day's events. Honor was all very well, but it wouldn't get his work done for him. We get the sense that for Mordecai, this was nothing special. Mordecai's nemesis, on the other hand, was completely mortified: "Haman hurried to his house, mourning and with his head covered" (Esth. 6:12). The tables had been turned. Earlier it was the Jews who mourned (Esth. 4:3), but now the balance of power was shifting.

Nor did Haman find much comfort when he got home. His wife and his other advisors had suddenly become the bearers of theological wisdom. Since Mordecai was of Jewish descent (or more literally "from the seed of the Jews"), Haman's chances of overcoming him were nonexistent: "And Haman told his wife Zeresh and all his friends everything that had happened to him. Then his wise men and his wife Zeresh said to him, 'If Mordecai, before whom you have begun to fall, is of the Jewish people, you will not overcome him but will surely fall before him'" (Esth. 6:13). Haman's fall, once begun, would inevitably continue. One wonders why they didn't share this nugget of revelation with Haman at the end of the previous chapter, when their counsel was the exact opposite, urging him to build a gallows for Mordecai. Perhaps they saw a divine portent in the events of that day, which clearly pointed ahead of itself to things to come, and the final, inevitable victory of Israel's God. Hindsight is a wonderful thing! As was typical, though, Haman's counselors did not explicitly acknowledge by name the one from whom this judgment would come.

Tragically, there was no change in Haman's course as a result of this insight. This was potentially a Psalm 2 moment for Haman. His idolatry had been exposed as empty, his hatred of the Lord's people shown to be vain. Now was the time to be wise, bow down, and kiss the son, submitting to the Lord and to his anointed one, lest he be destroyed along the way (Ps. 2:12). But Haman was given little time to reflect on his foolish ways: "While they were yet talking with him, the king's eunuchs arrived and hurried to bring Haman to the feast that Esther had prepared" (Esth. 6:14).

SEEING THE INVISIBLE HAND OF GOD

What can we learn from this chapter of Esther? In the first place, once again we see the invisible hand of God changing the course of history. Yes, it is an oxymoron to say that we see an invisible hand, but as with other invisible objects, sometimes the trail left in its wake is unmistakable. As we look outside through a window, we can neither see nor feel the wind blowing, but the bending of the trees tells its own story. So too, here in the Book of Esther, God's work of providence is so clear that even the pagans cannot miss its significance. Even Haman's friends are not so dense as to write off this day's events as mere coincidence: they know that all this must be attributed to the intervention of Israel's God, and that once he becomes involved in the world, the final outcome is never in doubt. Haman will now surely fall to destruction.

The text doesn't tell us how this knowledge came to Haman's wife and friends. Presumably they knew something of the history of their people's interactions with the people of Israel and their God in the past, but it is striking how quick they were to put two and two together and get the correct answer. Even though the answer was unpalatable to their personal convictions and preferences, Haman's wife and friends could read the unfolding events with true insight. Their swiftness to believe in the power and final victory of Israel's God is in marked contrast to the slowness of his own people to turn to him in their hour of need. As we saw in chapter 4, there was plenty of mourning and fasting among God's people when Haman's edict was announced, but precious little calling out to God on the basis of faith in his promises. Even in Mordecai's speech to Esther, in which he implored her to intervene with the king, he made no direct reference to God and his faithfulness as the source of ultimate confidence. The pagans seemed quicker to believe that Israel's God would act than his own people were![5]

What about us? Are we as quick to spot the hand of God at work as were Haman's wife and friends, or as slow to believe as his covenant people? We ought to have an unshakable confidence that, despite all appearances, God will act to bring about the salvation of his people. This confidence should drive us to act boldly in faith. Yet the reality is that we easily get thrown by circumstances that seem to be conspiring to bring about our downfall. Surprising as it may seem, we can learn a more godly response from Zeresh and Haman's friends.

GOD'S HAND IN THE INSIGNIFICANT

It is striking that such a seemingly insignificant event forms the turning point for the whole narrative.[6] It is not Esther's decision to stand up for God that turns the course of events around. Things continue to get worse for God's people even after that decision, all the way through chapter 5. But from the beginning of chapter 6 onward, the enemies of God's people are on the run and God's people are on the upswing—not because of their bold faith or fearless action, but simply because of a sleepless night. Esther is completely absent from this decisive chapter and Mordecai is merely a passive participant, but God is invisibly turning things around and restoring his people's fortunes. In a way, help is arising for the Jews from another place (see Esth. 4:14), in such a way as to make it clear that their deliverance is entirely from God!

Yet this decisive intervention by God's sovereignty does not make human actions meaningless. Esther will still get her moment to stand up for God and his people, and God will use her courageous stand to bring Haman's

---

5. Compare 1 Samuel 4, where the Philistines take God's power in history seriously, while the Israelites regard the ark as a mere totem to be manipulated.

6. Karen Jobes, *Esther* (New International Version Application Commentary; Grand Rapids: Zondervan, 1999), 158–59.

scheming to an end. Esther's faithfulness is important. But Haman's fate is inevitable by the end of this chapter, as even the pagans recognize, *before* Esther's subtle plans play themselves out. God's sovereign purpose works through his servants, but it does not depend upon their willing obedience. Rather, their obedience itself is part of God's wonderful work.

BOW NOW OR BOW LATER

This passage poses a serious warning to those who are not willing to bow the knee before God. Haman's fall was not predictable, humanly speaking. He seemed to have it all: fame, wealth, position, honor. Yet in the space of less than twenty-four hours, he was disgraced, and dead. How could this happen? Haman's wife and advisors were right in assessing the cause of that fall: it was because he had chosen to attack the seed of the Jews, and thereby to oppose Israel's God. Haman's fall may not have been humanly predictable, but it was scripturally predictable. God said to Abraham in Genesis 12:3, "I will bless those who bless you, and him who dishonors you I will curse." The blessing of the land was promised to Abraham and his seed (Gen. 13:15–16), so to oppose the seed of the Jews was necessarily to make oneself an enemy of God's promise. This enmity was what had brought the Amalekites, from whom Haman was descended, under God's curse in the first place. Back in Exodus 17, they assaulted God's people while they were journeying through the wilderness. Once that curse was pronounced, the Amalekites' ultimate fate was sealed.

Is it possible that we too are under God's curse? The Scriptures are clear that anyone who breaks God's law, even in the tiniest detail, is under God's curse (Gal. 3:10). This means that if we are relying on our own goodness, we are in serious trouble, even if we think our personal record is well above average. Even outward goodness stands condemned in God's sight, if it is done to further our own honor and not his. Nothing short of perfect obedience offered from a perfect heart meets God's standard, and all who fall short are under his curse. Outwardly, the marks of that curse may not be evident in our lives yet. We may be prospering in our business or career, surrounded by people who care about us and respect our integrity, enjoying the good life in every way, just as Haman was. But the seeds of our destruction are still germinating, like a hidden cancer that is waiting to burst out

81

and overwhelm our body's defenses. Our whole life has been built around serving an idolatry, feeding our own sense of what would make us feel honored in the sight of the world. Our fall could be just as sudden and as inescapable as Haman's, taking us from our present comforts to face a holy God in an instant. Are we ready for such an encounter?

Unlike Haman, we still have time to turn around. Whereas Haman had no sooner heard the prediction of his downfall than the king's eunuchs arrived and hurried him off to meet his fate, we still have time to reflect and repent. Where can we turn to avoid such a terrible end? There is only one place to go, and that is to turn to Israel's God and Jesus Christ, the true "seed of the Jews." Mordecai's honor before his enemies was more than just his reward from the Persian king for a job well done. It was also God's way of foreshadowing the Savior who was to come. The promise to Abraham of land and blessing was not just a general promise to take care of his descendants—his seeds (plural)—but a promise of ultimately bringing through Abraham the Seed (singular): Jesus Christ (see Gal. 3:16). In him, the blessings promised to Abraham would find their fulfillment not only for the descendants of Abraham, but even for their traditional enemies, the Gentiles. In Christ, the promised Holy Spirit descends on a new people made up of Jews and Gentiles so that they might receive together all of the blessings that God has planned for his people (Gal. 3:14). In Christ, there is hope even for former Hamans, those whose lives have been lived in enmity to God and his people.

THE MAN WHOM GOD DELIGHTS TO HONOR

Who is the man that God, the Great King, delights to honor? It is none other than this same Jesus Christ. One day Jesus will be at the head of a great victory parade, leading his enemies behind him. One day every knee will bow before him, willingly or not, and every tongue will confess that he is Lord, to the glory of God the Father (Phil. 2:10–11). All of our knees will bow before him one day, whether we like it or not. But why would we not bow before him even now, because of the great love he has shown us? For we who were once God's enemies, doomed like Haman to fall to destruction before him, can be adopted into his family through Christ.

How is this great reversal in our lives possible? Ironically, it is possible only because the way of Christ while he was here on earth was not the way of public recognition, but rather the reverse. Mordecai is both a type of Christ in his exaltation and a foil for Christ in his humiliation. Whereas Mordecai was dressed in royal robes, Jesus trod the road to the cross undressed, exposed to public shame. Whereas Mordecai was mounted on a royal horse, which itself was crowned with emblems of royalty, Jesus had to walk, bowed down by the weight of a heavy cross. The only crown in sight on that day was the crown of thorns that his enemies had made in order to mock him. Whereas Mordecai was proclaimed publicly as "the man whom the king delights to honor," Jesus was derided every step of that bitter way. "Hail, King of the Jews!" mocked the Roman soldiers (Matt. 27:29). "Crucify him," cried the crowd; "we have no king but Caesar" (John 19:15). "He is the King of Israel; let him come down now from the cross, and we will believe in him," said the chief priests and the scribes (Matt. 27:42). There was no public honor for Jesus on that day.

The mocking voices of the crowd and the public shame of the cross were not the deepest darkness that Jesus endured, though. It was the silence from heaven that was hardest to bear. The voice that once split the heavens, declaring at his baptism, "You are my beloved Son; with you I am well pleased" (Luke 3:22) was stilled. The voice that repeated at his transfiguration, "This is my Son, my Chosen One; listen to him" (Luke 9:35), had nothing to say. Though he cried out, "My God, my God, why have you forsaken me?" (Matt. 27:46), there was no answer, no response. Why not? Had God lost his delight in his own Son? Was Jesus no longer the one whom God delighted to honor? How could that be? The unimaginable became reality as on the cross Jesus endured the full measure of the shame and separation from God that our sin deserved. For we too have lifted our voices with the crowd to mock, saying in our hearts, "Yes, I know Christ was crucified, but all this means nothing to me as long as I don't have this idolatry satisfied." We too, like Peter at the high priest's house, have denied, either verbally or by our craven silence, that we ever knew him. We too have failed to give God the honor he deserves, seeking first our own kingdom and interests. We too have fallen short of the glory of God. It was our sin that required him to remain on the cross, exposed to public scorn, until his work of redeeming us by paying the full price for our sins was accomplished.

Honor Where Honor Is Due

How should we respond to this reality? Haman unwillingly declared Mordecai's honor. He was forced to declare his praise. So also some will unwillingly declare the honor of Christ on the last day. But should we who are his people be unwilling to sing his praises? Should we be among those who are slow to glorify God and give thanks to the Lamb that was slain for us? How could that be? How can we not exalt Christ in our hearts as Lord, even now? How can we grow tired of praising and shouting his excellence?

How too can we be slow to trust in God's providence, seeing that he has sent his beloved Son to the cross in our place? Will he not also, along with Christ, give us everything we need for our growth in godliness (Rom. 8:32)? Maybe we are still in an "Esther 5" situation at the moment, surrounded by enemies on every side, whose plans against us seem to be succeeding. Perhaps we are experiencing the pains and difficulties of living in a fallen world, a world that seems to exist in the grips of the evil empire. Yet even if we are misunderstood or mistreated, every wrong will be righted on the last day. Though the evil empire does its worst, it cannot prevail against those who have taken refuge in Christ (Ps. 2:12). Ultimately, its raging will be in vain. Read this and rejoice!

Indeed, if we are exalting Christ as Lord in our hearts, and are trusting firmly in God's providence to do what is good for our souls and to bring glory to himself, why are we so troubled? Why are we so filled with doubts and fears about our own futures, or the future of our children, or the future of our churches? God will accomplish his purposes, often slowly and imperceptibly, but nonetheless certainly. Sometimes he will do it through human agents who willingly submit to him. Sometimes he will do it by directing those whose hearts are at enmity to him, so that their sinful motives accomplish his perfect purposes. Sometimes he will do it through the collaboration of a whole series of seemingly trivial circumstances. But in the light of the great and precious promises of God, this we know for sure: our God will save his people. In the light of the cross, we know that his salvation cannot be thwarted. In the light of these heavenly realities, what is left for us to do but to bow our hearts and knees before him and sing his praises?

7

COMING OUT IN SUSA

Esther 7:1—10

Then Queen Esther answered, "If I have found favor in your sight, O king, and if it please the king, let my life be granted me for my wish, and my people for my request. For we have been sold, I and my people, to be destroyed, to be killed, and to be annihilated. If we had been sold merely as slaves, men and women, I would have been silent, for our affliction is not to be compared with the loss to the king." (Esth. 7:3–4)

Every other week, it seems, the press and television media are rocked by a startling new self-revelation from some celebrity. The process is called "coming out." For some, it relates to their sexuality; for others to their addiction to drugs; for still others to their relationships with their mothers. Invariably, though, it is more than we ever wanted to know about their private lives!

Queen Esther also had a deep, dark secret—her Jewishness—which she had kept under wraps ever since she was first taken into the royal harem back in chapter 2. She had followed Mordecai's advice to hide her ethnicity so faithfully, even when elevated to the level of queen, that five years later no one knew who her people were or her connection to Mordecai. Think about that. Everyone knew that Mordecai was Jewish: that is what triggered Haman's scheme to annihilate the Jews in the first place. But Esther had been under such deep cover that no one (with the possible exception of the odd household eunuch or two) had a clue. To hide her nationality that successfully while living so intimately among pagans, she must have broken virtually every law in the books of Moses. She certainly couldn't have observed the laws of ritual cleanliness, or of kosher food, or of special times and seasons of thanksgiving and fasting. She couldn't even have prayed to God publicly. She had blended in completely with the pagan colors of the empire.

Now it was time for Esther to come out of the closet. Haman's edict threatened the whole Jewish community and, for the sake of her people, she had agreed to go before the king to intercede with him for their lives. That was going to be a tricky proposition, for King Ahasuerus was a dangerously unstable individual.[1] One day, a person might be his best friend; the next day it would be "Off with his head!—and while you're at it, impale his body on a pole."

It was all the more tricky for Esther to intercede on behalf of the Jews since the edict she needed to have revoked had been put forward by Haman, who next to the king was the most powerful man in the empire. It was signed by him in the king's name and stood to benefit the royal treasury to the tune of half a year's taxes for the empire. This was not simply "Mission Difficult"; it was truly "Mission Impossible." All Esther had to offer in exchange was a pretty face—and behind it, a smart brain that had been working overtime. Thus, ever since she had agreed to intercede for her people back in chapter 4, she had been pursuing an intricate strategy with the king, inviting him and Haman to banquet after banquet. By almost revealing her request and then backing off, she persuaded the king three times to commit publicly in advance to give her whatever she wished, up to half his kingdom.

---

1. The Greek historian Herodotus describes Ahasuerus's response to the request of Pythius the Lydian that he might release the eldest of his five sons from the obligation of military service. Even though Pythius had earlier entertained him hospitably and contributed generously toward the costs of his war with Greece, Ahasuerus was so incensed by the request that he had Pythius's son cut into two pieces and made the army pass between them (Herodotus *Histories* 7.37–39). See also the events recounted in A. T. Olmstead, *History of the Persian Empire* (Chicago: University of Chicago Press, 1948), 266–67.

ESTHER'S REQUEST

Finally, the time had come to reveal all. So this time, when the king asked her what she wanted, Esther was ready to speak:

> So the king and Haman went in to feast with Queen Esther. And on the second day, as they were drinking wine after the feast, the king again said to Esther, "What is your wish, Queen Esther? It shall be granted you. And what is your request? Even to the half of my kingdom, it shall be fulfilled." Then Queen Esther answered, "If I have found favor in your sight, O king, and if it please the king, let my life be granted me for my wish, and my people for my request. For we have been sold, I and my people, to be destroyed, to be killed, and to be annihilated. If we had been sold merely as slaves, men and women, I would have been silent, for our affliction is not to be compared with the loss to the king." (Esth. 7:1–4)

Esther's words were as carefully chosen as her strategy had been. After the usual court niceties ("If I have found favor in your sight, O king, and if it please the king"), she asked for a twofold favor to match the king's twofold offer.[2] What she wanted for her gift was the sparing of her own life and the lives of her people. At this point, Esther came out of the closet far enough to link her own fate with the fate of her people. If they were destroyed, she would be destroyed. If they were spared, she would be spared. She didn't actually reveal which people she was talking about until the next chapter, but then Haman had never bothered to identify the people to be destroyed when he first asked for the edict. Haman, at least, would have had no doubt about what her request really meant, however. If her petition was refused by the king and the edict stood, Esther had now publicly added her own name to the list of those marked for slaughter.[3] She had irrevocably sided with her people, at peril of her life.

Esther also backed up her request with reasons. Why was her petition to the king necessary? It was necessary because she and her people had been sold to be destroyed, killed, and annihilated. Here Esther is simply quoting verbatim from the royal edict. If it had merely been a matter of enslavement,

---

2. Michael V. Fox, *Character and Ideology in the Book of Esther*, 2nd ed. (Grand Rapids: Eerdmans, 2001), 83.

3. Carey A. Moore, *Esther* (Anchor Bible; Garden City, NY: Doubleday, 1971), 73–74.

she said, she would not have brought it up at all. Esther was well aware that for Ahasuerus the empire's needs trumped issues of mere personal freedom. There was no constitutional right to life, liberty, and the pursuit of happiness in the Persian Empire. Indeed, there is a sharp irony in this sentence, since in a manner of speaking being sold as a female slave was precisely what had happened to her personally. She herself had been enslaved as the personal toy of the king. This was not the issue she was protesting, however. Of course the king's personal interests would far outweigh any such small injustices. To this point, the king was nodding happily along in agreement with Esther! Her logic appealed to him thus far. But genocide, said the queen, especially a genocide that may very well involve her personal death, is a different story altogether.

Notice how subtly Esther made her points. She skillfully used the passive mood in describing the edict.[4] She simply said, "We have been sold, I and my people," so as to avoid having to identify the guilty party (Esth. 7:4). First she wanted to make the king angry, and only then to unveil a target for his wrath, in the hopes that he would act before reflecting whether it was harder to find a new vizier or a new favorite wife. She was also softening the way for the realization that doing the right thing would hit the king in the treasury, yet at the same time affirming ahead of time (i.e., before he found out exactly how much it would cost him) that the good he could do would more than compensate for the personal loss he would suffer.

When one intercedes with the empire, one has no choice but to intercede on the empire's own terms. Esther could not simply appeal to the king's sense of right and wrong, and point out that genocide is evil, because he didn't think it was. Obviously the king was not troubled by the idea of genocide as such, or he wouldn't have signed the edict so carelessly in the first place. The only constitutional given in the empire was the right of the king to maximize his own interests. Therefore, Esther's case must rest on the fact that even though it would cost the king some inconvenience and financial loss, she did have his best interests at heart in making her request. After all, sparing this people also meant sparing her personally. Now we can see that the conditional clause with which she opened her request—"If I have found

4. D. J. A. Clines, *Ezra, Nehemiah, Esther* (New Century Bible Commentary; Grand Rapids: Eerdmans, 1984), 311.

favor in your sight" (Esth. 7:3)—is more than mere conventional court flattery. It is the heart of Esther's argument. If she has found favor in the king's sight, then an attack on her would also be an attack on his royal person.

AHASUERUS'S RESPONSE

The queen's argument hit home. The king's anger was stirred and he responded with another double-barreled question: "Who is he, and where is he, who has dared to do this?" (Esth. 7:5). A tempting answer for Esther might have been to say to the king what the prophet Nathan said in his confrontation with David: "You are the man!" (2 Sam. 12:7). After all, none of these events could have happened without the king's complicity. But that was not the goal of her speech. Not all injustices can be set right in the course of earthly events. As they say, politics is the art of the possible. So instead Esther focused the king's anger on the prime mover behind the edict, saying simply, "A foe and enemy! This wicked Haman!" (Esth. 7:6). Elsewhere, Haman was identified as "the enemy of the Jews," and that would be the ultimate reason for his demise (Esth. 8:1); however, this was not a reason that would have had any mileage with King Ahasuerus. Instead, Esther described Haman simply as "an enemy" because his offense before Ahasuerus was not really his enmity to the Jews, but only the fact that his edict had (unintentionally) threatened the king's favorite wife.

Haman was appalled by this turn of events, shocked into silence, "terrified before the king and the queen" (Esth. 7:6). He had been completely outsmarted by Esther's cunning strategy, and he could see that the king's fierce anger had been aroused against him. Meanwhile, the king stalked out into his garden: "And the king arose in his wrath from the wine-drinking and went into the palace garden, but Haman stayed to beg for his life from Queen Esther, for he saw that harm was determined against him by the king" (Esth. 7:7). Why did the king need to take a walk at this point? Not because he needed time to think or because he wanted to cool down. Haman, at least, was in no doubt what the king's verdict would be when he returned. Already as the king went out, Haman could see that Ahasuerus had determined to do him harm. Nor did that prospect particularly trouble the king. He was unlikely to lose any sleep over Haman's fate. What was troubling the king was more likely the issue of his own reputation. He had authorized Haman's edict, and his royal seal had ratified it. So how could he now, without losing face, punish Haman for promulgating a decree that he had approved personally? That was his tricky dilemma.[5]

When Ahasuerus returned to the banquet hall, he found that Haman had neatly solved his problem for him: "And the king returned from the palace garden to the place where they were drinking wine, as Haman was falling on the couch where Esther was" (Esth. 7:8). During the king's absence, Haman had tried to beg for his life from Esther. The one who had sought unwittingly to take her life, now wanted her to grant him his own. In order to emphasize his request, Haman had fallen down before her, thus neatly fulfilling the prediction of his wife that he would certainly fall to his ruin before the seed of the Jews (see Esth. 6:13). But Haman's falling down on Esther's couch gave the king precisely the excuse he needed to eliminate Haman without making any embarrassing public reference to the edict: "And the king said, 'Will he even assault the queen in my presence, in my own house?' As the word left the mouth of the king, they covered Haman's face" (Esth. 7:8). Ahasuerus can hardly have seriously believed that Haman was preparing to rape Esther in front of him, but it was a convenient charge that diverted attention from the real issue.[6] Ironically, the one who wanted to kill a Jew for not falling down before him was ultimately executed on a charge of falling down inappropriately before a Jew! And then came the cruelest irony of all: "Then Harbona, one of the eunuchs in attendance on the king, said, 'Moreover, the gallows that Haman has prepared for Mordecai, whose word saved the king, is standing at Haman's house, fifty cubits high.' And the king said, 'Hang him on that.' So they hanged Haman on the gallows that he had prepared for Mordecai. Then the wrath of the king abated" (Esth. 7:9–10). Thus Haman was taken out and his body was impaled on the massive pole that he himself had built just twenty-four hours before to execute Mordecai. What a difference a day makes!

With that the king's fury abated. Game over. Issue resolved. Threat to Esther removed. "Now that we've taken care of that little unpleasantness, what's for supper?" we can imagine Ahasuerus saying casually to Esther. Except that from Esther's perspective, it was far from over. Even though

---

5. Fox, *Character and Ideology*, 86.
6. Frederic Bush, *Ruth, Esther* (Waco, TX: Word, 1996), 433.

Haman personally had been dealt with, his edict still remained out there, like a ticking time bomb, just waiting to explode and destroy the Jews. Esther herself might be safe, guarded within the king's palace, but that wasn't what she had gone through this whole routine to achieve. At this point, she must still have wondered if she would be able to achieve her goal of rescuing her people.

DIVINE SOVEREIGNTY, HUMAN RESPONSIBILITY

In this chapter, we see the interplay between human responsibility and divine sovereignty. Esther's intricate plan was a necessary part of the process of bringing Haman to justice, a plan that required a combination of subtlety, boldness, and strength to carry it through. Yet Esther's plan by itself was not what turned around the fortunes of God's people. The writer of the story has shown us this by making the king's sleepless night the hinge on which the whole story turns. Prior to that point at the beginning of chapter 6, the fortunes of the Jews were heading steadily downhill. From that moment on, though, their prospects were transformed. The key event thus had nothing to do with Esther or Mordecai, but instead was a seemingly insignificant detail in which the hidden hand of providence may be discerned—though only with careful hindsight. Isn't that so often how it is in life? The intricate plans we lay can never come to fruition without God's providential blessing upon them. As Psalm 127:1 puts it, "Unless the LORD builds the house, those who build it labor in vain."

This chapter shows us the complementary aspect of that truth, however, which is that unless the builders labor, there won't be much of a house! It is thus significant that the pivotal chapter in the book, from which Esther is entirely absent, is bracketed by two chapters that show her diligently using all of the means at her disposal to bring about her desired end. God's sovereign act is the turning point, but God works through the faithful efforts of his people, just as much as through remarkable providences.

This is a very practical truth. Do we want to see our friends come to Christ? We can't reach their hearts and change them—only God can do that. But we can and should plan to talk to them about Christ, to introduce them to Christian friends, to invite them to church. Do we want to find God's leading for our lives? Progress may depend on his opening the key doors, but there is nothing wrong with our getting out there and knocking. Do we want to have a better marriage? Unless God changes our hearts and the hearts of our spouses, we may have no hope of lasting improvement, but that doesn't mean there is nothing we can do. Don't sit back and wait for God to work, if you are unwilling to put yourself out in pursuit of godly desires.

Most Christians err on one side or the other of this equation. Some are sit-back-and-pray types, whose motto is always "Leave it to Jesus." For such people, the tendency is to wait for God to drop a solution to all of their problems right into their laps. Others have activist personalities and are constantly saying, "If it is going to be, it's got to be me." For them, the tendency is to assume that the key to progress is following some three-step strategy. The Bible, however, sets before us the goal of the balance of prayer plus action, of leaning on Christ and leading people to Christ, of resting in the Lord and walking with him. Either one on its own is inadequate. Both together are the goal.

The truly wonderful part of God's plan, though, is that even when we get the balance wrong, he will still accomplish his holy will. Esther is the perfect example. Where is her balance? Would we say that she has a model prayer life? If she did, it is surprising that the biblical narrator has not shown us this, as we see so prominently in men like Daniel and Nehemiah. On the contrary, in chapter 4 we saw the Jewish community, among whom Esther was raised, fasting and moaning, but there is no word of them crying out to God. They may have gone through the religious motions, but there is no evidence of much true dependence on God. Yet God still delivered them, in spite of their inadequate theology. God chose to deliver his people through Esther's activity, in spite of the absence of any explicit evidence of her prayerful dependence on him.

God's Faithfulness to His Covenant

This assurance is a wonderful truth! God will certainly deliver his people, whether or not they are faithful. We can be sure of this truth because his action stems from his character, not ours. As Paul reminded Timothy, "if we are faithless, he remains faithful—for he cannot deny himself" (2 Tim. 2:13). It was possible to be certain all along that Haman would never ultimately triumph, not because we have confidence in the greater cunning of Esther, but because we have confidence in God's covenant promise to Abraham and his seed. God declared back in Genesis 12 that those who bless Abraham and his offspring will be blessed, while those who curse them will be cursed. Even a pagan like Haman's wife recognized the significance of that reality in the previous chapter, when she told her husband that since Mordecai was from the seed of the Jews, Haman would certainly fall to ruin before him (see Esth. 6:13). Haman was not simply taking on the Jews but their God. What we see in this chapter, then, is simply the outworking of the negative side of the Abrahamic covenant. Haman had assaulted the descendants of Abraham and would face the consequences. Being executed and impaled on the tree—the sign of a cursed death in the ancient Near East—was the consequence of his having offended God, the Great King, more than of his having offended Ahasuerus, the king of Persia.

This truth means that even at this point in the story, when everything still seemed to be hanging in the balance, the Jews had no need to fear. For if the negative consequences of the Abrahamic covenant were still in force, then surely so too was the positive goal of the covenant: that the Lord would be Israel's God and they would be his people. Patience might yet be required to see how exactly God would deliver his people from their enemies, but his commitment to do so was not in doubt. The Lord does not change.

What confidence this reality should give us! It should give us great hope for our children. The promises made to them in baptism are not simply our commitment to raise them to the best of our ability. Our ability to raise our children will frequently be flawed, sometimes enormously so. They inherit our sins and failings, sometimes magnified. If their spiritual destiny rested entirely, or even mainly, in our hands, they would have little or no hope of finding God. But our God has not simply committed himself to us; he has also committed himself to our children. On the day of Pentecost Peter declared that the promised Holy Spirit, the fundamental gift of the new covenant era, is not just for the descendants of Abraham, who by birth are near to God, but also for Gentiles, who by birth are far off, *and for our children* (Acts 2:39). Of course, having the promise of God does not allow us to be idle. We are not to sit back waiting for the Spirit to descend and smite little Joey with fire from on high. We scheme and plot and plan and draw our children to the gospel as earnestly and

93

seriously as we possibly can. But we also pray for them with boldness, for they are not outsiders to grace but insiders, those who can look to God's promises as made to them personally.

Likewise for our churches, we may have great hope. We don't have great hope because of the vast wisdom and ability with which God has gifted our elders, or because of the gifts and abilities of the pastors. If our hope rested in these things, we might as well shut the doors of the church right now. We could perhaps draw a crowd and build a large program based on these elements, but not a ministry that effects real spiritual change in the hearts of men and women. That only happens through the powerful work of the Holy Spirit. Rather than resting on human resources, our confidence rests on God's promise to build his church in such a way that the gates of hell will not prevail against it. Again, we cannot sit idly by, waiting for God to bring in the multitudes to our church. We are to be as skilled and active as we can be in presenting the good news to our neighbors and friends. But we also pray for them with boldness, knowing that God will surely accomplish through this church exactly what it is his purpose to do, in spite of our many sins and shortcomings.

Just as importantly, we may have hope in our struggle against sin. Our hope lies not in our own progress or personal strength. Not at all! We cannot pull ourselves up by our own efforts, and the further we progress in the Christian life, the more evident that becomes. As we grow in spiritual maturity, we see the depths of our sin and the deceitfulness of our hearts ever more distinctly. Yet we may have confidence that we will make progress in godliness because God has promised his Holy Spirit to be at work in our hearts, generating his fruits of righteousness and holiness. The work may not progress as fast as we would wish, but its progress is assured because God has promised it. We are not simply to sit back, to "let go and let God"; we are to strive with every fiber of our being toward the holiness for which God has designed us. But once again we do so with confidence, knowing that God will work his righteousness in us on the day we stand before him. In the meantime, he will also use our awareness of our own sin to drive us again and again to the cross in thanksgiving for his long-suffering and grace with such unprofitable servants as ourselves.

The Earthly Emperor and the Great King

But perhaps the most profound truth in this chapter of God's Word lies in the vivid contrast between the Lord our God and King Ahasuerus, between the heavenly King and the earthly emperor! King Ahasuerus is ignorant, shallow, fickle, and weak. He can be manipulated by Esther to do her bidding, just as he once was by Haman. He is apparently content to fabricate charges against his own right-hand man in order to avoid the personal embarrassment that the real charges would have caused. He has no concern for anyone except himself, no morality except his own personal interest. Yet this is the one in whom Haman placed his trust. Haman's life was built around the pursuit of power and achievement, and he achieved both to the full extent that this was possible within the bounds of the empire. He had reached the top of his career path. No one apart from the emperor himself matched Haman's glory and status. Yet all that he had gained disappeared completely in the space of a few minutes, along with his life itself. At the end of his life, what did he have to show for all his striving after wealth and recognition?

Such is the downward path of all who have placed their trust in the empire. Our fall may not be as dramatic as Haman's was, but if our trust is in things that will burn or rust, or things that can be stolen or destroyed, then ultimately they will let us down. Even good things, such as the love of family and friends and the respect of our colleagues, cannot survive the test of the grave. If that is all we have, then when all is said and done, we have nothing. So why would we build our lives around nothing?

God's people are those who have built their lives around the only truth that will last, the truth of a King who is utterly different from Ahasuerus. We have a King who doesn't need to be manipulated and cajoled to do what is right. Our King does what is right because he himself is righteous—he cannot do anything other than the right. We have a King who instead of being consumed with himself and his own interests has staked his name and reputation upon a people whom he would always call his own, even when it was costly for him to do so. We have a King who, far from inventing charges against us, took the charges that we had deservedly incurred for failing to serve him as we ought and laid them upon his dearly beloved Son. It was our King's own Son who was taken and impaled on a tree, bearing our curse all the way to death (see 2 Cor. 5:21). Our King's wrath was poured out in full upon his own Son on the cross.

And if God's fury has been poured out in full upon Christ, now there is none left for us (see Gal. 3:13). If our debt has been paid in full, now we are free to go. What is more, we are free to come into the King's presence as a dearly beloved son or a precious daughter, welcomed for Christ's sake (see 1 John 3:1). No one and nothing can separate us from the love of this King (see Rom. 8:38–39). He won't love us today and leave us to hang tomorrow, no matter what we do. Why not? It is because his love for us rests in his character, not in ours.

Furthermore, the basis for our appearing before the Father is not "if I have found favor in your sight," but rather, "if Christ has found favor in your sight." Our destiny is bound up in Christ's, if we are Christians. Having loved us and given his Son for us, while we were still sinners (Rom. 5:8), will God the Father give us up now that we are justified by the blood of his Son (see Rom. 5:9)? Can his enemies snatch us out of his hand? Can Satan's accusations remove us from his care? Can death itself drag us out of his presence? Not with a King like the one we serve. No one and nothing can take us away from his great love. There is no condemnation for us, if we are in Christ Jesus, if our faith and trust are placed in him as Savior and Lord (see Rom. 8:1).

Do you know the sure and certain love of that King? Some have built their entire lives around their career, or their family, or their reputation, or their own personal goodness. It's not enough. Perhaps you have experienced a Haman-like fall, and for the first time you are beginning to see that success is not sufficient. Perhaps you haven't yet had that experience. One day, though, we will all inevitably discover that it is the truth. Whatever we give our lives to apart from the true and living God, we will invariably find out sooner or later that it is not enough. But why would we give our lives to anything or anyone other than this God who has loved us so much? Why wouldn't we want to follow such a King, who is so kind and gracious and good to his people? Why wouldn't we bow down before him willingly and surrender our whole lives to him, for richer or for poorer, for better or for worse, in sickness and in health, whatever it takes? He has loved us so much; is he not worthy of all our praise and indeed of our very hearts?

All who believe this gospel need to hear over and over again those precious words: "No condemnation; Christ has found favor before the Father for you." Christ has made peace between us and God, a peace that nothing in heaven or on earth can destroy. Is he not worthy of receiving afresh today all our praise from the bottom of our hearts? Is he not worthy of all of our trust? What a wonderful King we serve!

8

IT AIN'T OVER

Esther 8:1—17

Then Esther spoke again to the king. She fell at his feet and wept
and pleaded with him to avert the evil plan of Haman the
Agagite and the plot that he had devised against the Jews. When
the king held out the golden scepter to Esther, Esther rose and
stood before the king. And she said, "If it please the king,
and if I have found favor in his sight, and if the thing seems right
before the king, and I am pleasing in his eyes, let an order be writ-
ten to revoke the letters devised by Haman the Agagite,
the son of Hammedatha, which he wrote to destroy the Jews
who are in all the provinces of the king." (Esth. 8:3–5)

*I*t was that great baseball philosopher Yogi Berra who came up
with the memorable slogan, "It ain't over till it's over." It was,
perhaps, Yogi's own version of the more highbrow saying,
"The opera isn't over till the fat lady sings"—which anyone who has ever
endured a full-length Wagnerian opera will recognize as a fairly accurate
plot summary.

So too, this biblical soap opera, *The Days of Esther's Life*, is not yet at its
conclusion. Many issues have been resolved already. The villainous Haman
has met his comeuppance—literally, with the aid of his own seventy-five
foot pole. Esther and Mordecai also receive their reward at the beginning of

Esther 8, in the shape of Haman's confiscated estate and a promotion for Mordecai: "On that day King Ahasuerus gave to Queen Esther the house of Haman, the enemy of the Jews. And Mordecai came before the king, for Esther had told what he was to her. And the king took off his signet ring, which he had taken from Haman, and gave it to Mordecai. And Esther set Mordecai over the house of Haman" (Esth. 8:1–2). However, Haman's edict to exterminate the Jews had not yet been reversed: it was still hanging over their heads like the proverbial sword of Damocles. Perhaps it would yet turn out that the laws of the Medes and the Persians really could not be changed, and all of Esther's efforts would have been wasted. Much still hangs in the balance at this point in the story.

COMPLETELY OUT OF THE CLOSET

Before we proceed further with the story, though, it is interesting to observe what happened when Esther finally came completely out of the closet about her ethnicity and her relationship to Mordecai. Far from being disturbed by the revelation that Esther was Jewish, the king's response to the news was to promote Mordecai into Haman's former position as vizier over the empire. This fact should make us wonder once again about the wisdom of Esther's entire chameleon strategy. Not only was it morally dubious (to say the least) for Esther to hide her Jewishness, since it required her to live as a practical pagan for five years, but now it turns out that even pragmatically it may have been a mistake. Perhaps if Esther had revealed her Jewishness and her connection to Mordecai back in chapter 2, the whole threat to the Jewish community might have been circumvented. The king might even have promoted Mordecai to the rank of vizier at that point, after he uncovered the attempt on the king's life, and Haman might never have risen to power at all.

Does that scenario seem far-fetched? If so, remember how odd the connection is between chapters 2 and 3 of the Book of Esther: Mordecai saved the king's life, the deed was carefully recorded in the royal annals, and the king promoted . . . (in the very next verse) Haman. Perhaps the idea that Mordecai could have been promoted earlier is not so bizarre as it seems, at least in the thinking of the narrator of the story. Far from bringing about

Wow

99

the desired result of safety, then, Esther's hiddenness may have been what unwittingly opened the door to danger for her whole people.

Of course, we are never told what might have been, either in real life or in this story. Certainly God chose to unfold events through precisely this scenario, even through Esther and Mordecai's sin, so that his redemptive power would become abundantly clear. Whatever may have been the case with Esther, though, it is certainly true that very often we are led into sin because we are afraid of dangers that will never materialize. How often have we failed to bear witness for our faith because of the fear of what others will think, only to discover when we finally timidly open our mouths that the response is not at all what we feared? How many potential dangers and difficulties paralyze us with fright and faithless worry, but then evaporate in front of us like the morning mist? How often are we led into sin by those worries? It is worth reminding ourselves that the sin we think will smooth our path in fact often complicates our lives in unforeseen ways and leads us into even greater difficulties than the ones we feared. The way of the transgressor is not only morally wrong, but frequently it is also far harder than the way of obedience would have been.

Esther's Second Request

Whatever the "might have beens" in Esther's case, the reality was that the edict to exterminate the Jews was still in force. King Ahasuerus may have thought that everything had been taken care of with the disposal of Haman, but in fact it hadn't. So Queen Esther had to go once more before the king to plead for her people's lives. This time cool, calculating strategy was abandoned as Esther threw herself down in front of the king, weeping and pleading[1] with him to make Haman's evil plot go away: "Then Esther spoke again to the king. She fell at his feet and wept and pleaded with him to avert the evil plan of Haman the Agagite and the plot that he had devised against the Jews" (Esth. 8:3). Whereas before she had retained her royal dignity, always appearing as the stately queen before the king, now she threw herself down like a common beggar, crying and asking desperately for mercy for her

---

1. The verb is often used with reference to God and connotes intensity and importunity. See Michael V. Fox, *Character and Ideology in the Book of Esther*, 2nd ed. (Grand Rapids: Eerdmans, 2001), 92.

people. The similarities and differences with Haman in the previous chapter are striking: he fell down before Esther, but his concern was simply to plead for his own life, and he was unsuccessful in his petition (see Esth. 7:8). Esther fell down before King Ahasuerus to plead not for her own life, but for the lives of her people, and she was granted what she asked.

Once again, as in chapter 5, the king stretched out his golden scepter to Esther and received her. This time her request was immediately delivered, without manipulative games. Her words were still carefully chosen, however:

> When the king held out the golden scepter to Esther, Esther rose and stood before the king. And she said, "If it please the king, and if I have found favor in his sight, and if the thing seems right before the king, and I am pleasing in his eyes, let an order be written to revoke the letters devised by Haman the Agagite, the son of Hammedatha, which he wrote to destroy the Jews who are in all the provinces of the king. For how can I bear to see the calamity that is coming to my people? Or how can I bear to see the destruction of my kindred?" (Esth. 8:4–6)

Esther prefaced her request with a long preamble in four parts: "If it please the king, and if I have found favor in his sight, and if the thing seems right[2] before the king, and I am pleasing in his eyes" (Esth. 8:4). Two of these clauses dealt with whether the matter to be discussed was acceptable to the king, while the other two asked whether Esther herself was acceptable. These two themes were inextricably linked, for the only real reason for the king to grant her request was his favor toward her. Esther made no reference to right and wrong, justice and injustice. Those were not categories that registered with the empire. All she could do was to appeal to Ahasuerus's own self-interest, as it related to her: "If you *really* love me and want me to be happy, you have to grant my request." Her people's destiny hung upon the king's response to her personally. If watching her people and kindred[3] being destroyed would cause her great pain, how could anyone who loved her endure that?

---

2. *Kasher*, from which we get the English word "kosher." There is not a little irony in Esther, newly out of the assimilationist closet, asking the pagan king to do the "kosher" thing!

3. The twofold designation matches (and reverses) her twofold concealment of "her people and her kindred" in Esther 2:10, 20.

AHASUERUS'S RESPONSE

King Ahasuerus's immediate response was less than satisfactory, however: "Then King Ahasuerus said to Queen Esther and to Mordecai the Jew, 'Behold, I have given Esther the house of Haman, and they have hanged him on the gallows, because he intended to lay hands on the Jews'" (Esth. 8:7). The king said, in effect, "Look, I gave you all this money and killed your enemy for scheming against your people.[4] What more could you possibly want?" Ahasuerus assumed that Esther was just like him: concerned only about herself and her own interests. But even though Esther had once concealed her identity because her only thought was to protect herself, now that she had identified with her people, she had a new perspective that stretched beyond her own narrow self-interests. Salvation for herself was not enough if it came without salvation for her people.

Seeing that his initial answer was not exactly what Esther was looking for, Ahasuerus went on to tell her that she and Mordecai could write whatever they wanted in the king's name and seal it with the king's signet ring, because, after all, the king's edicts could not be revoked: "But you may write as you please with regard to the Jews, in the name of the king, and seal it with the king's ring, for an edict written in the name of the king and sealed with the king's ring cannot be revoked" (Esth. 8:8). So King Ahasuerus could not undo his former edict because it was irrevocable, but he had no problem with Mordecai and Esther writing a contradictory edict, which would then also become irrevocable. May the best edict win! What is more, even after he had once been manipulated by his top official into signing a deadly edict, Ahasuerus personally encouraged his new vizier to send out another edict, sight unseen. Isn't that rather silly of him? Of course it is—but that's the whole point. The empire is so law-bound that it is tied in impenetrable bureaucratic knots, and its emperor cares absolutely nothing about his people. What a world we live in!

Mordecai had now been granted the power that Haman earlier possessed so that he could counteract Haman's edict. He didn't waste any time, but immediately sent out an edict of his own to the 127 provinces of the empire:

---

4. This was not, of course, the official reason for Haman's execution given in the previous chapter, but the conversation between Esther and the king is strictly "off the record."

The king's scribes were summoned at that time, in the third month, which is the month of Sivan, on the twenty-third day. And an edict was written, according to all that Mordecai commanded concerning the Jews, to the satraps and the governors and the officials of the provinces from India to Ethiopia, 127 provinces, to each province in its own script and to each people in its own language, and also to the Jews in their script and their language. And he wrote in the name of King Ahasuerus and sealed it with the king's signet ring. Then he sent the letters by mounted couriers riding on swift horses that were used in the king's service, bred from the royal stud, saying that the king allowed the Jews who were in every city to gather and defend their lives, to destroy, to kill, and to annihilate any armed force of any people or province that might attack them, children and women included, and to plunder their goods, on one day throughout all the provinces of King Ahasuerus, on the thirteenth day of the twelfth month, which is the month of Adar. A copy of what was written was to be issued as a decree in every province, being publicly displayed to all peoples, and the Jews were to be ready on that day to take vengeance on their enemies. So the couriers, mounted on their swift horses that were used in the king's service, rode out hurriedly, urged by the king's command. And the decree was issued in Susa the citadel. (Esth. 8:9–14)

Mordecai's language deliberately echoed that of the original edict in order to highlight their parallel nature. The main difference is that these messages were not only committed to couriers, but to couriers riding on specially-bred fast horses; the message must get through in time, even to the most distant parts of the empire.

What Mordecai's edict mandated was measure-for-measure retaliation by the Jews against their enemies. They could kill those who attacked them, along with their families,[5] and then plunder them, just as their enemies had planned to kill the Jews and their families and take their plunder. This was not merely self-defense, but neither was it a license for indiscriminate slaughter: the verb used in verse 13 to describe the action for which the Jews are to be prepared is *naqam,* which always indicates punitive retribution for a prior

5. The NIV obscures the issue by making "their women and children" in 8:11 refer to the Jews who are under attack, not the families of their aggressors. However, most English translations and commentators follow the natural reading of the Hebrew which, in parallel with Haman's edict, permits slaughter of the families and the taking of their plunder. So, for example, Fox, *Character and Ideology*, 99–100.

wrong.[6] Those who, like Haman, sought to destroy the seed of the Jews, in accordance with his edict, would themselves share Haman's fate. The authority of the empire now backed up the threats of the Abrahamic covenant against those who sought to harm the descendants of Abraham. However, it was the Jews themselves who would have to carry out the sanctions of the covenant in a kind of holy war against their enemies.

GLORY FOR SHAME, JOY FOR SORROW

Once the edict had gone out, so too did Mordecai, leaving the king's presence dressed in royal splendor: "Then Mordecai went out from the presence of the king in royal robes of blue and white, with a great golden crown and a robe of fine linen and purple, and the city of Susa shouted and rejoiced" (Esth. 8:15). Whereas after the issuing of the first edict he went clothed in sackcloth and ashes, unable even to go in before the king, now after the second edict he emerged from the presence of the king clothed in glory. Nor was this merely a temporary glory of the kind he received in chapter 6, as a reward for his previously unrewarded faithful service. Now the attire was Mordecai's by right as second only to the king. He had become a walking work of the empire's art, clothed with a richness that paralleled the decorations at Ahasuerus's great feast back in Esther 1 (compare Esth. 1:6).

Nor was this the only reversal of earlier events. After the issuing of Haman's edict, the city of Susa was thrown into confusion (Esth. 3:15), but after Mordecai's edict was published the city rejoiced (Esth. 8:15). The Jewish community that had responded to the first edict with four kinds of distress—mourning, fasting, weeping, and wailing (4:3)—now responded to the second with four kinds of delight: "light and gladness and joy and honor" (Esth. 8:16). In particular, the fasting and sorrow of chapter 4 were turned into feasting and joy by the announcement of the edict.

The most poignant transformation of all, however, is surely the concluding note of the chapter: "And in every province and in every city, wherever the king's command and his edict reached, there was gladness and joy among the Jews, a feast and a holiday. And many from the peoples of the country

---

6. Fox, *Character and Ideology*, 101. On this term, see also Joyce G. Baldwin, *Esther* (Tyndale Old Testament Commentaries; Downers Grove, IL: InterVarsity, 1984), 100–102.

declared themselves Jews, for fear of the Jews had fallen on them" (Esth. 8:17). How ironic! No sooner had Esther conquered her fear and revealed her true identity with respect to her Jewishness than many of the pagans around her apparently chose to pretend to be Jewish, motivated by precisely the same type of fear. Some may indeed have been genuinely converted, motivated to join God's people by the fear of the Lord. But others were motivated more by their fear of the Jews.[7]

Once again, we should notice how much of our behavior is driven by perceptions about what the future holds rather than by reality. The actual fortunes of the Jews did not change significantly throughout the story. Their livelihoods were not ruined by Haman's edict; there were no instant pogroms, leading to killing and looting. Nor were their futures radically transformed by the new edict, which simply gave them the right to defend themselves and their property. Yet they had *thought* that their lives were threatened by Haman, and so they fasted and mourned. Now they *felt* that threat to have lifted, and so they responded with joy. The empire in which they lived was no better a place at the end of the book than it was in the beginning, but compared to their outlook in the middle of the story, it was a wonderful new world. It is the same experience we have when we go to the doctor for a routine physical and he points out a spot on the X-ray. For weeks we may torment ourselves with a variety of imagined futures, until a second opinion gives us an all-clear. Our health hasn't actually changed over this period, up or down, but our emotional responses surely have, going up and down like a yo-yo.

RIGHT TO REJOICE?

But should the Jews have been so quick to rejoice at the news of the second edict? The empire had not changed, even though Mordecai was now the vizier. Today they had a friend in high places, to be sure, but Haman's fate illustrated the insecurity of that position. What was to prevent Mordecai from suffering a similarly rapid demise from power, and the people from finding themselves right back in fasting mode? It made sense for them to rejoice only if their deliverance was not simply one of the random oscilla-

---

7. Frederic Bush, *Ruth, Esther* (Waco, TX: Word, 1996), 449.

tions of the wheel of fortune, but rather the expression of a more fundamental principle in the universe. Rejoicing was warranted only if their deliverance was an expression of God's unshakable commitment to protect his
own people and to bring judgment upon their enemies, as promised in the
Abrahamic covenant: "I will bless those who bless you, and him who dishonors you I will curse" (Gen. 12:3).

We might expect, then, that the Jews' praise would be God-directed. Once
again, though, this vertical dimension to their thankfulness is not exactly
prominent. Just as their earlier fasting and wailing didn't seem particularly
heaven-directed, neither do their rejoicing and feasting. It seems that there
was plenty of relief that disaster had been averted, but precious little genuine praise for the One who averted it by the directing hand of his providence. The same is often true of us, though, isn't it? When life goes badly,
we are so quick to become anxious and despairing about the future and so
slow to bring our concerns before God in believing prayer. Meanwhile, when
life goes well and our trials are removed, we rejoice and celebrate the good
news of deliverance, but all too often forget to give thanks to the One to
whom it is due. What a narrow vision of the world we have!

MORDECAI'S HOLY WAR

So far though, we have not addressed the fundamental moral question
that the passage raises in the minds of many readers. It is this: "Was Mordecai right to issue an edict that permitted the Jews not just to defend themselves against their enemies, but to carry the battle to them, executing not
only combatants but their women and children too?" Does this Scripture
suggest that genocide is permissible and right when carried out by the Jews
and reprehensible only when carried out by their enemies? It seems as if
there is a moral double-standard here.

In order to understand these events, we need to see that what Mordecai
was authorizing in his edict was a form of holy war. Haman's edict against
the Jews was not merely a matter of personal animosity; it was an expression of the age-old enmity between the Amalekites and God's people. That
connection is underlined for us twice in this text by the designation of
Haman as the Agagite, the descendant of King Agag, who was king of the
Amalekites in the time of Saul (Esth. 8:3, 5; see 1 Sam. 15). Even in Saul's

time, the conflict between the Israelites and the Agagites had been a long-standing enmity. The Amalekites first attacked the Israelites at Rephidim, when they were on the way out of Egypt in the time of Moses. That unprovoked attack led to a commitment on God's part that the memory of the Amalekites would be erased from under heaven (Ex. 17:14–16). King Saul's attack on Agag in 1 Samuel 15 was part of that ongoing war between God's people and his enemies, the Amalekites, rather than a personal vendetta. Yet Saul failed to carry it through completely, a failure that led to the present difficulties of God's people. Now Mordecai planned to finish what his ancient kinsman (see Esth. 2:5) had left incomplete. His edict was a continuation of that same ongoing struggle, of holy war. That is why even though Mordecai's edict, in line with Haman's, gave the Jews the right to plunder their defeated enemies, the text makes it very clear that they refrained from doing so (Esth. 9:10, 15–16). This was holy war, and therefore the spoils were not theirs to take.[8]

What, then, is holy war? In holy war, the Israelites acted as the agents of God's righteous judgment against sinners. At Jericho and certain other cities during the conquest of Canaan, they were instructed to destroy the city and to kill all its inhabitants outright (Josh. 6:21). They functioned as a kind of human equivalent to the fire and brimstone from heaven that destroyed Sodom and Gomorrah, along with all of its residents, young and old, or the flood of Noah's day, which wiped out an entire generation of humanity. In all of these cases, the people were not destroyed because they happened to be in the wrong place at the wrong time, but because they were sinners steadfastly opposed to God. The sentence for such opposition to God is death, and it applies to all, regardless of age or gender.

Fortunately, God does not always carry out his sentence immediately. God reveals himself as "The LORD, the LORD, the compassionate and gracious God, slow to anger, abounding in love and faithfulness, maintaining love to thousands, and forgiving wickedness, rebellion and sin" (Ex. 34:6–7 NIV). Out of the midst of the flood, he rescued Noah and his family; out of the midst of Sodom and Gomorrah, he rescued the family of Lot; out of Jericho, he delivered the household of Rahab. Yet God is also the one who "does

---

8. In clear contrast to 1 Samuel 15, where Saul and the people violated the terms of holy war by taking the best of the people and the best of the sheep and cattle for themselves.

not leave the guilty unpunished; he punishes the children and their children for the sin of the fathers to the third and fourth generation" (Ex. 34:7). As one writer comments concerning Sodom and Gomorrah: "The Lord waits long to be gracious, as if he knew not how to smite. He smites at last as if he knew not how to pity."[9]

Holy war was not executed just against non-Israelites, however. When Achan violated the terms of holy war at Jericho by coveting and taking some of the spoil, he found himself and his family liable to the same destruction (see Josh. 7). Similarly, the later devastation of Jerusalem by Nebuchadnezzar and the exiling of God's people from his land were the result of their long-standing unholiness (2 Kings 24:2–4). The land that had once vomited out the Canaanites for their lengthy history of sin now spat out the covenant people. Holy war targets sinners for destruction, whatever their ethnic affiliation.

Yet holy war was not a universal practice in the Bible, not even throughout the Old Testament. It is distinctively part of the Mosaic era of redemptive history. Jesus rebuked James and John for their desire to call down fire from heaven on the Samaritan village that would not welcome Jesus (Luke 9:54–55). He taught them and us in no uncertain terms that this kind of holy war is not part of our calling as Christians. We are not engaged in an evangelical *jihad* in which we take up the sword and tell our non-Christian neighbors to convert or die.

It is important that we see why we are not called to this kind of holy war. It is not because holy war was somehow wrong in its original historical context, or was a sub-Christian procedure, unworthy of the followers of Christ. It is not even because holy war seems out of date and old-fashioned, a barbarous and uncivilized practice. We have not abandoned holy war simply because we have become modern people and have grown more civilized. Rather, we have abandoned holy war in its Old Testament form because we live in a different era in the history of redemption. We live in the era of the outpouring of grace, in which we fight with spiritual weapons to bring the gospel to the nations, defeating God's enemies by seeing them graciously transformed into his friends. Now we fight with the sword of the Spirit, the Word of God, which instead of turning live foes into dead corpses can trans-

9. Robert S. Candlish, *Studies in Genesis* (Grand Rapids: Kregel, 1979 reprint), 327.

form dead sinners into live saints. Now we wrestle in prayer, seeking God's enlivening work in the hearts and souls of our friends and neighbors.

What gives urgency to our task, though, is the fact that God's nature hasn't changed and his edict of death against rebellious sinners still stands. All men and women, young and old, must ultimately bow the knee before Christ or be eternally damned. There is no middle ground: we are either part of the Lord's people or among his enemies, and the wrong allegiance will be eternally fatal. The Mosaic-era practice of holy war was itself a foreshadowing within history of the last judgment, a warning to men and women everywhere not to presume upon God's grace and mercy, just as the physical blessings of the Promised Land foreshadowed the blessings of the age to come. There is still a judgment to come, when Christ himself will go out dressed in a blood-stained robe as the rider on the white horse, armed with a sharp sword with which to strike down the nations (Rev. 19:11–15). Holy war is not obsolete; it has just been temporarily suspended during this era of grace.

ESCAPING GOD'S JUDGMENT

God's judgment can still be escaped. Unlike Haman's edict, which would have allowed for no escape for God's people, Mordecai's edict condemned only those who attacked the Jews and their families. Those who were not hostile to God's people were not condemned by the edict. Many people from other nations joined the Jews and thereby avoided the fate of their enemies. The message was clear: there is a way out of judgment through identification with God's people.

How can that be, though, given that God's own people are themselves as guilty of rebellion and sin as those who are not God's people? How can any of us stand in the presence of a holy God, when we ourselves have rebelled against him in thought, word, and deed? Who will deliver us from the edict of death that still stands against us in the heavenly court? What we need is an Esther of our own, someone who will put aside personal interests and safety and risk dignity, honor, even life itself, in order to plead our case before God, the Great King.

Such a mediator is ours in Jesus Christ. He left the glories of heaven and took on the form of a servant, not simply humiliating himself, but going all the way to death for us. Long before the day in which he will don a blood-

109

soaked robe to go and wreak vengeance on his enemies, he first soaked robes in his own blood to protect those who are his own people. God put his own Son under the curse of holy war, and cut him off because of our sin. As the prophet Isaiah predicted, he had no family or descendants of his own (see Isa. 53). He was bruised for our transgressions, wounded for our iniquities, dishonored for our glory, and plunged into darkness that we who are rebellious sinners might see the light. This is the Grand Reversal to which all the reversals in Esther's story point.

But the death of Jesus Christ on the cross, crucial though it was, is not the end of the story. It wasn't over when the women gathered at the tomb to mourn. It wasn't over until the angels sang, celebrating Christ's resurrection and his ascension to glory. What is more, he now stands before the Great King of the cosmos, pleading with the Father for all of his spiritual children. There he says, "Father, this is one of my people! How could I bear to see the destruction of this one for his sin? Yes, I know that is what each deserves— but I died so that this one might live!"

How does the Great King respond? Not for him the answer of Ahasuerus in Esther 8:11: "I don't care. Do whatever you think best." No, he says to his Son, "Welcome them in! Bring them into my presence forever, because of the love I have for you. Your people are my people. Your spiritual family shall be clothed in glory and honor, with all of the splendors of heaven, because of your faithful obedience. Their sorrows and pains will soon be forgotten, their fasting swallowed up in feasting, their darkness turned forever to glorious light." The Father delights to honor the servants of his Son (see John 12:26).

Every Lord's Day is a day of feasting when we celebrate the great reversal of our eternal fate. Are we celebrating that reality in our hearts Sunday by Sunday? Like the pagans of Esther's time, people still go to church and identify with the covenant community for all kinds of different reasons (see Esth. 8:17). Just being in church on a Sunday is no evidence of our genuine status as belonging to Christ. We must ask ourselves directly, "Am I trusting in Christ's death in my place? Am I a genuine part of his community today? Will he say of me personally on the last day, 'This one is one of mine'?"

If the answer to these profound questions is yes, then where are our joy and our peace? The Jews celebrated their deliverance, even though they still lived in a hostile empire in which their fortunes could change for the worse again at any moment. How much more, then, should we celebrate, since in Christ our eternal fortunes have been definitively changed in an irreversible way. God's edict of life for all who trust in Christ can neither be revoked nor challenged. There is no other edict that can be issued to countermand it. God's settled decree is "There is therefore now no condemnation for those who are in Christ Jesus" (Rom. 8:1). No one and nothing in all creation can ever separate us from his love. So let us daily celebrate our deliverance with unshakable and glorious joy! Let the peace that comes from Christ's completed victory daily guard our hearts and minds against the vicissitudes of our experiences in the fallen world! Look forward to the day when the end will indeed come, when we too will be able to sing along with all the redeemed saints to the praise of God the Father and the risen Lamb.

9

A World Turned Upside Down

Esther 9:1—10:3

Now in the twelfth month, which is the month of Adar, on the thir-
teenth day of the same, when the king's command and edict were
about to be carried out, on the very day when the enemies of the
Jews hoped to gain the mastery over them, the reverse occurred: the
Jews gained mastery over those who hated them." (Esth. 9:1)

reat literature is filled with great reversals. Take Shakespeare's
plays, for example. Whether it is a tragedy like *Romeo and Juliet*,
where the characters' blossoming prospects of love and happiness are dashed and turned to sorrow, or a comedy like *Twelfth Night*, where
impending disaster is averted and it all turns out happily in the end, there
is almost always a dramatic turn in the course of events.

The Book of Esther is, as we have seen, similarly built around a great reversal of fortunes. Whether Esther is a tragedy or a comedy depends on one's
perspective. For Haman and his allies, it is a great tragedy, as all of their
schemes to triumph over the hated Jews come to nothing. For Esther, Mordecai, and the community of God's people, however, it is a comedy in every
sense, with the transformation from imminent disaster to a situation where
everyone may live happily ever after and laugh at earlier fears.

A REVERSAL DECLARED

This theme of reversal becomes explicit in the very first verse of Esther 9: "Now in the twelfth month, which is the month of Adar, on the thirteenth day of the same, when the king's command and edict were about to be carried out, on the very day when the enemies of the Jews hoped to gain the mastery over them, the reverse occurred: the Jews gained mastery over those who hated them" (Esth. 9:1). Finally, the day of decision for the Jewish community in the Persian Empire had dawned on the thirteenth of Adar. The conflicting edicts of Haman and Mordecai against and in favor of God's people were now put into play, raising the question of which edict would win the day. The writer doesn't leave us in suspense for long. On the contrary, he tells us at the very outset how the day turned out: the tables were turned. Those who had hoped to dominate and destroy the Jews were themselves destroyed. Suspense has been deliberately eliminated so that the writer can highlight the main point of the chapter: a reversal has been brought about in the fortunes of God's people. The end of the story shows those who had been powerless, the Jews, in complete power, dominant over their enemies on the very day when their enemies had hoped to be dominant over them. After this verse, the rest of the book is wrap-up.

That it is wrap-up, however, does not mean that it is unimportant. The lengthy denouement to the story shows us three things: it describes the reversal in detail (Esth. 9:2–16), it shows how the reversal is to be celebrated in perpetuity (9:17–32), and then, in a concluding postscript (10:1–3), it invites us to reconsider the reversal's ultimate impact.

A REVERSAL DESCRIBED

First we have the outworking of the reversal described in detail:

The Jews gathered in their cities throughout all the provinces of King Ahasuerus to lay hands on those who sought their harm. And no one could stand against them, for the fear of them had fallen on all peoples. All the officials of the provinces and the satraps and the governors and the royal agents also helped the Jews, for the fear of Mordecai had fallen on them. For Mordecai was great in the king's house, and his fame spread throughout all the provinces, for the man Mordecai grew more and more powerful. The Jews

113

struck all their enemies with the sword, killing and destroying them, and did as they pleased to those who hated them. In Susa the citadel itself the Jews killed and destroyed 500 men, and also killed Parshandatha and Dalphon and Aspatha and Poratha and Adalia and Aridatha and Parmashta and Arisai and Aridai and Vaizatha, the ten sons of Haman the son of Hammedatha, the enemy of the Jews, but they laid no hand on the plunder. (Esth. 9:2–10)

Israel's victory was nothing short of comprehensive, as the extensive detail shows. All the Persian officials and royal bureaucracy supported the Jews out of the fear of Mordecai. His position ensured the success of his edict, rather than that of the disgraced and deposed Haman. As a result, the Jews were free to slaughter and destroy all their enemies, just as their enemies had planned to do to them. In the acropolis of Susa, the center of power in the empire, they killed five hundred men in one day. The large number slain within the acropolis itself highlights the extent of the opposition to the Jews in positions of influence and power. Included in the slaughter were all ten of Haman's sons, whose importance is highlighted by listing each and every one of their names.[1] The holy war against this Agagite had been carried through effectively, unlike King Saul's half-hearted assault on his ancestor (1 Sam. 15). Haman had no seed left to carry on his unholy war against the seed of the Jews. With the death of his sons, the loss of his position, and the confiscation of his estate in the previous chapter, all of the things in which Haman boasted in Esther 5 are now gone, along with his own life.

Nor was a single day enough for a victory of this magnitude. When the information of the scale of the slaughter in his capital came to Ahasuerus, he seemed more impressed than perturbed by the news: "That very day the number of those killed in Susa the citadel was reported to the king. And the king said to Queen Esther, 'In Susa the citadel the Jews have killed and destroyed 500 men and also the ten sons of Haman. What then have they done in the rest of the king's provinces! Now what is your wish? It shall be granted you. And what further is your request? It shall be fulfilled'" (Esth. 9:11–12). In fact, the king was so impressed that he repeated, unsolicited, his offer to Esther to grant her petition and her request. Whatever she wanted would be given to her—and what she wanted was not a fur coat or a dia-

---

1. The Masoretic text highlights this feature by arranging the names in columns, as it does with the names of the kings defeated by Joshua in Joshua 12.

mond, but more time for pressing the destruction of those who had organized themselves against the people of God. Esther requested one more day
for the Jews to carry out the edict, and for the sons of Haman to receive dis-
honor as well as death: "And Esther said, 'If it please the king, let the Jews
who are in Susa be allowed tomorrow also to do according to this day's edict.
And let the ten sons of Haman be hanged on the gallows.' So the king commanded this to be done. A decree was issued in Susa, and the ten sons of
Haman were hanged" (Esth. 9:13–14). This too was part of the practice of
holy war, as it had been carried out by Joshua: the leaders of the defeated
enemies were not only killed, but their bodies were also hung on trees as a
sign of their being under God's curse (see Josh. 8:29; 10:26).

Was this additional day of killing a vindictive and vengeful gesture on
Esther's part, or merely a pragmatic and realistic attempt to secure the
position of the Jewish people? In fact, it was neither. What Esther was doing
was pressing through toward completion the practice of holy war against
the self-declared enemies of God. That this was her understanding of what
was going on is made abundantly clear by the refrain repeated at the end
of verse 15: "The Jews who were in Susa gathered also on the fourteenth
day of the month of Adar and they killed 300 men in Susa, but they laid
no hands on the plunder" (Esth. 9:15; cf. 9:10, 16). Even though Mordecai's edict had permitted the taking of plunder, which was merely normal
practice in warfare, the Jews refrained from enriching themselves through
this conflict because it was holy war, so the spoils were not theirs to take.
The same reserve was shown by the Jews in the countryside around the
empire, who likewise took part in the war against God's enemies but kept
themselves from the spoil: "Now the rest of the Jews who were in the king's
provinces also gathered to defend their lives, and got relief from their enemies and killed 75,000 of those who hated them, but they laid no hands
on the plunder" (Esth. 9:16). Once again, the failures of King Saul's cam-
paign against Agag were being reversed (see 1 Sam. 15:14–19). The end
result that flowed from the events initially set in motion by Haman's edict
was that God's enemies were comprehensively defeated throughout the
empire. Instead of being destroyed, as Haman intended, God's people
received rest from those who hated them. The world was indeed turned
upside down.

A Reversal Celebrated

It was not enough to win the victory, however; the victory also had to be celebrated. Sometimes in the closing moments of a sporting event, the commentator will say, "It's all over but the shouting." The saying means that the action on the field of play is effectively finished; all that remains as the clock winds down is the celebration in the stands. The shouting is also an important part of the victory in holy war. The shouting provides the opportunity to give praise where praise is due, and go on record with thankfulness to God for victory won and rest received. So it was that after the Egyptians and their chariots were buried in the Red Sea, Moses led the people in a song of praise to God (Ex. 15). So also, after the victories at Jericho and Ai, Joshua led the people in covenant renewal at Mount Ebal (Josh. 8:30–35). And after the Lord delivered his people under Deborah, she led them in thanksgiving (Judg. 5). Indeed, many of the psalms are psalms of acknowledgement, in which the psalmist records his thanks publicly for God's deliverance. In some cases, thanksgiving became a lasting ordinance. The most striking example is Passover, the annual festival at which God's people were commanded to remind themselves and their children of God's protection during the final plague and his deliverance of them from Egypt (Ex. 12).

These unique and repeated festivals of thanksgiving provide the context and background against which to read the story of the establishment of Purim:

> This was on the thirteenth day of the month of Adar, and on the fourteenth day they rested and made that a day of feasting and gladness. But the Jews who were in Susa gathered on the thirteenth day and on the fourteenth, and rested on the fifteenth day, making that a day of feasting and gladness. Therefore the Jews of the villages, who live in the rural towns, hold the fourteenth day of the month of Adar as a day for gladness and feasting, as a holiday, and as a day on which they send gifts of food to one another (Esth. 9:17–19).

Seen against the backdrop of other Old Testament festivals, the horizontal aspects of the festival of Purim are striking. It was established as an ordinance by edicts from Esther and Mordecai, not from God:

116

And Mordecai recorded these things and sent letters to all the Jews who were in all the provinces of King Ahasuerus, both near and far, obliging them to keep the fourteenth day of the month Adar and also the fifteenth day of the same, year by year, as the days on which the Jews got relief from their enemies, and as the month that had been turned for them from sorrow into gladness and from mourning into a holiday; that they should make them days of feasting and gladness, days for sending gifts of food to one another and gifts to the poor. . . .

Then Queen Esther, the daughter of Abihail, and Mordecai the Jew gave full written authority, confirming this second letter about Purim. Letters were sent to all the Jews, to the 127 provinces of the kingdom of Ahasuerus, in words of peace and truth, that these days of Purim should be observed at their appointed seasons, as Mordecai the Jew and Queen Esther obligated them, and as they had obligated themselves and their offspring, with regard to their fasts and their lamenting. The command of Queen Esther confirmed these practices of Purim, and it was recorded in writing. (Esth. 9:20–22, 29–32)

In the festival of Purim the Jews, both far and near,[2] bound themselves to feast, rejoice, and give presents to one another and gifts to the poor. This celebration was to endure forever, rather like the laws of the Medes and the Persians, which never pass away. What the people were to remember was Haman's plot and the king's intervention to deliver them:

So the Jews accepted what they had started to do, and what Mordecai had written to them. For Haman the Agagite, the son of Hammedatha, the enemy of all the Jews, had plotted against the Jews to destroy them, and had cast Pur (that is, cast lots), to crush and to destroy them. But when it came before the king, he gave orders in writing that his evil plan that he had devised against the Jews should return on his own head, and that he and his sons should be hanged on the gallows. Therefore they called these days Purim, after the term Pur. Therefore, because of all that was written in this letter, and of what they had faced in this matter, and of what had happened to them, the Jews firmly obligated themselves and their offspring and all who joined them, that without fail they would keep these two days according to what

2. Here there may be an explicit allusion to Isaiah 57:19, with its promise that God would heal his people and provide peace to all, both far and near.

was written and at the time appointed every year, that these days should be remembered and kept throughout every generation, in every clan, province, and city, and that these days of Purim should never fall into disuse among the Jews, nor should the commemoration of these days cease among their descendants. (Esth. 9:23–28)

Nowhere in any of these instructions do we find any obvious word about God's people binding themselves to praise God for his deliverance and remind their children of this demonstration of God's faithfulness, as was central to a feast like Passover. It seems as if they could have obeyed Mordecai and Esther's edict to the letter and gone through the whole day without thinking about God even once. Just as with their lamenting and fasting in chapter 4, the vertical dimension seems to have been absent from their praise. They could simply give their neighbor an "Esther is the Reason for the Season" T-shirt and settle down on the couch for a big meal.

Does that make celebrating the feast of Purim wrong? Does the writer want his hearers to abandon the festival as being an unauthorized feast? Almost certainly not. After all, the heart of the feast of Purim, as the Bible reports it, was exactly right. It was a memorial of the time when the Jews got rest from their enemies, when their sorrow was turned to joy and their mourning to celebration (see Esth. 9:22). The theme of gaining rest from one's enemies is a motif with rich overtones in the Old Testament. It was a prerequisite for the building of the temple in Deuteronomy 12:10 and the sign of the completion of the conquest under Joshua (Josh. 11:23). These themes came together in 2 Samuel 7, where as the Lord established David's kingdom and gave him rest from his enemies, the king started thinking about building the temple. How could anyone possibly remember the turning around of darkness into light and the receiving of rest from one's enemies without thinking about God? How could anyone possibly celebrate Purim without seeing what God had done? The poor who are raised from the dust and the needy who are lifted out of the ash heap and seated with princes should need little urging to join in praising the Lord (see Ps. 113:5–9).

This is particularly true if we read more carefully what Mordecai actually wrote in his letter to the Jews establishing Purim. Esther 9:24–25 literally says: "For Haman, the son of Hammedatha, the Agagite, the enemy of all Jews, had plotted against the Jews to destroy them, and he had cast the Pur (that is, the lot) to harass them and to destroy them. But when it[3] came before the king, he said in writing, 'Let his evil plot which he has plotted against the Jews return upon his head'—so they impaled him and his sons upon the tree." These verses have caused commentators some difficulty, because they raise the question, "When exactly did Ahasuerus issue this supposed decree to deliver the Jews and return Haman's evil upon his own head?" This version doesn't seem to square exactly with the portrayal of events in the previous chapters, in which it was Mordecai who issued the decree that saved the Jews, without much assistance from King Ahasuerus. This observation has led some scholars to think that what we have in Esther 9 is a "cleaned-up," public version of events, designed to give more credit to Ahasuerus than was really his due.[4] But perhaps the jarring mismatch between the letter and the events of the story is actually a hint to think more deeply about which king is in view in Mordecai's letter. Ahasuerus's name is nowhere in the letter, because it was not Ahasuerus that really saved the Jews, and he was not the king whose intervention changed the course of history! It was the Great King, God himself, who reversed the fortunes of Haman and the fortunes of the Jews. His decrees, written in the heavenly scrolls, were the ones that really could not be reversed! So Mordecai's letter could be read by the Persians as glorifying King Ahasuerus, but the alert reader was pointed to a higher hand.

The trouble with annual festivals is that in the midst of the busyness of organizing the celebration, alertness can easily go out of the window. Just how easy it is to celebrate the turning of darkness into light and the receiving of rest without ever thinking about the God who accomplished them becomes clear every year as December rolls around. Crowds of people hear songs that declare the message of the incarnation far more clearly than the hidden message of Mordecai's letter. They join in singing "Joy to the world, the Lord is come!" without ever thinking in the slightest about why the world should rejoice. We too may send presents to one another and give gifts to

3. The feminine pronoun here could refer either to the plot or to Esther. I have taken it as referring to the plot. See Joyce G. Baldwin, *Esther* (Tyndale Old Testament Commentaries; Downers Grove, IL: InterVarsity, 1984), 108–9.

4. Michael V. Fox, *Character and Ideology in the Book of Esther*, 2nd ed. (Grand Rapids: Eerdmans, 2001), 119–20.

the poor, through donations to the Salvation Army and toy drives for charity. We too may feast and celebrate, year after year, without fail. We don't even need to bind ourselves to obey an edict from our community leaders, since the advertisers ensure the seasonal focus far wider and more intensive coverage than Mordecai's imperial messengers could ever have done! Yet in all of the getting and giving, in all of the eating and feasting, where is God? Do we remember exactly what we are supposed to be celebrating? In the midst of celebrating the coming of light into the world to transform our darkness, have we completely forgotten who that light is and how that reversal was accomplished?

It is the same with all our other annual celebrations: Thanksgiving, Easter, New Year, even our birthdays. In the midst of all of the busyness of celebrating, in all of the feasting and giving, where is God? Do we remember the one who in love has redeemed us from futility and death? Do we stop to give thanks where thanks is really due, to our gracious heavenly Father? When we celebrate life's good times, we so easily forget the greatest gift of all.

A Reversal Reconsidered

The edict to celebrate the feast of Purim forever is not the end of the story though. Tacked on the end, rather awkwardly, is the little postscript of chapter 10:

> King Ahasuerus imposed tax on the land and on the coastlands of the sea. And all the acts of his power and might, and the full account of the high honor of Mordecai, to which the king advanced him, are they not written in the Book of the Chronicles of the kings of Media and Persia? For Mordecai the Jew was second in rank to King Ahasuerus, and he was great among the Jews and popular with the multitude of his brothers, for he sought the welfare of his people and spoke peace to all his people. (Esth. 10:1–3)

What are these verses doing there? How do they round out the story? They serve to put into perspective the great reversal of the Book of Esther by showing us how much remained unchanged after all.

The postscript starts out with the notice that King Ahasuerus imposed tribute throughout the empire, to its most distant shores. Mordecai the Jew and Esther, daughter of Abihail,[5] might now be the ones writing the edicts in Haman's place but Ahasuerus was still king. His own personal interests remained paramount, no matter what the cost to his loyal subjects.

Some commentators try to put a positive spin on the notice of new taxation by seeing a parallel with the taxes Joseph imposed on the Egyptian economy after he was elevated to power (Gen. 47:13–26). For them, the point is that doing the right thing by the Jews is actually good for the royal economy.[6] However, it is one thing to celebrate the taxation of the hated Egyptians and quite another to be happy about a new imposition on your own back! This is especially true when it is clear that the money raised will not be spent on education and the public welfare of the people, but on the personal interests and whims of the emperor. If the emperor was really short of cash, he could always have melted down one or two of the couches we were shown in his gardens in Esther 1. In fact, the imposition of taxes on the empire is itself another reversal, but this time a negative one. At the time of Esther's coronation as queen, there was a general remission of taxes (Esth. 2:18). Now, even though Esther is more queen than ever, the earlier blessings are reversed. The more things change, the more they stay the same in the empire of Ahasuerus.

This brief notice invites us to go back and reconsider the extent of the reversal that has happened for the Jews. Yes, the Jews have received rest from their enemies all around . . . except for one enemy, Ahasuerus himself. It was his callous indifference that enabled Haman's edict to be signed into law in the first place, because he believed his vizier's statement that it was not in his best interests to give this people rest (i.e. leave them alone; Esth. 3:8). Haman received his just deserts, and God the Great King intervened to give his people the rest that King Ahasuerus would have denied them. King Ahasuerus himself remained untouched, however. He was still in charge, still exercising his power and might in his own interests.

That being the case, the present fate of God's people rested on Mordecai. It was surely good news for God's people that now Mordecai was second in rank to Ahasuerus, in a place where he was able to seek good for his people and speak peace to all his seed. The position once filled by the enemy of the

5. Now her Jewish heritage has become something to be celebrated, not hidden.
6. So Jon D. Levenson, *Esther* (Old Testament Library; Louisville: Westminster John Knox, 1997), 132.

Jews was now occupied by their friend. This was good news, but it was not yet the best of news. When they truly have rest from their enemies all around, their king will surely no longer be named Ahasuerus, but will be a king who embodies the virtues described in Psalm 72, especially the pursuit of justice and righteousness. True rest would come when the one who seeks their good and speaks their peace is not second in rank to anyone, but himself reigns as the true king. In other words, the text itself shows us that the great reversal of the Book of Esther is not yet the Great Reversal of full redemption. It was a great deliverance, to be sure, but any deliverance that rests on the influence of a single individual who must inevitably grow old and die, in an empire that has not been radically transformed, is at best only partial and temporary. We need a greater reversal yet, one which results in the coming of the true King, the Prince of Peace, whose reign will never end!

THE GREATEST REVERSAL

The feast of Purim, when properly understood, is more than just a reminder to God's people of his past ability to intervene decisively even while remaining hidden to all but the eye of faith. It also pointed beyond itself to show us the need for a greater deliverance yet to come. The events celebrated by Esther's generation and their descendants provided a foreshadowing within history of the judgment of the wicked and the deliverance of God's people, but neither of these was comprehensively accomplished. More than seventy-five thousand of the enemies of God's people were slain, while Mordecai and Esther rose to positions of considerable influence and power. Yet at the same time, one of the people most directly responsible for their danger, King Ahasuerus, escaped scot-free. God's people near and far rightly celebrated their deliverance from immediate extinction, but at the end of the day, the power of the empire was left largely intact.

What we have not yet seen in Esther's day, then, is the complete fulfillment of the ancient prophecy: " 'Peace, peace, to those far and near,' says the LORD. 'And I will heal them.' But the wicked are like the tossing sea, which cannot rest, whose waves cast up mire and mud. 'There is no peace,' says my God, 'for the wicked' " (Isa. 57:19–21 NIV). In the Book of Esther we see the tossing sea temporarily driven back through God's grace and providence, but not yet finally stilled. That awaited the coming of one greater even than

Mordecai, one who would be the Prince of Peace, for whom Isaiah looked. This coming one would still the raging sea of wickedness once and for all, and would proclaim full and final peace to those who were far away and peace to those who were near (see Eph. 2:17).

Yet he did so not by waging comprehensive holy war on the historic enemies of God's people, the Gentiles, and destroying them utterly, but rather by destroying the ancient enmity between them and God (Eph. 2:14). He came not as a mighty warrior but as the Prince of Peace. In Christ, former Amalekites and Jews are now brought together into the glorious peace that flows to the one new people of God. Yet our peace has a great cost. Peace was established for us by God declaring holy war on his own Son. This is what was happening on the cross: God the Father laid upon his Son Jesus the guilt of all the sins of those who would become his people. As 2 Corinthians 5:21 put it, "[God] made him to be sin who knew no sin." Having laid our sin on his shoulders, God the Father then poured out the full measure of his wrath against sin upon him. All of the ugliness and pain of the entire history of holy war were concentrated into six hours of awful agony and the burning darkness of the cross. His body was not merely tortured and brutalized by the Romans to the point of death, but was exposed to cosmic shame by being hung on the cross. Like Haman and his sons, Jesus' body was hung on a tree, the ultimate sign of God's judgment curse (see Deut. 21:23). On the cross Jesus fully bore God's curse upon our sin. Why? So that we might receive peace through his righteousness and have rest from all our guilt and sin and access into the life-giving presence of God.

BECOMING PURIM PEOPLE

What a difference understanding our forgiveness in Christ makes in our lives. Now we have peace with God. We have a peace that transcends any peace this world has to offer because it rests not on a Mordecai to plead our case before a king like Ahasuerus, but on Jesus, who brings us constantly into the presence of the King of kings. Jesus is the one who seeks our good and speaks peace to us as his seed (see Esth. 10:3).

To be sure, life often still looks as it did in the days of Mordecai and Esther, and we are tempted to respond in the same way as the Jews of their generation did, without reference to God. At times, we appear to be in the midst of the tossing sea and in danger of being overwhelmed by the mire and the mud. Perhaps a Haman seems to be in control of our personal destiny, and so we weep and wail. Then things turn around and a Mordecai or an Esther appears for us and life becomes better, so we feast and celebrate and say to one another, "It doesn't get any better than this." Studying our patterns of feasting and fasting may reveal where our priorities and hopes lie. But the eye of faith is constantly looking beyond the visible circumstances of this world to the unseen heavenly reality, where even now Christ is enthroned for us.

The Book of Esther calls us to analyze our fasting and our feasting to help us diagnose our hearts. What things cast us down to the depths of despair? What things lift us up to the heights of exultation? Even the way we celebrate the festivals of our religious calendar—such as Thanksgiving, Christmas, and Easter—can be a powerful diagnostic tool. What do we have to have to make these celebrations "right"? What things cause us anxiety and stress every year because we are nervous that they won't get done? Do we have to have a large pile of presents at Christmas? Do we have to have certain foods cooked just right at Thanksgiving? Do we require the presence of certain family members around the table at Easter? For many people, there are things that they are inordinately stressed out about each year, because they feel that everything has to be just right.

Why does the level of domestic stress rise dramatically over the holiday period? It is because the festival itself exposes our idolatries. I remember throwing a ridiculous tantrum one Christmas because I received a model ship kit from an aunt, while my sisters received adorable stuffed animals. There was nothing wrong with the gift. However, it wasn't what I wanted, and my self-idolatry became exposed for all to see! But it is not just children whose idolatries are on display year after year at Christmas. Adults, too, show their hearts by what thrills them and what disappoints them. We too are condemned by the tantrums we throw because people and presents haven't lived up to our expectations.

It is not just our festival tantrums that expose our hearts, though. Even our seasonal feelings of happiness and satisfaction may expose our hearts. It is not just the worst Thanksgiving ever, when we burn the turkey and throw a plate, which shows our trust is placed in the wrong thing. It may even be the best Christmas of our lives, when everything we put on the table is perfect, and our spouse bought us the most thoughtful present ever. Is that all it takes for the festival to satisfy our hearts? Is our definition of the best festival ever really so horizontal that it holds no need for God's work of creating gladness in our souls? Our hearts are sometimes condemned by what we rejoice in, as well as what we worry about.

How then might we celebrate these feasts properly? To be sure, Christmas and Easter are not commanded in Scripture, to be celebrated on a particular day at a particular time of year. We cannot insist that Christians celebrate the incarnation on or around December 25, or that we celebrate the resurrection on a particular Sunday in the spring. The date is not important. But if the reversal of Purim was worth celebrating annually, as a reminder of God's intervention in history, how much more should those who understand the Greatest Reversal of all celebrate. How much more should we find ourselves on our knees with thankfulness to God, not simply that life has gone well for us this year (if it has), but because death has been transformed into life for us in Christ. With the birth of Christ, light has come into the world, a light that can never be extinguished. Through the death of Christ on the cross and his resurrection from the dead, peace has definitively been given to us, a peace that no circumstances can ever add to or take away from. In Christ, we have rest from all our efforts to win God's favor in our own strength, a resting on his righteousness given to us as a free gift. Don't forget the real significance of the feast in the midst of the seasonal busyness!

But don't forget to feast either! We have something to celebrate at these festivals. There is nothing wrong with exchanging gifts and hanging seasonal decorations at Christmas, enjoying turkeys and pies along with an abundance of other good things at Thanksgiving, decorating eggs and eating lamb at Easter. We should celebrate God's goodness to us as God's people have always done, with good food and good fellowship. In the midst of that fellowship, though, don't just invite neighbors and friends to share the joy. Remember those who are poor, both those who are poor in things and those who are poor before God. Our times of feasting should be times for sharing with the less fortunate, for looking out for the lonely, for welcoming outcasts and strangers into our families. These are times of special opportunity for sharing the gospel good news with those who have never heard it, rich or poor, that they too may receive God's peace. These are times for pointing all to Christ, the true light of the world, the true Prince of Peace. The celebration of his birth, the opening move in the greatest reversal of all, is something that will truly never pass away, until his kingdom comes in all its fullness. The celebration of his death and resurrection, the climax of God's plan of salvation, is something that Christians will never tire of observing, until he returns again in his glory.

Indeed, we have something to celebrate every Sunday as we gather together with God's people. The Puritans who refused to celebrate Christmas and Easter annually did so not because they were against celebration. On the contrary, they wanted to stress the fact that we celebrate the Great Reversal every Lord's Day as we gather with his people. For them, every Sunday was Christmas, every Sunday was Easter, every Sunday was Thanksgiving. There should constantly be a note of celebration and joy in our worship too, for we remember the death from which we have been spared. A somber tone may be appropriate for a funeral, but not for a feast day! Our tongues should be filled with such rejoicing that we can hardly wait to burst into songs of praise to celebrate the great victory that our God has won for us, turning death into life, darkness into light, the prospect of hell into the assurance of heaven.

The kingdom of Ahasuerus has passed away, though the evil empire still remains around us in different forms. Here on earth, we are constantly still involved in a life-and-death struggle with the forces of evil. But it will not always be so. The day is coming when our King will return to claim his throne and the days of the evil empire will end. The day is coming when the angels will cry out at last, "The kingdom of the world has become the kingdom of our Lord and of his Christ, and he shall reign forever and ever" (Rev. 11:15). On that day, we too, like the elders in heaven, will fall on our faces and cry out, "Worthy is God the Father and the Lamb that was slain, by whose blood we have been redeemed for God from every tribe and language and people and nation" (see Rev. 5:9). To which, all creation will simply add, "Amen!"

THE LORD REDEEMS

10

THE ROAD TO NOWHERE

Ruth 1:1–5

*In the days when the judges ruled there was a famine in the land,
and a man of Bethlehem in Judah went to sojourn in the country
of Moab, he and his wife and his two sons. . . . They lived there
about ten years, and both Mahlon and Chilion died, so that the
woman was left without her two sons and her husband."*
(Ruth 1:1, 4–5)

*I*n every life there are certain defining moments, key crossroads along the way. On the one hand, there are certain times when a person consciously chooses his or her destination. There are occasions like the one that the writer M. Scott Peck recalls when he had to make a choice between going down the path everyone else was following and taking another path—what he called "the road less traveled."[1] The remainder of his life was, as Peck remembers it, the result of having chosen to take that less-traveled road.

On the other hand, though, there are also times in life when it seems that your destination has chosen you. These are the occasions when life gives us no choice at all, but thrusts us willy-nilly down a path that, however well or little traveled, we would never have chosen for ourselves. No one chooses to

1. M. Scott Peck, *The Road Less Traveled: A New Psychology of Love, Traditional Values and Spiritual Growth* (New York: Simon & Schuster, 1978).

have her husband die, leaving her a widow with young children. No one chooses to have a crippling accident or a life-threatening disease with permanent consequences. These too can be defining moments in a life. But all of us—whether defined by the choices we have made or the choices life has made for us—are on a journey through life, a road that is heading toward some destination or other. Where are you going?

The first chapter of the Book of Ruth is the story of choices made and choices seemingly thrust upon people, about roads traveled or left untraveled. It is about the long-term consequences of the decisions we make. Often the consequences are not those we expected and anticipated, but our lives nonetheless bear the mark of the decisions we have made and the defining moments we have faced. The Book of Ruth shows us that our actions have consequences. However, our lives are not simply the consequence of the various decisions we have made and events that have occurred, as if the universe were a giant supercomputer into which we feed all of the variables and come out with a predictable answer. There is a mysterious X-factor that is evident in the Book of Ruth—a variable that has the power to change everything. It is the grace of God, which directs the outcomes of those decisions and events according to his sovereignty and good purpose for his people. That grace is not always evident to the players in the game at the time. But it is always there, whether acknowledged or unacknowledged. Ultimately, for Christians, the grace of God is always the defining element of our lives.

IN THE DAYS WHEN THE JUDGES RULED

The Book of Ruth starts with a description of the times in which the events took place: "In the days when the judges ruled there was a famine in the land, and a man of Bethlehem in Judah went to sojourn in the country of Moab, he and his wife and his two sons" (Ruth 1:1). This is not merely a date-stamp to locate the moment in history in which the characters lived, as if the writer had started out, "Fourscore and seven years ago . . . there was a famine in the land." Rather, it is a theological description of the character of the times in which these events take place. It is like Charles Dickens's beginning to *The Tale of Two Cities*: "It was the best of times, it was the worst of times"—only there was little that was good about the times of the judges. During the days of the judges, everyone did as seemed best in his own eyes, for there was no king in the land (Judg. 21:25).

There is a repeated cycle (or, more precisely, a downward spiral) of events in the Book of Judges. At the beginning of each cycle, God's people rebelled against him and sinned. Next, God acted in judgment against them. Then the people repented and cried out to the Lord. At least they did this the first few times they passed through the cycle. Later on in the Book of Judges, though, this step of repentance is missing. Finally, at the end of each cycle, the Lord sent a deliverer to rescue his people, and they experienced some measure of rest.

As the Book of Judges progresses, however, there is a change in the nature of the deliverers who are sent and the deliverance God's people receive. The first judge, Othniel, is a squeaky-clean hero. The last judge, Samson, systematically undermines our expectations of what a deliverer ought to be. Called to be a Nazirite at birth, separated for God from defiling influences, he systematically breaks every vow that was made on his behalf. Instead of avoiding contact with everything dead, he scoops honey from the corpse of a lion (Judg. 14:9). Instead of avoiding contact with the Philistines, he wants to marry one (Judg. 14:1–2). Instead of avoiding fermented drinks, he participates in a drinking party with his future Philistine in-laws (Judg. 14:10). Samson ends his life bringing judgment on God's enemies, but establishing no rest for God's people.

The final chapters of the Book of Judges (Judg. 17–21) stand outside this downward spiral and show us in graphic detail a nation that had comprehensively lost its way, becoming every bit as bad as the pagan nations that were the previous inhabitants of the Promised Land. Except for those times when God periodically sent a deliverer to rescue his people and turned their hearts back toward him, the days of the judges were a bleak, dark time of disobedience on the part of God's people. Such disobedience was inevitably followed by God's judgment resting upon their land, just as the covenant with Moses had threatened (Deut. 28:15–68).

ELIMELECH'S CHOICE

It was in these difficult days that a man moved his family out of Israel: "The name of the man was Elimelech and the name of his wife Naomi, and

131

the names of his two sons were Mahlon and Chilion. They were Ephrathites from Bethlehem in Judah. They went into the country of Moab and remained there" (Ruth 1:2). Unfaithfulness to God had once again resulted in a famine in the land.[2] The ultimate irony had occurred: Bethlehem, whose very name means "House of Bread," was a place of no food. In that situation, Elimelech had a choice to make, a road to choose. He could stay in Bethlehem, the empty breadbasket of Judah, mourning the sin that surrounded him and trusting God to provide for him. Alternatively, he could leave the Promised Land behind in search of greener fields, in this case the fields of Moab, where food was more abundant.

Elimelech's choices were not equal choices, theologically speaking, in the way that the choice of city in which to live might be for us. We can perhaps serve the Lord equally well in New York or New Orleans, in Atlanta or Acapulco or Amsterdam. However, God had delivered his people from Egypt and brought them to the land of Canaan as a special place for them to live. God had called Elimelech to live in Bethlehem. He therefore had no business leaving there to go anywhere, least of all Moab. For Israel, Moab was known for several things, none of them good. The Moabites had originated out of an incestuous relationship between Lot and his older daughter (Gen. 19:30–38); their king Balak had hired Balaam to curse Israel when they came out of Egypt (Num. 22–24); their women had been a stumbling block to Israel in the wilderness, seducing them to the worship of false gods (Num. 25); and they had recently oppressed the Israelites in the days of Eglon (Judg. 3). Does this sound like the place to go in order to raise a godly family?

Before he left the Promised Land and went to a place like Moab, Elimelech's very name should have given him pause, for it literally means "My God is king." It appears, however, that God was no more king in Elimelech's heart than he was in the hearts of his fellow countrymen (see Judg. 21:25). There was no king in Elimelech's life, and therefore, like so many others in the days when the judges ruled, he chose to do what was best in his own eyes. Instead of following the path of repentance and faith, trusting the Lord to provide for his needs, he moved to follow what seemed to be the best prospects of supporting his family, humanly speaking. He chose the road to Moab.

---

2. For the implied connection between the unfaithfulness of the people and the famine, see K. Lawson Younger Jr., *Judges, Ruth* (New International Version Application Commentary; Grand Rapids: Zondervan, 2002), 414.

Which road will each of us choose? Very often in those defining moments in life where we get to direct our own course for the future, the factors that weigh most heavily in our decisions are those that seem most likely to provide us with comfort and security. The bottom line in our lives is rarely God's will, as it is revealed in his Word, especially if it seems to cut directly across our best prospects for happiness and success. We rarely think seriously about the impact our choices will have on our ability to raise a Christian family in a world that is often less than ideal. Like Elimelech, we act as the sovereign of our own lives, making the choices that seem best in our eyes, without reference to God and without serious thought about the long-term implications. Many bear the label "Christian," yet their Christianity has no real impact on life-defining decisions, just as Elimelech bore the name "My God is king" yet lived in a way that made it evident that God wasn't his king at all. The roads we choose for ourselves often make our deepest heart commitments plain for all to see.

THE ROAD TO NOWHERE

The road to Moab turned out to be the road to nowhere. That reality was not immediately apparent, of course. But then it rarely is.

At first it seemed as if Elimelech had made the sensible choice. While his kinsmen back home were suffering and hungry, there was food in Moab. Like the prodigal son in the story Jesus told (Luke 15:11–32), Elimelech's stay in the far country went well at the outset. He was able to support his wife and two sons in comfort, and after a while Moab became home. It's not clear when in the process that happened. Perhaps there never was a conscious decision to settle there permanently. Verse 2 literally says, "They went to the fields of Moab, and they were there." Unlike their plan in verse 1, it doesn't say, "they sojourned there," as if, like Abraham before them, they consciously were temporary residents in a country not their own. Nor does it say "they settled there," as if they had now consciously decided that the move was permanent. They just existed there, perhaps not really thinking about what the future might hold.[3] Like so many, they now seemed simply to be drifting through life without any grand plan.

---

3. The Hebrew in verse 2 is *wayyihyu*, which comes from the verb *hayah*. The verb in verse 1 is *gur*, while "to settle" would be *yashab*.

Somewhere along the road, however, being in Moab took on a more permanent cast: "But Elimelech, the husband of Naomi, died, and she was left with her two sons. These took Moabite wives; the name of the one was Orpah and the name of the other Ruth. They lived there about ten years" (Ruth 1:3–4). Now after Elimelech's death the remnant[4] of the family had a decision to make. They could repent and go back home to their own land and their own God, or they could stay where they were in exile. Tellingly, their choice was to stay. They still rated their prospects more highly in Moab than in Judah; they felt more at home in the land of compromise than in the land of promise. As a result of that road not taken, Naomi's sons then took Moabite women as wives (Ruth 1:4), even though the law of Moses had commanded them not to do so (Deut. 7:3).[5] After all, they probably thought to themselves, who else was there to choose from? Once entered upon, the road to continued and deepened disobedience is often smoothly paved and provides little resistance.

This too is often the way it is for us. Choosing to step outside God's revealed will may come at the end of a lengthy period of wrestling with our consciences. Yet remaining on the outside may well require less effort. The prodigal's decision to leave home was a deliberate one; remaining in the far country after all his money had been squandered required only an absence of thought. Indeed, sometimes the biggest obstacle to returning home is our pride. We hate the thought of having to return to our homes and our families with our lives in tatters and having to admit that our previous choice was wrong. Somehow, it seems easier to bear the pain of continued emptiness than to confess our pursuit of fullness in the wrong place.

Even after Elimelech had died, though, Naomi was still reasonably well situated in life. She had her sons, after all. They were young and married and had every prospect of providing future descendants to take care of her in her old age. For ten years, everything seemed to be proceeding sufficiently accord-

---

4. Perhaps not coincidentally the theologically significant word "remnant" (*she'erit*) comes from the same root as the verb "to be left behind" (*sha'ar*). Daniel Block comments that *sha'ar* "often refers to those who have survived the wrath and judgment of God" (*Judges, Ruth* [New American Commentary; Nashville: Broadman & Holman, 1999], 628).

5. Block points out that the uncommon idiom used for taking wives here (*nasa' nashim*) highlights the illegitimate nature of their marriages (*Judges, Ruth*, 629).

ing to plan, although the barrenness of both of her son's wives ought surely to have been recognized as a sign that God was not blessing the family.

Worse was to come for Naomi. "Both Mahlon and Chilion died, so that the woman was left without her two sons and her husband" (Ruth 1:5). In the space of half a verse, Naomi's whole world came crashing down around her, and she was left alone, a remnant of one under the judgment of God. Who would now support a foreign widow in her declining years? No family meant no food, and government-sponsored welfare programs were scarce in Moab. She was a stranger in a strange land, an aging, single woman of no significance in a family-oriented culture, with no one to care for or about her. So Naomi faced another defining moment in her life. It was time to make another choice—though this time, it hardly seemed like much of a choice at all. She would have to swallow her pride and go back to God's people, in Bethlehem, where she had heard that there was now food again (1:6). God's blessing had finally returned to Bethlehem. After experiencing the bitter emptiness of the land of compromise, the time was long overdue for the prodigal daughter to go home.

Danger: God at Work

Typically, we think the knowledge that God is at work in our lives is a comforting truth. Sometimes that is indeed the case. However, in the days when the judges ruled, God's activity included both judgment and blessing. Those who rebelled against him and did what seemed right in their own eyes consistently saw life turn sour for them, just as God had warned. By contrast, those who truly repented and turned to him found him more than ready to forgive.

This same pattern is at work in the opening verses of the Book of Ruth. In the first place, although it is easy to overlook since it is in the background of the text, the pattern of judgment followed by blessing came to Israel: "Then she arose with her daughters-in-law to return from the country of Moab, for she had heard in the fields of Moab that the Lord had visited his people and given them food" (Ruth 1:6). The famine which the people in Bethlehem had been experiencing because of their sins was finally lifted (Ruth 1:6). Given the setting in the days of the judges, this can only mean that God's people repented and saw his favor restored. This is the crucial

135

backdrop against which to read Naomi's personal experience of exile and return. Bethlehem had repented and experienced God's grace and favor; would the same experience be Naomi's?

Such a positive outcome was certainly not inevitable. Naomi, along with her husband and children, had set out on a road of disobedience, and they had experienced the reality of God's judgment. Elimelech, Mahlon, and Chilion were all dead as a result. There was no hope of repentance and return for them. Yet God in his grace had not left her family completely without survivors. A remnant remained, giving hope that there might be a future after all. God's judgment on sin is reliable, for his Word is faithful, but even more consistent is God's desire to restore wandering sinners to himself. Grace is always God's last word.

This is both a challenging and comforting truth for us. To be sure, God's actions of blessing and curse are not normally as physical and tangible in our lives as they were during the period of the Mosaic covenant, in which Naomi lived. We don't see God's favor and disfavor as directly expressed in terms of abundant prosperity when we are faithful and exile when we are unfaithful. Israel uniquely experienced these physical blessings and curses as a foreshadowing of the final rewards and judgments to come on the last day. Yet the spiritual realities to which those signs pointed remain the same. The way of unfaithfulness to God continues to be the way of death.

Not everyone who abandons the way of the Lord will return. Some who once seemed to be part of God's people prove that they were never really his, as they abandon the path to life and fall away (see 1 John 2:19). That is why the fear of the Lord is the beginning of wisdom and the way to life in all its fullness. In fact, were it not for the mercy and power of the Lord, all of us would end up like Elimelech, Mahlon, and Chilion: dead and buried without trace and without memory, the victims of our own bad decisions and foolish choices. Left to ourselves, we would all fall away in an instant. Fortunately for us, however, God's grace transcends our rebellion, and not only leaves the door open for us to retrace our steps, but stirs our hearts to see our folly and the welcoming arms that await our return. So the Spirit of God stirred Naomi's heart to leave the land of rebellion, swallow her wounded pride, and start out at last on the long road home.

Even though she was hardly blameless in these events, Naomi nonetheless had a future because of the grace of God. Naomi was not a woman of character simply caught up in a juggernaut of events outside her control. She couldn't blame Elimelech for everything that transpired, especially since she had the opportunity to return home when he died. She was personally responsible for at least some of her troubles. Yet however far she had wandered from her home, the beginning of the road to return was only one step away. Here too there is hope for us; even for those who have chosen the way of rebellion and persisted for a long time in the way of rebellion, there is still a way home. In the grace of God, the road to nowhere may yet turn out to be the first leg of the long journey home.

THE ROAD HOME

The Book of Ruth addresses us as people who are just like Elimelech and Naomi. Like them, we often find that the grass seems greener in the fields on the Moabite side of the fence. The temptation to abandon the bread of heaven for this world's provisions is very strong, especially during times when the bread of heaven seems scarce. The option of choosing the land of compromise (in this case Moab) instead of faithfully persevering by faith in the land of promise is a constant theme in the Old Testament. The food that the unpromised land offers seems very real, very tangible, and easily available in contrast to the promises of God, which constantly test our faith and our trust.

Like believers in Old Testament times, we continue to struggle in this area. Often we exhibit a fundamental lack of trust in God's goodness. Perhaps we complain about the job God has given us, or the spouse that we married, or the family (or lack of family) that God in his providence has allotted to us, and we fantasize about greener fields elsewhere. Perhaps we have to confess that we have even turned our back on the Lord's way and have journeyed to the fields of Moab that seemed to offer better bread. But God's grace not only brings in those who were always outsiders to his people, like Ruth, but also extends to those who have rebelled against him from the inside and pursued forbidden paths. No matter what we have done and how long we have done it, there are forgiveness and hope for us. Indeed, the very fact that we have come, whether willingly or unwillingly, to see the emptiness of the fields of Moab is itself a hopeful sign of the Lord's work in our hearts.

The reason for our hope is God's faithfulness to his people. God is committed to save for himself a people of his own. He does this not by searching for perfect paragons of virtue, but rather by reaching down to rebellious sinners and transforming them from the inside out. This is usually a slow work, as it was in Naomi's case, but God is not in a hurry. This slow work often involves painful paths, as God strips away the things in which we have placed our trust instead of him. All along the hard road to heaven, though, the love of God draws us and drives us to himself and will not let us go.

The father of the prodigal son did not sit in his living room with his feet up, waiting for his errant son to come crawling home on his hands and knees. On the contrary, he ran to meet him on the road (Luke 15:20). So too God has not left us to make the journey home alone. In Christ, God comes running to meet us. Whereas Elimelech left the place of famine to seek a false blessing in Moab, Jesus Christ left the glories of heaven to bring us a true blessing on earth. Elimelech and Naomi sent themselves into exile from the land of promise, trying to build their own kingdom rather than waiting for God to do it; Jesus, though, went into exile from his Father's presence so that he might rescue us from our own kingdom-building and grant us a true and living future in his kingdom. The God who empties us and strips away, however painfully, those precious things in which we are trusting knows what it is to be stripped of all of his possessions, left alone and abandoned by his friends, and hung empty on a cross. Every tear of loss that God inflicts on us is a tear whose cost he himself understands.

The pain of God's chastening work is therefore never harsh; it is never more than is absolutely necessary to turn us to himself. It is measured and designed to show us the emptiness of the paths we have chosen for ourselves, so that we may return to his ways. What is more, when we do return to him, we discover that it is his delight to fill the void we have created. The Father delights to clothe the naked prodigal, exults to honor the humiliated prodigal, thrills to feed the starving prodigal, and rejoices to celebrate with the downcast prodigal. He takes the proud and brings them low, but once we have recognized our inner poverty, he delights to exalt us and seat us with princes (see Ps. 113:7–8). What an awesome God he is! How great are his mercy and grace!

11

GRACE AT THE BOTTOM OF THE BARREL

Ruth 1:6–22

*But Ruth said, "Do not urge me to leave you or to return from
following you. For where you go I will go, and where you lodge
I will lodge. Your people shall be my people, and your God
my God. Where you die I will die, and there will I be buried.
May the LORD do so to me and more also if anything
but death parts me from you." (Ruth 1:16–17)*

"O love that will not let me go . . . ," wrote the hymn writer George Matheson. Yet there are times when we may be tempted to wish that God *would* let us go. There are moments in life when God's pursuit of us seems like that of a persistent mosquito, constantly buzzing around our heads and causing us pain, and we are utterly powerless to shake him off. Certainly, Naomi was thinking of God in those terms in the second half of Ruth 1. Having departed from the Promised Land with a husband and two sons to go to the greener fields of Moab, she had been left utterly bereft of support by their death. Moab was no longer a viable place for her to live; she had no choice but to return home. There was food at last in Bethlehem, and perhaps she too, widow that she was, might yet be able to eke out the rest of her miserable existence there.

GOING HOME

But what should Naomi do about her two Moabite daughters-in-law, Orpah and Ruth? At first, they all set out to go back to Judah together. But was the choice Naomi was making, to go home to Bethlehem, the right choice for them as well? This was the dilemma Naomi faced on the road out of Moab:

> Then she arose with her daughters-in-law to return from the country of Moab, for she had heard in the fields of Moab that the LORD had visited his people and given them food. So she set out from the place where she was with her two daughters-in-law, and they went on the way to return to the land of Judah. But Naomi said to her two daughters-in-law, "Go, return each of you to her mother's house. May the LORD deal kindly with you, as you have dealt with the dead and with me. The LORD grant that you may find rest, each of you in the house of her husband!" Then she kissed them, and they lifted up their voices and wept. And they said to her, "No, we will return with you to your people." But Naomi said, "Turn back, my daughters; why will you go with me? Have I yet sons in my womb that they may become your husbands? Turn back, my daughters; go your way, for I am too old to have a husband. If I should say I have hope, even if I should have a husband this night and should bear sons, would you therefore wait till they were grown? Would you therefore refrain from marrying? No, my daughters, for it is exceedingly bitter to me for your sake that the hand of the LORD has gone out against me." (Ruth 1:6–13)

What should these women do? Should they stay or should they go? While Bethlehem had once been Naomi's home, it was never theirs. Her people were not their people. And if Orpah and Ruth came with her, it would mean two more mouths to feed on a fixed and limited budget, two more bodies to clothe and house, all the while dependent on the charity of family members.

What made it far worse for Naomi to contemplate, though, was the fact that these two were foreigners who would hardly be welcome in polite society in Bethlehem. They were Moabite women who by their very presence would be a constant reminder to Naomi and all those around her of her sin in abandoning the Promised Land and marrying her sons outside the covenant people. Every time she saw their foreign faces, she would be confronted with the heavy hand of God's judgment upon her in the loss of her husband and her sons. It was in some ways similar to the situation of a young woman who has lived a rebellious life away from home and has a child outside of marriage. Adoption may be a hard choice, but if she keeps the child when she returns home, she (and everyone around her) may be constantly reminded of her sin by the child's presence. Unless grace is powerfully present in the situation, the child could easily be viewed as an embarrassing intruder.

No wonder, then, that Naomi thought it far better for these women (and for her) that they should go back to their parents' houses, to live on the charity of their own people and find new husbands among their kinsfolk. Why should they choose their own road to nowhere and come along with her to a land that was not their own? "Go home, my daughters!" said Naomi. "Return to your own people and your own gods. There is no hope in coming with me; with my people, there will be no future prospects of marriage and a family." For Orpah and Ruth, going with Naomi would be choosing the road to nowhere, embracing the path that led to emptiness.

EMPTINESS REJECTED, EMPTINESS EMBRACED

Orpah made the sensible choice and went back home: "Then they lifted up their voices and wept again. And Orpah kissed her mother-in-law, but Ruth clung to her" (Ruth 1:14). Orpah was fond of her mother-in-law, but she didn't allow her emotions to cloud her decision. "You have to use your head as well as your heart when choosing the road to travel," she reasoned. Who could fault her logic or blame her choice? If there was no special blessing to be found in the land of promise (and Naomi's whole life had been lived on that basis), then the best prospect of blessing for Orpah and Ruth was with their own people. Here was their best chance of achieving some significance through husbands and families of their own.

Orpah looked her situation in life clearly in the face and made the necessary decisions by using exactly the same logic that Naomi had followed earlier: the fields of Moab looked far greener than the land of Israel. With that simple, sensible choice she marched off, out of the pages of the Bible. She went back to her people, and back to her gods. Yet though she certainly didn't see it that way, there was nonetheless a cost to her logical choice. Who now remembers Orpah? She rejected the road to emptiness, but at the same time unknowingly turned aside from the one road that could have led her to a life of lasting significance and meaning. The world's wise choice to avoid emptiness leads in the end to a different kind of oblivion.

Then there was Ruth. Ruth was a nobody, an outsider, a Moabite of all things.[1] There was nothing kosher about Ruth. She knew she would be about as welcome in Bethlehem as a ham sandwich at a bar mitzvah. Conventional wisdom shouted for Ruth to follow the way of Orpah, the most likely way of worldly security and significance. But Ruth was not Orpah and there was nothing conventional about her. She would not let Naomi go on alone to her empty future. She clung to her; here the text uses the same verb (*davaq*) that is used in Genesis 2:24 to describe the bond that exists in marriage. It is a word that describes loyalty to a covenant commitment. Ruth was glued to her mother-in-law, and nothing and no one could send her away. Naomi said, "See, your sister-in-law has gone back to her people and to her gods; return after your sister-in-law" (Ruth 1:15). But in a crescendo of commitment, Ruth poured out her heart to Naomi: "Do not urge me to leave you or to return from following you. For where you go, I will go, and where you lodge, I will lodge. Your people shall be my people, and your God my God. Where you die I will die, and there will I be buried. May the LORD do so to me and more also if anything but death parts me from you" (Ruth 1:16–17).

Each of these statements ratchets up the level of her commitment a notch higher. Ruth was not merely relocating her home to go somewhere geographically less pleasant, as if someone were willing to move from sunny Southern California to the unbearable heat of Death Valley. That would be noble self-sacrifice; this is far more. She is committing her life to Naomi, body and soul, for better or for worse, for richer or for poorer, in sickness and in health. In so doing, she is also committing her life to Naomi's God, whom she calls as a witness by his personal name, the Lord. She is even willing to die and be buried in Naomi's land—the land of Naomi's God, not the gods of the Moabites. Given the intimate connection between land and deity in the ancient Near East, and the importance of proper burial for a restful

---

1. Ruth's foreign ethnic origins are stressed in the frequent use of the appellation "Ruth the Moabite" to describe her. See Robert L. Hubbard Jr., *The Book of Ruth* (New International Commentary on the Old Testament; Grand Rapids: Eerdmans, 1988), 137.

afterlife, this was the ultimate commitment in the ancient world. She further binds herself to do this with an oath of self-imprecation. If she reneges on her promise, she invites the Lord—Naomi's God—to stretch out his hand to strike her down. Here is an astonishing act of surrender and self-sacrifice. Ruth was laying down her entire life to serve Naomi.

CALL ME MARA!

In response, Naomi said . . . nothing: "And when Naomi saw that she was determined to go with her, she said no more" (Ruth 1:18). No "Thank you" graced Naomi's lips. There was no "I'll be really glad for some company on this difficult road." Literally, the Hebrew says, "When Naomi realized that Ruth was determined to go with her, she stopped talking to her." Having listened to one of the most emotionally moving speeches in the whole Bible, in which Ruth pledged herself completely to Naomi, she could make no response other than a hard silence.[2]

Isn't Naomi's silence an astonishing response to her daughter-in-law's words? Our own response to Ruth's words is instinctively to frame them and hang them on the wall. We quote the words in marriage ceremonies and are choked up by their implications, so profoundly touching do they seem to us. Yet these were far from welcome words for Naomi in her state of bitterness. She had nothing to say to this unwanted outpouring.

Is this interpretation too hard on Naomi? Does it read too much into her silence? For confirmation that this was indeed her line of thinking, consider what she said when she and Ruth finally reached Bethlehem, and the townswomen gathered around her:

> So the two of them went on until they came to Bethlehem. And when they came to Bethlehem, the whole town was stirred because of them. And the women said, "Is this Naomi?" She said to them, "Do not call me Naomi; call me Mara, for the Almighty has dealt very bitterly with me. I went away full, and the LORD has brought me back empty. Why call me Naomi, when the Lord has testified against me and the Almighty has brought calamity upon me? (Ruth 1:19–21)

2. So also D. N. Fewell and D. M. Gunn, " 'A Son Is Born to Naomi!': Literary Allusions and Interpretation in the Book of Ruth," *Journal for the Study of the Old Testament* 40 (1988): 104.

As she returned to Bethlehem Naomi summed up her experience while she had been away. "Don't call me Naomi ("Pleasant") any more," she said. "Instead, call me Mara ("Bitter"). I went away full, but the Lord has brought me back empty. I left here with everything; now I'm left with absolutely nothing." But if Naomi evaluates her present situation on her return to Bethlehem as having absolutely nothing, what does that make Ruth? Less than nothing? She certainly doesn't rate much higher in Naomi's estimation at this point.[3]

It is equally striking that when the women of Bethlehem welcomed Naomi home, they didn't even deign to notice her companion. The narrator has neatly highlighted their deliberate omission: "The *two of them* went on until *they* came to Bethlehem. And when *they* came to Bethlehem, the whole town was stirred because of *them*. And the women said, 'Is *this* Naomi?'" In other words, everyone in Bethlehem could see that there were two people there, but instead of asking the obvious question ("Who are these two? Naomi, who is this with you?"), the townswomen simply said, "Is this Naomi?" neatly sidestepping the question of who her embarrassing appendage might be.[4] There almost seems to have been an unspoken communal conspiracy not to mention the Moabitess.

Note also that Naomi was not broken and repentant over her Moabite experience. She may have been returning to the Lord's land in body, but she was not exactly returning to the Lord with a broken spirit and a contrite heart. Mara, "Bitter," was exactly the right name for Naomi now. It was a name with a history, a history of God's people rebelling at his perceived lack of provision for their needs. It was at Marah in the wilderness on the way out of Egypt that the children of Israel grumbled against the Lord because they couldn't drink the water (Ex. 15:23–24). This was only a few days after the Lord had parted the Red Sea and delivered them from the chariots and horsemen of Egypt, but all of that meant nothing in the face of their very present thirst.

Like her ancestors, Naomi's heart was angry with God for the way her life was turning out. She was experiencing the pain of life in the desert and felt

3. Similarly, K. Lawson Younger Jr., *Judges, Ruth* (New International Version Application Commentary; Grand Rapids: Zondervan, 2002), 428.
4. The slightly awkward syntax in Ruth 1:22 ("So Naomi returned, and Ruth the Moabite her daughter-in-law with her, who returned from the country of Moab") also serves to place a certain distance between Naomi and Ruth in their return from Moab.

that the judgments that had befallen her were all God's fault. The Lord had "testified against" her (Ruth 1:21); that is, he had called her to account at the bar of his courtroom.[5] Her losses were attributable directly to the Almighty's acts of judgment against her. In response, her heart had grown hard and bitter toward him, both recognizing and at the same time resenting his power in her life. At this point, there was no whisper of acknowledgement in her heart of her own responsibility in choosing the path of disobedience that had led her away from the Promised Land in the first place. Naomi was simply resentful that the greener pastures of Moab, outside the land of promise, had actually turned into a desert in her experience. The prodigal daughter may now have been back home in her Father's land physically, but she was back only because she didn't see any prospect of continued survival among the pigs in the far country. Her body may have made the journey home, but her spirit was still far from restored.

THE ONE WAY TO LIFE

So what does this passage say to us? In the first place, it addresses us as people who are just like Orpah and Ruth. Like Orpah and Ruth, there was nothing kosher about us when we were born. On the contrary, we were outsiders to the gospel, outsiders to grace, by nature objects of God's wrath, even if we grew up in a Christian home. By nature, we were dead in our transgressions and sins, as Paul puts it (Eph. 2:1). We all need a new birth—to be born of the Spirit, as Jesus told Nicodemus—in order to enter the kingdom of God (John 3:5).

Like Orpah and Ruth, as natural-born outsiders, we cannot simply slide into the kingdom. We are all faced with a crucial choice at some point in our lives, a dividing of the ways. We can continue to seek our security and significance in the world's way, as Orpah did. We can seek to find meaning and value in our career, our family, our health, or our wealth. Or, alternatively, we can choose the way of Ruth.

Up to a point, Orpah's approach to life may work, granting us everything we ask of it. Who knows what happened to Orpah when she went home? Perhaps she met her Mr. Right, had a pack of children, and lived happily

---

5. For the legal usage of this idiom, see Hubbard, *Ruth*, 126.

145

ever after in Moab. So too, for many people life works out relatively well, giving them in reasonable measure the things that they have sought. But in the process of pursuing the Moabite option, Orpah missed out on the one thing of true value in life: a living relationship with the Lord, the one true God. She chose with her eyes, just as Naomi and Elimelech had earlier, opting for the way of the world instead of the way of faith. Whether she found what she was looking for in Moab or not really doesn't matter. Either way, she missed the pearl of great price. She failed to find friendship with Israel's God, the only God that there is. The saddest part of Orpah's story is that she probably never even knew what she was missing.

Alternatively, we can follow Ruth's pattern and choose the gospel way to true life. It is a daunting path that can be taken only by faith, by throwing oneself on the mercy and favor of Israel's God. As outsiders, we have nothing to offer him except our emptiness. Ruth embraced that emptiness, and trusted that Naomi's God would be her God also. This road necessarily passes through the way of the cross, the way of dying to self and to our own interests. In one sense, the gospel road is the easiest path in the world, for we bring to it nothing except our own need. In another sense, though, it is the hardest path, for the cross is a continual stumbling block to anyone who wants to bring anything to contribute to one's own salvation. The way of the cross means constantly dying to self-interest, putting the needs and desires of others first, whether or not their response is one of gratitude and thanks. It means pouring out our lives for others, even in the face of their bitterness of spirit.

That this is our experience of the way of the cross should not surprise us, for it was the experience also of the one whose life defined the way of the cross, Jesus himself. When we take up our own cross, we are simply following where he has led. He too was rejected by the people whom he came to serve, a man of sorrows and acquainted thoroughly with grief. He carried that burden all the way to Calvary, where he laid down his life for bitter and hard-hearted unbelievers like us. That reality is what should strengthen us to keep on the road that he has trodden first for us, even in the face of opposition and thankless ingratitude.

Choosing the way of Ruth not only means identifying with Israel's God, however; it also means identifying with the stubborn, recalcitrant, and frequently offensive flock that he calls his own. Ruth found no warm welcome either from Naomi or from the women of Bethlehem. Yet she committed herself to Naomi and her kin. So too we may often find the Lord's people to be a disappointing bunch, exhibiting fewer of the fruits of the Spirit than we would like. The new Israel may have far too much in common with the old Israel for our taste. Yet flawed as the people of God are, if the Lord is to be our God then his people must be our people, too. We will each add our own sins and flaws to the mix, of course, yet the impact that Ruth's faithful service had on Naomi and Bethlehem should not be missed. One person who is totally committed to the Lord and to the community of his people, even a young believer, may make a lasting difference to the life of the flock.

MISSION TO MOAB?

Like Naomi, we naturally tend to lack a fundamental concern for the Moabites all around us. Naomi, it appears, had little concern for the spiritual condition of her Moabite daughters-in-law. She had found them functionally adequate, and she wished them well in their new lives back in Moab.[6] Presumably they had been good wives for her sons, keeping them fed and warm and generally happy. Naomi's relationship with them was superficially warm and friendly (unlike the relationships some women have with their daughters-in-law!). However, underneath that superficial relationship, Naomi had no deep concern for their souls.

Perhaps Naomi simply assumed that Orpah and Ruth wouldn't be interested in Israel's God. They were Moabites, after all; they had their god and she had hers. Who was she to impose her own understanding of God on her neighbors? They seemed to be good moral people, and she was living in a pluralistic society where everyone attended the temple of the god of one's own choice. The vision of reaching out to her neighbors and incorporating them into the covenant community was lost on her, even when the opportunity leapt up and struck her in the face.

She at least had some excuse for her reticence. Although the mandate to be a blessing to all nations had been given to Abraham, in the days of the

---

6. Naomi's wish that *the Lord* would grant them rest with their husbands in Moab is, perhaps, merely a conventional turn of phrase on her part (see Ruth 1:9). If she is aware of the implications of her request, however, she is asking the Lord to grant them exactly what she and Elimelech never found: rest outside the covenant community. Her thinking still shows the marks of confusion as to the way to true blessing.

judges that mandate was rather dimly understood. Few were looking for opportunities to make converts to the covenant community from those around them. But in the light of Matthew 28:19, where Jesus told us to go and make disciples of all nations, what is our excuse? Who are the Moabites we see day after day, the people all around us who we so quickly assume are not going to be interested in the gospel? Perhaps if we sought to testify to them of God's goodness to us in Jesus Christ, we might discover more interest in the gospel than we ever imagined. Our problem is that all too often we have as little real care for our friends and neighbors as Naomi had for hers.

Part of Naomi's difficulty, of course, was that she wasn't a very good member of the covenant community herself. There was no distinctive holiness about her; on the contrary, she herself was sinfully on the run from the land of obedience. Those who are consciously living a life of disobedience to God are not typically eager to defend and explain their faith to others! Yet isn't it striking (and encouraging to us all) that even though at that moment she wasn't looking out for Ruth's spiritual interests, or even looking for God herself, nonetheless God was still able to use her, in spite of her attitude, as a means to draw Ruth to himself? Fortunately, God's mission to rescue sinners is not limited by our flaws, failings, and foibles! God will call to himself those whom he chooses, sometimes through the most bizarre messengers and unlikely combinations of circumstances. It is his work from beginning to end.

Marah Redeemed

We are often like Naomi in another way as well. Like her, when the circumstances of life go badly for us, we are tempted to assume that it is because God is out to get us. We easily view God as the cosmic policeman, just waiting beside the highway of life for an opportunity to pull us over and give us a ticket. When life is hard, even when the difficulties are a direct result of our own sin, we swiftly attribute our pain and loss to the harshness of God's wrath. Whether it is closed doors in our career path, financial difficulties, or shattered relationships, our first resort is often to blame God's harshness for our pain.

The result of that attitude in our hearts may be that our lives become filled with such bitterness that we completely miss the providential marks of God's continuing goodness to us in the midst of our difficulties. Like Naomi, we may be so busy complaining about our emptiness that we miss the fact that God has emptied our hands only in order to fill them with something so much better. Without Naomi's emptiness, she would never have left Moab behind and returned to the land of promise. Had she stayed contentedly "full" (as she thought) in Moab, Naomi would have missed out on the far greater blessing of a prime place in the history of redemption. She was so caught up in what she had lost, however, that she could not yet see the far greater treasure she had been given in Ruth, a token of God's grace to her.

We too, like Naomi, often cling desperately to small treasures, or even ridiculous nothings, when God has intended us for larger vistas. C. S. Lewis put it like this:

> Indeed, if we consider the unblushing promises of reward and the staggering nature of the rewards promised in the Gospels, it would seem that the Lord finds our desires, not too strong, but too weak. We are half-hearted creatures, fooling about with drink and sex and ambition when infinite joy is offered us, like an ignorant child who wants to go on making mud pies in a slum because he cannot understand what is meant by the offer of a holiday at the sea. We are far too easily pleased.[7]

God sometimes takes away the things that have become precious to us because they are supporting us in our life of sin and hardness of heart toward him. Alternatively, he sometimes takes away things that were good in themselves because he wants to use our lives as a powerful testimony of the sufficiency of his relentless grace in the midst of our weakness and loss. Invariably, though, he has not brought these trials and losses into our lives because he hates us and is seeking to afflict us, or to get even with us for our sin. On the contrary, if we are his children, he loves us and through this loss wants us to receive something far more precious than all of the trinkets to which we become so desperately attached. He wants to give us more of himself.

Why do we find this truth so hard to understand? Why do we so often miss the small marks of God's goodness to us in the midst of our pain, such as surrounding us with believing friends and family members and a church

---

7. *The Weight of Glory and Other Addresses* (Grand Rapids: Eerdmans, 1965), 1–2.

that loves us? We undervalue the little tokens of God's goodness because we have neglected the big mark of God's goodness. Why should Naomi *not* have been bitter, even after all she had experienced? Why should she *not* have viewed herself as the victim of God's afflictions? As part of the covenant people, she should have been able to look back on God's goodness to his people in bringing them out of Egypt and into the Promised Land in the first place. If God dealt with his people like that in the past, even though he knew ahead of time how they would trample and despise his grace, would he not also be merciful and patient and gracious toward a repentant sinner who came home humbly confessing her wrongs?

Even calling herself Mara should have caused Naomi to ponder more deeply the events that took place in that wilderness location, where in spite of his people's grumbling, God nonetheless turned the bitter water into sweet, and thereby demonstrated that he was "the LORD, your healer" (Ex. 15:26). Was that deliverance from their pain a reward for their goodness? Certainly not! It was a landmark measure of God's unfailing goodness and mercy upon an undeserving, rebellious, and grumbling people. Marah was not just the definitive place of grumbling bitterness, it was also the place where God's grace to grumblers was definitively displayed.

If Naomi had pondered that truth from the history of the covenant people, it might have brought new hope in her life! In addition, if Naomi felt that she was presently located in her own personal Marah, she could have remembered that the next stop on the wilderness road for the people of the exodus was not more of the same, but Elim, the place of rest, with its twelve springs of water and seventy palm trees (Ex. 15:27). God's people didn't have to wait for the conquest of the Promised Land to experience a measure of relief; even along the desert road there were brief oases of comfort that God had provided in his goodness for his people. In the midst of her pain, though, Naomi had completely forgotten the history of God's faithfulness.

REMEMBERING GRACE, FINDING HOPE

If Naomi in her self-pitying myopia failed to look back to God's grace in the exodus as the source of her hope, what about us as we face our own trials? What do we need to remember? The gospel is the fundamental answer to Naomi's need and to our own. Tremendous asset that she will prove to be, Ruth is not the final answer to Naomi's needs. Ruth is simply a pointer to the gospel, a small symbol of God's grace that pointed Naomi to the great symbols of God's grace. The gospel is the fundamental answer, both for our lack of trust in God and for our lack of concern for the nations.

In the first place, the gospel answers our doubts that God really has our best interests at heart. Who left his Father's house to come and live with us, even to the point of death? Against whom did the Almighty's hand truly go out in bitter judgment, even though he had no sin of his own that would have deserved such punishment? Jesus is the answer Naomi needs, and Jesus is the answer that we need. Jesus is our Immanuel: he took God's Old Testament declaration that "I will be with you" and lived it out to the fullest extent. He left the glories of heaven in order to say to us, "Where you go I will go, and where you lodge I will lodge. Your people shall be my people, and your God my God" (Ruth 1:16). Even death was not shirked in his identification with us; he died and was buried, just as we are. In his grace, he has clung to us, uniting our souls with his in eternal union.

As a result of that covenantal bond of union between Jesus and his people, no one and nothing—not even death—can now separate us from Christ. Jesus died on the cross both as the ultimate demonstration of God's love for his people and as the ultimate means by which God would bring all of his prodigal sons and daughters back to the true Promised Land, heaven itself. Though we have each gone astray like Naomi in search of bread that does not satisfy, God has not simply cut us off in his anger and wrath as we deserved. Though the Lord could justly have dealt bitterly with us, he instead poured that wrath out on Christ on the cross so that we—rebellious insiders and alien outsiders alike—might be invited in. In Christ, we are welcomed to feast at the banquet we had by our disobedience forfeited, pursuing instead the empty tables of this world.

In the light of that tremendous gospel reality, how can we now doubt from day to day God's love for us? How can we ever doubt God's desire for our best? Though he takes us through deep waters of pain and suffering and loss (and we should expect that he will, for that is his enduring pattern with his people), it is only so that he may break our fascination with our earthly mud pies. He wants to replace our deplorable desire to play with dirt with a deep longing for something much better: the true bread of heaven. In Christ, he not only gives us a profound and growing desire for fellowship with him; ultimately, he will also satisfy it in his presence forever.

Second, the gospel shows us that this grace is not merely for covenant insiders who have lost their way. It is now for men and women from all nations and backgrounds, the unclean as much as the kosher, the unwashed as well as the religious. Black and white, male and female, Jewish and Gentile, all are one in Christ Jesus (Gal. 3:28). There are no more Moabite outsiders in the light of the cross. All are welcome to come, whatever their background, and to be received into the family of God. The grace of God that we have received is to be extended by us to others, so that all may hear the good news of redemption in Christ.

It is deeply convicting that in Ruth it is the former pagan who has more passion for Israel's God than has the child of the covenant, who heard of his dealings with his people from her earliest days. Perhaps those of us who have grown up in church can easily lose sight of the awesome preciousness of the grace of God, and cease to be amazed at his love for us. It becomes familiar and loses its freshness, whereas those to whom this is new news are more easily moved by it.

Whether we grew up in the church or were converted as adults, can we be content to have only a little passion for our God and for the spread of his fame? Can we mutter a conventional blessing on those who still have not heard of Christ and leave it at that? For some, the call of God will be for them too to leave comfort, family, home, and country to take the gospel across cultures. They will become part of a new people for the sake of the gospel, laying down their lives daily that others may hear Jesus speak through them. It is a difficult and costly calling, but at the same time it is a powerful testimony when someone completely abandons his or her own culture and enters a new one for Christ.

For most of us in this modern world, though, the other cultures have come to us where we live. The Moabites are now our neighbors, waiting to see if we are concerned enough about them to minister to them in Christ's name. We don't have to leave our towns and neighborhoods to encounter other nations and people groups. Yet if we are truly to minister to them, it will still cost us time and effort, interest and concern, as we seek to bring the gospel to bear within a different cultural context.

How glorious it is to have these opportunities to share the gospel across cultures! For on the last day, the assembly before God will be made up of people from all nations. Moabites and Americans, Japanese and Jews, former Muslims and former atheists, all of them washed by the blood of the Lamb and made one in Christ Jesus. What a glorious field we are called to harvest, and what an awesome gospel we have been given to share!

12

A REFUGE FROM THE STORM

Ruth 2:1–23

> *But Boaz answered her, "All that you have done for your*
> *mother-in-law since the death of your husband has been fully*
> *told to me, and how you left your father and mother and your*
> *native land and came to a people that you did not know before.*
> *The LORD repay you for what you have done, and a full reward*
> *be given you by the LORD, the God of Israel, under whose wings*
> *you have come to take refuge!"* (Ruth 2:11–12)

Have you ever hit rock bottom? Sometimes we feel as if we are not simply scraping the bottom of the barrel but have already taken the barrel, held it upside down, shaken it, and discovered that there is absolutely nothing left in it. Further scraping would be a fruitless task, because there is nothing left to scrape. That is where Naomi and Ruth found themselves in the beginning of Ruth 2. From her state of fullness at the beginning of the book, where Naomi had a husband and two sons to support her and take care of her, Naomi had been reduced to a state of emptiness with no one around her to help her. The only one left was her pesky Moabitess daughter-in-law, Ruth, and she wasn't too sure whether Ruth was more of an asset or an embarrassment.

THE BOTTOM OF THE BARREL

It had not been Naomi's idea for Ruth to come back to Israel with her. The last thing she wanted was one more mouth to feed and one more body to clothe. This was especially the case when that particular body would be a constant reminder of Naomi's sin in abandoning the Promised Land with her husband years before in search of the greener fields of Moab. Ruth was also a constant reminder of Naomi's sin in marrying her sons to foreign women, outsiders to the covenant. No, she had *told* her to go back home to her own people and her own gods in Moab (Ruth 1:8)!

Naomi had done her best to dissuade Ruth. She had said, in effect: "Go back with Orpah and leave me alone in my guilt and bitterness against the Lord!" (Ruth 1:11–13). "This is all the Lord's fault—his hand has afflicted me and brought misfortune upon me," she had said. "You don't know what you are committing yourself to. I appreciate all of your fine words about going where I go, staying where I stay, and dying where I die. That is all very romantic and makes for a fine speech, but really, why go with me? Why should a healthy young woman like you keep company with a doomed old albatross like me who is returning to the land of a God who has been so determined to get even with me for my shortcomings? Why would you even want such a God? Better by far to go back home to your own people and live out the rest of your life as best you can."

This would seem to be the line of Naomi's urging to Ruth while they were still in Moab. But Ruth would not listen to her pleas. Ruth would not be turned aside from her commitment to Naomi, and along with it, her commitment to cut all her ties with her own people and her old gods. Henceforth, she would be part of Naomi's people and serve her God.

This odd couple returned to Bethlehem. The afflicted Jewess and her thoroughly non-kosher daughter-in-law took the road to what looked like a bleak future, in which they would have to depend on family charity and whatever food they could scrounge for themselves. But in the midst of the darkness at the very end of Ruth 1, there was a tiny sliver of light. They arrived in Bethlehem "at the beginning of barley harvest" (Ruth 1:22). In this little notice, the narrator hints that Naomi is not reading events correctly. Perhaps she could not really be expected to see clearly in the midst of her bitter tears. But whereas Naomi saw the progression of the chapter as being

155

from fullness to emptiness in her own life, the movement for her people had been the opposite. They had gone from famine as the story opened to the brink of a new harvest in the Promised Land. There was food once again in Bethlehem. God's hand of judgment had been lifted from his people. Now if that trajectory from emptiness to fullness was possible for Naomi's people, perhaps her own future was not as dark as she imagined it to be. Even if God's face was turned aside from her at present, as she thought, perhaps his favor could yet be restored to her.

Naomi's problem is like the struggle many of us experience. In the dark night of our souls, we imagine and worry about the worst possible scenario. In fact, we often conjure up contradictory worst case scenarios to worry about, events that cannot all happen to us. We persuade ourselves that God has abandoned us and that we have no prospects. How much unnecessary turmoil do we put ourselves through! God doesn't promise to give us the grace to survive all the scenarios we can dream up—but only to give us the grace to enable us to make it through whatever he actually brings into our lives. In fact, much of what we worry about turns out in the end not to be part of God's plan for us after all; our worry was wasted work! Of course, Jesus told us this himself when he said, "Which of you by being anxious can add a single hour to his span of life?" (Matt. 6:27).

GLEANING IN THE FIELDS

In the meantime, though, there was the pressing issue for Ruth and Naomi of what to eat. And there was a likely solution: "Now Naomi had a relative of her husband's, a worthy man of the clan of Elimelech, whose name was Boaz. And Ruth the Moabite said to Naomi, 'Let me go to the field and glean among the ears of grain after him in whose sight I shall find favor.' And she said to her, 'Go, my daughter'" (Ruth 2:1–2).

Provision was made in the law of Moses to take care of the poor through a kind of "Welfare to Work" program. The poor were not simply to depend on handouts from the state. Rather, they were allowed to glean in the fields after the harvesters and around the edges, picking up the scraps that were left behind. Indeed, farmers were required to leave the edges of their fields unharvested so that there would be a better possibility for the poor to eke out a subsistence living in this way (see Lev. 19:9–10; Deut. 24:19–20). Even

156

though this law was part of God's covenant with his people at Sinai and is no longer directly applicable to farmers in our society, the general principle behind it is one our society would do well to heed. We should strive to make it possible for the poor through hard work to provide for their own needs and the needs of their dependents.

Gleaning was hard work; it was hot work; it was not necessarily safe work either, since not every landowner would fulfill the provisions of the law. It was perhaps especially dangerous for a foreign woman, a Moabitess, who had no clan connections to protect her or to call on in distress. So when Ruth volunteered to go out and glean to provide food for the two of them, she was making herself vulnerable not just for her own sake but for Naomi's too (Ruth 2:2). She was stepping out in faith that somewhere out there was a generous, God-fearing landowner who would make room for the poor. Faith doesn't simply sit around waiting for provision to drop down from heaven; we are called to do what we can, and as we do, to trust that God will provide for our needs.

It is not clear why Naomi did not also go out and glean. She was perhaps in her fifties at this point in the story and evidenced no obvious crippling disability that made her unable to go out and work. Was there nothing she could have done in the field to help in their need? Two certainly would have been safer than one and might have expected to bring home at least a little more food. It is tempting to imagine that her bitterness caused her to sink into depression and despair. Certainly her terse response to Ruth's request to glean ("Go, my daughter") does nothing to dispel that impression. She has apparently consumed all her energies in worrying and has none left to try to do anything that might actually resolve her problems.

Whether or not despair is what drives Naomi's inaction, it is certainly a problem in our own experience. When we stop believing in God's goodness and give ourselves over to doubt and worry, we easily sink into a despairing inactivity. This can lead to a downward spiral in which our inactivity makes our situation worse and deepens our despair, which in turn makes us feel less inclined than ever to step out into what we believe to be a hostile world. The key to breaking that cycle is grasping hold of God's covenant commitment to do us good. If we can once look to the cross and grasp the height and depth of the love of God for us in Jesus, then how can we doubt his desire to give us everything necessary for life and godliness? If we feel the smile of the Father's favor toward us in Christ, in spite of our history of sin and failure, then we will be encouraged to step out again in faith. We will still not know what the future holds, yet if we know that the one who holds the future cares for us, that first step upward on the long road back to obedience becomes possible again.

DIVINE COINCIDENCE

As it turned out, there *was* a God-fearing landowner in Bethlehem who cared for the poor: a man named Boaz, who was a distant relative of Naomi's. What a coincidence! Ruth had no obvious reason to pick one field over the next, but she ended up in Boaz's field: "So she set out and went and gleaned in the field after the reapers, and she happened to come to the part of the field belonging to Boaz, who was of the clan of Elimelech" (Ruth 2:3). The text tells us that it was literally "as chance chanced," or as we might say, "as luck would have it." Only, as the narrator is inviting us to see, there was no such thing as luck driving this chain of events. This was all part of a higher plan. It was nothing less than a divine appointment that brought Ruth to the fields of Boaz. There were no angelic visions to direct her to the right field or voices from heaven to guide her. Nevertheless, as she trusted in the Lord, he directed her steps unwittingly to exactly the right location (see Prov. 16:9).

In due course, the divine appointment-maker also brought Boaz to his fields to see how the harvest was progressing:

> And behold, Boaz came from Bethlehem. And he said to the reapers, "The LORD be with you!" And they answered, "The LORD bless you." Then Boaz said to his young man who was in charge of the reapers, "Whose young woman is this?" And the servant who was in charge of the reapers answered, "She is the young Moabite woman, who came back with Naomi from the country of Moab. She said, 'Please let me glean and gather among the sheaves after the reapers.' So she came, and she has continued from early morning until now, except for a short rest." (Ruth 2:4–7)

Very often in the Bible, a person's first words tell you something significant. Boaz's first words certainly do. He greeted his servants by saying, "The LORD be with you," to which his workers responded in kind, "The LORD bless you"

(Ruth 2:4). The narrator has included this interchange so that we can immediately tell that Boaz honors the Lord in his work and is respected by his workers. But as Boaz looked out over the scene before him, something struck him. Among the gleaning poor was an unfamiliar figure. He therefore asked "Whose is she?"—not "*Who* is she?" as if he expected a name, but "Whom does she belong to? Where does she fit in society?" (see Ruth 2:5). The foreman replied, in effect, "Oh she's that foreigner who came back from Moab with Naomi—you know the one. She's an outsider; she doesn't really belong anywhere. But I can tell you, she's worked like a dog in this hot sun all day."[1]

Boaz indeed knew the one of whom the foreman spoke. He had heard all about Ruth abandoning her people and her land for Naomi's sake, and now he found her hard at work in his field for the sake of her mother-in-law. In spite of the difference between their social standings, Boaz spoke to her as a person ("my daughter") and he made her a generous offer:

> Then Boaz said to Ruth, "Now, listen, my daughter, do not go to glean in another field or leave this one, but keep close to my young women. Let your eyes be on the field that they are reaping, and go after them. Have I not charged the young men not to touch you? And when you are thirsty, go to the vessels and drink what the young men have drawn." Then she fell on her face, bowing to the ground, and said to him, "Why have I found favor in your eyes, that you should take notice of me, since I am a foreigner?" But Boaz answered her, "All that you have done for your mother-in-law since the death of your husband has been fully told to me, and how you left your father and mother and your native land and came to a people that you did not know before. The LORD repay you for what you have done, and a full reward be given you by the LORD, the God of Israel, under whose wings you have come to take refuge!" (Ruth 2:9–12)

Can you imagine the impact these words must have had on Ruth, the outsider? These were the first kind words she had heard since she left Moab. More than that, they were a blessing that sought God's favor upon her, as if she too were a member of the covenant community. Boaz recognized the sincerity of Ruth's words to Naomi when they left Moab. He saw that she

---

1. The exact translation of Ruth 2:7 is difficult. See Daniel Block, *Judges, Ruth* (New American Commentary; Nashville: Broadman & Holman, 1999), 657–58 for the various options. Most probably, however, the focus is on Ruth's hard and persistent work since she arrived in the morning.

was turning her back not just on her homeland, but also on her former gods, and looking to the Lord for refuge. He therefore prayed for the Lord to grant her the protection that she was seeking. Here was the gracious and warm response that her commitment to Naomi on the Bethlehem road had deserved but never received.

No wonder Ruth was comforted, then, if perhaps a little overawed by Boaz's generosity. She said, "I have found favor in your eyes, my lord, for you have comforted me and spoken kindly to your servant, though I am not one of your servants" (Ruth 2:13). Ruth, the outsider, had been made to feel welcome to come in. The one who came seeking Israel's God had for the first time been made to feel that there might be a place for her among the followers of God. Why should anyone, especially a man of standing in the community like Boaz, take such kind notice of a foreign woman like herself, who was a nonentity (or worse) in everyone else's eyes?

Boaz's kindness was not limited to mere words, however. Rather than leave her at a distance at the mealtime, as she would have expected, he invited her to draw near: "And at mealtime Boaz said to her, 'Come here and eat some bread and dip your morsel in the wine.' So she sat beside the reapers, and he passed to her roasted grain. And she ate until she was satisfied, and she had some left over" (Ruth 2:14). Though Ruth had probably brought little or nothing to eat, Boaz provided her a share of his own food: special treats of bread dipped in sour vinegar and roasted grain so that, heaven of heavens, for once she had enough to eat. The joy of having enough to eat is a hard concept for us to grasp in our affluence, for we are used to satisfying our appetites three times a day, with snacks in between. But for a foreign widow to be able to eat to the point where she was full and still have some left over to take home . . . what a feast!

Boaz even commanded his men to be deliberately careless in their harvesting, so that this poor widow would have an abundance to carry home with her:

> When she rose to glean, Boaz instructed his young men, saying, "Let her glean even among the sheaves, and do not reproach her. And also pull out some from the bundles for her and leave it for her to glean, and do not rebuke her." So she gleaned in the field until evening. Then she beat out what she had gleaned, and it was about an ephah of barley. And she took it up and went

into the city. Her mother-in-law saw what she had gleaned. She also brought out and gave her what food she had left over after being satisfied. And her mother-in-law said to her, "Where did you glean today? And where have you worked? Blessed be the man who took notice of you." (Ruth 2:15–19)

No wonder Naomi was astonished at what Ruth had gathered: she brought home a whole ephah! Most of us are not used to visualizing ephahs, and as a result, we are not particularly impressed by Ruth's haul. It may clarify the issue if we recognize that Ruth brought home somewhere between twenty-nine and fifty pounds of grain, or several weeks' worth of food for the average worker. To put it more vividly in our culture, the bag she brought home was the size of a colossal bag of dog food!

Do we welcome outsiders like Ruth, the non-kosher people, the people who do not naturally fit in our community, the way that Boaz did? It is doubtful whether many rich men in Bethlehem would have looked over the laborers harvesting their fields, instantly picked out a single foreigner, and identified her as someone new. So also, perhaps, many of us scan the rows of people in our church and completely miss all of the Ruths in our congregation because we are only looking to make friends with people who are like us. We cast an eye over our neighborhood or community and completely overlook those who are outcasts and strangers, the immigrants and the homeless, the poor and the needy. We have eyes but do not easily see what Boaz saw, because we are not looking for the poor and the outcast.

Whom do you see? Are you consciously looking for those who are on their own? Do you have eyes to see the poor and needy in your own neighborhood, the outcasts and neglected in your own church, or do they remain invisible to you? Boaz went far above and beyond his mere duty in order to take care of the poor and include this outsider. He took time and care to build ties of relationship with her, and paid the costs of her provision out of his own pocket. Do we have a similar heart of compassion for those who seem to have little or nothing to offer us in return?

A HEART SOFTENED BY COVENANT FAITHFULNESS

When Ruth returned home, there was plenty to eat, and also plenty to talk about:

> So she told her mother-in-law with whom she had worked and said, "The man's name with whom I worked today is Boaz." And Naomi said to her daughter-in-law, "May he be blessed by the LORD, whose kindness has not forsaken the living or the dead!" Naomi also said to her, "The man is a close relative of ours, one of our redeemers." And Ruth the Moabite said, "Besides, he said to me, 'You shall keep close by my young men until they have finished all my harvest.' " And Naomi said to Ruth, her daughter-in-law, "It is good, my daughter, that you go out with his young women, lest in another field you be assaulted." So she kept close to the young women of Boaz, gleaning until the end of the barley and wheat harvests. And she lived with her mother-in-law. (Ruth 2:19–23)

All of a sudden, faced with the mound of food that Ruth had brought home, the practical evidence of God's goodness to her, Naomi's attitude began to change. First, her heart began to soften toward God. She cried out, "The LORD bless him! He has not stopped showing his kindness to the living and the dead" (Ruth 2:20 NIV). Who, though, is the "he" in this sentence? Who is the one who has not stopped showing kindness, or covenant faithfulness (*hesed*), to the living and the dead? Grammatically, the subject could be either the Lord or Boaz—but since Boaz has had no history of dealings with Naomi, in context it surely has to be the Lord whom Naomi is describing. Suddenly, Naomi was beginning to see that the Lord was not out to get her. In fact, he was still able and willing to smile upon her, to show her covenant faithfulness, in spite of her history of sin and rebellion. Ruth's one-day outing, in which she went out empty and came back full because the Lord went ahead of her, persuaded Naomi that perhaps she had been too quick with her bitterness. The Lord was able and willing to provide for their physical needs after all. Nor was it only her needs that were being met: the word "living" is plural, encompassing both Naomi and Ruth. For the first time since leaving Moab, Ruth is included in the family of Naomi to whom the Lord will show his faithfulness.[2]

Interestingly, God did all this through the means he himself had set up in the law: through someone willing to act as a "kinsman redeemer" (Ruth 2:20). A kinsman redeemer was obliged to buy back his relatives if they fell into debt and had to sell themselves into slavery (Lev. 25:25–55). Under cer-

---

2. "The living and the dead" is a merism—two opposites that encompass everything in between—covering the whole of Naomi's family. The "living" (plural) are Naomi and Ruth, while the "dead" are clearly Elimelech, Mahlon, and Chilion (Block, *Judges, Ruth*, 673).

tain circumstances, the kinsman redeemer also had an obligation to marry the widow and raise up a child for a brother who had died childless (Deut. 25:5–10). In this way, the inheritance would continue to be associated with the name of the man who had died.

Those legal precedents do not seem to address this case directly, however. Boaz was not a brother to the dead man, and describing him as a kinsman redeemer in this case seems to mean he had some kind of general familial obligation toward Naomi.[3] In addition, the law didn't address the issue of foreigners who had illegally married into the family and what obligations, if any, a kinsman redeemer had toward them. There were plenty of loopholes Boaz could have slipped through and absolved himself of any legal responsibility, had he so wished. But Boaz was not concerned simply with the obligations of the law. He had a heart that had been touched by God's covenant faithfulness, and it overflowed in covenant faithfulness to those around him. Covenant faithfulness (*hesed*) is a key term in the Book of Ruth and in the Bible generally. It is a hard word to translate because it includes so many things: love, grace, mercy, kindness—all of the positive acts of devotion that flow out of a covenantal relationship. It describes the acts of loyalty and faithfulness that a healthy relationship inspires, acts that inevitably go far beyond duty and obligation.[4] Covenant includes God's kindness to his people and their consequent kindness to one another. Boaz's generosity to Ruth is a model of *hesed* in action.

The reference to Boaz as redeemer, moreover, points our eyes beyond him to the figure of the Redeemer. The earlier grammatical ambiguity over whether it was Boaz or the Lord who was showing favor to Ruth and Naomi was profound rather than accidental. Boaz was the means that God used in a small way to show Naomi his goodness. Her bitterness, which had hardened and deepened under what she saw as the lashes of God's judgment, at last began to melt when brought face to face with an undeniable experience of his goodness and grace. She began to recognize that, contrary to what she had earlier thought, the Lord had not stopped showing his covenant faithfulness (*hesed*) to her and Ruth.

3. For the legal issues, see Robert L. Hubbard Jr., *The Book of Ruth* (New International Commentary on the Old Testament; Grand Rapids: Eerdmans, 1988), 48–51.

4. For a fuller description, see K. D. Sakenfeld, *Faithfulness in Action: Loyalty in Biblical Perspective* (Philadelphia: Fortress, 1985).

There is even a hint of repentance in Naomi's strong urging of Ruth to heed Boaz's counsel to stay from now on in his fields, rather than going into the fields of another, lest she come to any harm (Ruth 2:22). This may seem a rather obvious response to such a generous offer. Why would anyone in her right mind not stay in Boaz's field after all his past kindness? Who would go elsewhere? But that is precisely the point! Naomi and Elimelech had displayed exactly that kind of foolish blindness so many years before: they ignored the Lord's constant faithful provision in the past to his people and went to someone else's field. Instead of staying in the land God had promised to his people and trusting in his covenant faithfulness, they went to the fields of Moab (Ruth 1:1)[5] in search of greener grass. Now Naomi could see clearly how foolish that decision had been. She was thus warning Ruth not to repeat her own pattern of sin: "Stay in the fields of the one upon whom the Lord's blessing rests. Don't go wandering off as I did!"

But food was only one of the things that Ruth lacked. She had not simply given up her best prospect of physical sustenance by going with Naomi, she had also—to all human appearances—given up the prospect of marriage and a home of her own. Even though she now had food, she still needed a husband, a lack that is emphasized by the closing statement of the chapter: "She lived with her mother-in-law" (Ruth 2:23). Why state the obvious? It is because that simple remark highlights the fact that she wasn't living with a husband. One need still remained for Ruth.

However, if God has faithfully provided so abundantly for Ruth's need of food, will he not also supply her needs in this other area? This is especially true since we recall that the function of a kinsman redeemer was not simply to provide financially for his destitute relatives but, if necessary, to provide them with offspring to inherit as well. If Boaz has been willing to meet one need, even to his own cost, might he not perhaps be willing to meet the other as well? This thought is the link that connects this chapter with what follows.

---

5. The same phrase (literally, "the fields of Moab") also occurs in the Hebrew of Ruth 1:2, 6, and 22, though unfortunately it has not been preserved in most English translations. On this unusual form, see M. A. Grisanti, "sadeh/saday," in *New International Dictionary of Old Testament Theology and Exegesis*, ed. Willem VanGemeren, 5 vols. (Grand Rapids: Zondervan, 1997), 3:1218.

God's Perfect Timing

In the background of the Book of Ruth, a clock is ticking. We may not notice it at first because our ears are not attuned to the calendar of redemptive history, but it is striking when we notice it. Naomi and Ruth arrived back in Bethlehem at the beginning of the barley harvest (Ruth 1:22); in other words, they came home at the time of the feast of Passover, when the grain harvest began (see Deut. 16:9). What better time for an exodus from the fields of Moab to the Promised Land? It was the beginning of the year in the Jewish calendar, the fitting time for a fresh start by God's grace. By the end of chapter 2, the end of the barley harvest had arrived (Ruth 2:23); seven weeks had passed by and it was time for the festival of first fruits, which was part of the feast of weeks, or Pentecost. By this time, Ruth and Naomi have experienced the first fruits of God's deliverance in the gift of Boaz's grain, but they have not yet seen the fullness of what God had planned for them.

Ruth not only experiences the first fruits of God's grace, but in a profound sense, she *is* the first fruits. In the fullness of time, Pentecost, which was the harvest festival par excellence in Israel, was the day that God chose to pour out his Spirit on Jews and Gentiles alike, bringing them together into the one new people of God (Acts 2:1–39). Ruth's incorporation by faith into God's people was a foreshadowing of the much greater harvest that God one day would reap among the Gentiles as his grace extended more fully to the nations. Focused in as they were on their own needs, Naomi and Ruth probably didn't hear the redemptive clock ticking, but the narrator wants us to hear that sound and reflect on the perfection of God's timing.

For us, too, a clock is ticking. We who have received the first fruits of our salvation await its fullness (Rom. 8:23). Often, we are so preoccupied with the challenges of surviving from one day to the next that we are inclined to forget the clock's relentless beat. When we do think about it, our redemption seems slow in coming. Yet we ought not to forget that in God's perfect time, our present groaning will give way to shouts of joy, as we receive our full adoption as the sons and daughters of God. Quieting our hearts and focusing our attention on the reality and certainty of the inheritance that is stored up for us in heaven will feed our hope and encourage us to persevere patiently until the sands of God's time run out.

165

THE GLORIES OF GOD'S GRACE AND COVENANT FAITHFULNESS

The apostle Paul says, "My God will supply every need of yours according to his riches in glory in Christ Jesus" (Phil. 4:19). Sometimes it doesn't seem that way, though, does it? Sometimes it may seem as if God has turned his face away from us and closed his ears to our prayers. It may even seem that he has stopped showing us his faithfulness, his *hesed*, after all. Yet the Book of Ruth is a glorious testimony to Paul's statement: God will meet *all* our needs. In her grief and confusion, Naomi had misunderstood God and misjudged Ruth. She had failed to see that the Lord is the God who welcomes the outsider. She had forgotten that he is the shepherd who does not stop showing his covenant faithfulness to the wandering sheep. She didn't remember that he is the Father who waits with open arms to welcome back the prodigal daughter.

We who live in the New Testament era should see the constant faithfulness and glorious grace of this God even more clearly than Naomi did. In the Scriptures, we have written down for us the rich history of God's long-suffering with his rebellious children. We know more fully that the Father stands with open arms and open heart, scanning the horizon for the returning prodigal, eager to welcome her home. He doesn't just allow us grudging admission to glean in his field; he invites us to his table to partake in his feast.

In addition, we see more clearly what the prodigal's return would cost the Father. In order to receive home the wandering sinner, it would cost the Father nothing less than the death of his Son on the cross. It would cost the Father the unthinkable agony of pouring out his wrath and anger against sin on Jesus, God the Son. No mere duty could force God to pay that price. Nothing less than his faithfulness to his covenant purposes, his overwhelming love for us, and his desire to have us as part of his people, could inspire such sacrifice.

What Naomi and Ruth most needed was not simply a redeemer to rescue them from their earthly poverty and danger, nor even a husband for Ruth. Rather, they needed a heavenly Redeemer to rescue them from their sin. The cost for Naomi and Ruth to have their deepest need supplied was for Jesus—the ever-living One—to taste death in their place. The cost for us to have our deepest need met, our need for salvation, was for the Sinless One to be made sin for us, so that in him we might become the righteousness of God (2 Cor. 5:21). Out of his covenant faithfulness, God willingly paid the price in full!

Is your heart constantly ignited by the glorious grace and covenant faithfulness of this God? We should trust in Christ alone for our daily bread instead of wandering off to search for crumbs in the field of another. The temptation is real for us to doubt his good provision for our needs and to look to ourselves or to others to provide for us. We are easily cast into despair and bitterness when we find ourselves scraping the bottom of life's barrel, and we turn our backs on the bread of life in favor of bread that will not satisfy.

The remedy for our hard and bitter hearts in the midst of our distress is to ponder God's awesome grace and covenant faithfulness. If we fix our eyes on the glorious grace of God, and his costly answer for our deepest need, then we will not so quickly doubt that he will meet all of our other needs. Since the Lord has shown us this covenant faithfulness, will he not order all things well in our lives? In sickness or in health, in poverty or in riches, for better or for worse . . . all of these conditions come to us as part of our Father's plan. No, even the bitterest parts of our lives are given to us as part of his perfect plan for us and must in some way work for our blessing.

What is more, these hardest of providences come to us from our Redeemer's nail-scarred hand. The Jesus who commits himself to be with us in the midst of our trials knows what it is to suffer. As a result, he is able to be our Refuge in the storm, the one under whose wings we may come and take shelter. He is our Redeemer from and through all kinds of difficulties. Follow the path he sets before you, holding firmly to your faith and knowing that his covenant faithfulness will never leave you nor forsake you. His *hesed* never ceases; his mercies never come to an end; they are new every morning (Lam. 3:22), and will accompany us every step along the hard road of life, until our faithful God welcomes us into our heavenly home.

13

RUTH'S REDEEMER

Ruth 3:1—18

*At midnight the man was startled and turned over, and behold,
a woman lay at his feet! He said, "Who are you?" And she
answered, "I am Ruth, your servant. Spread your wings over
your servant, for you are a redeemer." And he said, "May you be
blessed by the LORD, my daughter. You have made this last
kindness greater than the first in that you have not gone after
young men, whether poor or rich." (Ruth 3:8–10)*

A good man is hard to find. It has always been this way. How can a woman of character, especially an outsider like Ruth, go about the task of finding a husband to support her and take care of her? Nowadays she might run an advertisement in the *Bethlehem Times*: "Widowed Moabitess seeks hardworking man of character for long walks in the barley fields and quiet evenings by the fire. Must like children." It was a tricky task, yet Naomi decided that for Ruth's sake it needed to be undertaken.

This thought in itself seems to be a mark of progress in Naomi's thinking. Through most of the first two chapters of the book, Naomi has been preoccupied with three people: me, myself, and I. She had turned inward, consumed by grief and bitterness, cut off from those around her. Even Ruth's passionate commitment of devotion in chapter 1 seemed unable to touch her heart. While Ruth went out to glean, Naomi stayed at home. Yet now she is starting to think of someone else's needs rather than her own.

What seems to have happened is that over the course of these chapters, as she experienced God's goodness and continued faithfulness (*hesed*) to her, her heart began to soften. Through the hard work of Ruth and the generosity of Boaz, she found new hope. Perhaps she even began to see that she had been too quick to blame God and to assume that when things went badly in her life it was because God was out to get her. Perhaps she began to recognize her failure to take responsibility and to repent of it. Repentance inevitably draws our attention away from ourselves and out toward others. Bitterness drives us inward in self-absorbed depression, while true repentance enables us and motivates us to start to serve other people's needs.

NAOMI'S WONDERFUL PLAN FOR RUTH'S LIFE

Naomi now started to consider Ruth's needs. Living with her mother-in-law could never be an ideal situation (Ruth 2:23). Ruth needed a husband and a home of her own. This was not exactly a new observation: it was, after all, the reason why Naomi had told Ruth to go home in chapter 1, back to a place where she might be more likely to find such a place of rest with a husband of her own. Naomi had even asked the Lord to provide such a place for both of her daughters-in-law in Moab (see Ruth 1:9). She told Ruth that this was still what she wanted. "My daughter," she said, "should I not seek rest for you, that it may be well with you?" (Ruth 3:1). But who in Bethlehem would provide a place of rest for an outsider, especially a foreigner like Ruth? In Numbers 25, Moabite women led the Israelite men into sexual immorality and idolatry. Indeed, the very origins of Moab were in an act of drunken incest between Lot and his older daughter (Gen. 19:31–38). It is not surprising, therefore, that the image of Moabite women in Israel was far from positive. Taking on a Moabite wife would probably have been at least socially awkward, if not worse. A man might end up as a social outcast, spurned by decent society. Who would be willing to undertake such a risk?

Naomi thought she knew the answer: "Is not Boaz our relative, with whose young women you were? See, he is winnowing barley tonight at the threshing floor" (Ruth 3:2). Boaz was a man of character (Ruth 2:1). He was a relative of Naomi. He was a man who had already shown himself willing to make costly provision for the poor and the needy. Indeed, the reference to him as "a close relative of ours, one of our redeemers" in the previous chapter (Ruth 2:20) may already have started Naomi's mind moving in the direction of Boaz's marriage potential as a solution to all of their problems.[1]

But how exactly could a woman make such a delicate proposal? Ruth could hardly walk up to Boaz in the middle of the field, drop to one knee and say, "Marry me!" Moreover, it was now close to the end of the wheat harvest, six to eight weeks after the first encounter between Ruth and Boaz, and there seemed to be little progress in their relationship. However, Naomi had an idea how to jumpstart things. She said to Ruth, "Wash therefore and anoint yourself, and put on your cloak and go down to the threshing floor, but do not make yourself known to the man until he has finished eating and drinking. But when he lies down, observe the place where he lies. Then go and uncover his feet and lie down, and he will tell you what to do" (Ruth 3:3–4). That night, when the winnowing was over and the workers had finished eating and drinking, Boaz would be sleeping out with the pile of grain, guarding it through the night. Naomi's instructions to her daughter-in-law went along these lines: "Ruth, get washed, put on your best clothes, splash on some perfume, and apply some makeup. Go see where he lies down, and then lie down next to him. He will tell you what to do next" (see Ruth 3:2–4).

It is not hard to imagine some of the things that a man might conceivably want to do next in such a situation. Has Naomi been reading too many racy women's magazines during the long days when Ruth was out gleaning, with their lead articles about how to use feminine charms to snare a husband? Naomi's instructions to Ruth are extremely ambiguous, and even more so in the Hebrew original, where virtually every word in verse 4 is capable of more than one sense. Did Naomi really intend for Ruth to seduce Boaz, perhaps because she is still thinking of her as "the Moabitess," and expecting her to behave like the cultural stereotype? If that is the case, then Naomi is an example of seeking a good goal in the wrong way. Her goal would then be a worthy one, to find a place of rest for Ruth by means of the legal remedy God had provided in the person of the kinsman redeemer. However, her strategy for reaching that goal in that case would be less than ideal, being

---

1. Daniel Block, *Judges, Ruth* (New American Commentary; Nashville: Broadman & Holman, 1999), 676.

based on human manipulation rather than faith in God. On this reading, Naomi is making progress but is still some way from the goal of full trust in God.

On the other hand, it is also possible that Naomi did not intend for a sexual encounter to take place between Boaz and Ruth. She may simply have been making a desperate attempt to extend an invitation to Boaz to act as kinsman redeemer for the family. In that case, the purpose of the deliberate verbal ambiguity in Naomi's speech would have been to highlight the potential for Ruth's action in presenting herself to Boaz to be misunderstood. Ruth was putting both her reputation and personal safety in grave danger. Boaz had earlier warned Ruth of the risks that a foreign woman might encounter even gleaning in the fields by day (Ruth 2:8–9). How much greater would the danger of harm be if she were to present herself alone to a man in the middle of the night!

Both interpretations of Naomi's speech are plausible, and both heighten our suspense. Ruth was ready to act. She said to Naomi, "All that you say I will do." Then she "went down to the threshing floor and did just as her mother-in-law had commanded her" (Ruth 3:5–6). But what will happen next?

A DANGEROUS ENCOUNTER

Ruth agreed to her mother-in-law's plan and put it into effect—up to a point. Later that night, she found herself alone watching events at the threshing floor: "And when Boaz had eaten and drunk, and his heart was merry, he went to lie down at the end of the heap of grain. Then she came softly and uncovered his feet and lay down" (Ruth 3:7). The party was over, and it had been a good evening. After a long day of work, and a long night of feasting, Boaz must have been feeling very good about life. So he went and lay down at the end of the grain pile and fell fast asleep. In the middle of the night, though, something disturbed him—perhaps the cold air on his now exposed lower extremities. He rolled over, reaching for his blanket, and discovered to his amazement a woman there. "At midnight the man was startled and turned over, and behold, a woman lay at his feet!" (Ruth 3:8).

Under the circumstances, "Who are you?" was a natural enough question for Boaz to ask. Ruth responded, "I am Ruth, your servant. Spread your wings over your servant, for you are a redeemer" (Ruth 3:9). Here is where Ruth's actions diverged from her mother-in-law's instructions. Instead of leaving the situation dangerously ambiguous, as a woman of character Ruth wanted to make her intentions clear right from the outset. Her goal was a commitment to marriage, not a single night of passion. In the ancient world, such a commitment was symbolized by the gesture of covering someone with the corner of one's robe, roughly equivalent to the giving of an engagement ring in our culture (compare Ezek. 16:8).[2]

Ruth wanted Boaz to marry her and thus to provide a refuge for her and Naomi, just as a kinsman redeemer would. As we noted in chapter 12, a kinsman redeemer was a person who had an obligation to buy his relatives back if they sold themselves into slavery to pay off their debts. Under certain circumstances, the kinsman redeemer would also be obligated to marry his brother's widow in order to raise up a family for the dead man, a family that would inherit his property. Clearly, there was no legal obligation on Boaz to act in this way. Otherwise, this kind of elaborate strategy would not have been necessary. Ruth could simply have walked up to Boaz in the marketplace and said, "You are my kinsman redeemer; do what you are supposed to do." Boaz was a man of character; surely he would have followed through on his obligations in spite of the personal and social cost. What Ruth was asking Boaz to do, though, was to act according to the spirit of the law of the kinsman redeemer, even though he was not under any legal obligation. She appealed to him to be the family member who, at his own cost, would act to rescue those whose future had been blighted, even though he didn't have to do so.

Ruth's request required more than a little chutzpah on her part. It was entirely countercultural for a woman to propose to a man, or a younger person to an elder, or a field worker to a field owner. Indeed, Naomi's plan had called for her simply to be silent at this point and to let Boaz take the initiative (Ruth 3:4). However, whether out of faith or fear, or a simple inability to keep her mouth shut, Ruth blurted out her whole heart in response to Boaz's rather less searching question.

2. See K. Lawson Younger, Jr., *Judges, Ruth* (New International Version Application Commentary; Grand Rapids: Zondervan, 2002), 462.

As a strategy, Ruth's words left a great deal to be desired. Naomi's more open-ended scheme had a variety of possible outcomes that might each have reached the same goal, through more or less morally acceptable pathways. But Ruth knew that her future didn't ultimately depend on her ability to formulate a cunning plan and execute it. God was overruling all things for good and, amazingly enough, Boaz agreed to her audacious request. His first words to her—"my daughter"—show that he had not been misled by the potential ambiguity of the situation (Ruth 3:10), still less that he had any intention of taking advantage of her. On the contrary, he declared himself willing to take the risk that marriage to Ruth entailed. He was willing to pay the social and financial costs of welcoming this despised outsider into his family.

Indeed, Boaz complimented Ruth on having chosen him rather than going after a younger man. He said, "May you be blessed by the LORD, my daughter. You have made this last kindness greater than the first in that you have not gone after young men, whether poor or rich" (Ruth 3:10). A younger man would have had a better prospect, humanly speaking, of providing Ruth with children of her own, and thereby with significance. But Ruth knew that Boaz, as a man of character, could be counted upon to take care of Naomi as well as her. So Boaz rightly saw Ruth's adoption of Naomi's plan as yet another act of covenant faithfulness on Ruth's part. Just as she had left her own household and her own family to be with Naomi, so now when Naomi asked her to follow this dangerous plan she did it, even though it was at great personal risk. She was indeed a woman of character.

It is noteworthy that Proverbs 31, which in the ordering of the Hebrew Bible comes right before Ruth, describes a woman of character whose "works praise her in the gates" (Prov. 31:31). Using similar language, Boaz says, "And now, my daughter, do not fear. I will do for you all that you ask, for all my fellow townsmen know that you are a worthy woman" (Ruth 3:11). More literally, Boaz says, "all the gate of my people knows that you are a woman of worth." The idiom is usually lost in translation, but what we see in Ruth is precisely a "Proverbs 31" woman in the flesh: her deeds have indeed been praised in the city gates!

How did Ruth achieve this reputation among the Bethlehemites, when just a few short weeks earlier she had been ignored and slighted as an insignificant foreigner? She didn't gain a good reputation by pushing herself forward and blowing her own trumpet. Rather, she made herself Naomi's servant and worked without complaint in the heat of the harvest to help her mother-in-law to survive. Such humble devotion to duty did not escape people's notice—although we wonder if an opinion poll taken at the town gate would have revealed quite the unanimity that Boaz graciously suggested. As we will see in the next chapter, there was at least one man in Bethlehem who was still far from captivated by Ruth's worth.

FAITHFULNESS REWARDED

At this point in the story a complication arose. Although Boaz was a close relative of Naomi's, apparently there was another redeemer who was even closer. As Boaz explained to Ruth, "Now it is true that I am a redeemer. Yet there is a redeemer nearer than I. Remain tonight, and in the morning, if he will redeem you, good; let him do it. But if he is not willing to redeem you, then, as the LORD lives, I will redeem you. Lie down until the morning" (Ruth 3:12–13).

By rights, this other redeemer had a better claim to perform this service for Naomi and her family. This must have been a bitter blow to Ruth, who at this point was surely feeling that things had been progressing rather well. We can almost hear Ruth wondering aloud to herself whether now she is going to have to repeat the threshing floor encounter with some other man. But no, Boaz would take care of this unwanted and unexpected complication. In the morning, he would approach the man and sound him out. If the other man wanted to redeem her, then well and good. But if he were not absolutely delighted[3] to undertake this service, then Boaz swore that he would do it himself. One way or another, Naomi and Ruth would certainly be taken care of.

In the morning, before it was light enough for her reputation to be unfairly tarnished, Boaz sent Ruth away, but not before giving her a gift: "So she lay at his feet until the morning, but arose before one could recognize another. And he said, 'Let it not be known that the woman came to the threshing floor.' And he said, 'Bring the garment you are wearing and hold it out.' So

---

3. The ESV and NIV have "if he is not willing . . . ," but Boaz's language seems stronger, implying that he regards it as a high privilege to be able to help Ruth and Naomi in this way.

she held it, and he measured out six measures of barley and put it on her. Then she went into the city" (Ruth 3:14–15). Six measures of barley! If we are not excited by that announcement, it is simply because we don't realize that six measures comprises eighty pounds of barley![4] Boaz put it all in Ruth's cloak, lifted it up, and put it on her back so that she could carry it home (Ruth 3:15).

Obviously Ruth was no frail waif of a creature. If she could pick up eighty pounds of grain and carry it back from the threshing floor into the city, then she was clearly a woman of substance indeed—a big, strong girl. But this abundance of seed is not just a generous financial contribution from Boaz toward Ruth and Naomi's physical needs. It is a symbolic expression of Ruth's greater need for seed (a child), which we will finally see fulfilled in the next chapter.

Perhaps it is also significant that Ruth received only six measures, not seven. In biblical symbolism, the number six sometimes stands for incompleteness, whereas seven stands for completeness. Thus the world was created in six days, yet it was incomplete without the seventh day, the Sabbath. Given the significance of the concept of "rest" in this chapter of the Book of Ruth (see 3:1), it may be that the narrator was signaling the fact that even this generous gift of seed is, by itself, similarly incomplete. Ruth is still looking forward to receiving the final installment of "seed" that will accomplish her rest!

In the Morning: It Was Ruth!

Chapter 3 ends much the way that chapter 2 had ended, with Ruth returning home to share with Naomi news of her adventures: "And when she came to her mother-in-law, she said, 'How did you fare, my daughter?' Then she told her all that the man had done for her, saying, 'These six measures of barley he gave to me, for he said to me, "You must not go back empty-handed

4. This assumes that the unspecified measures here are seahs (so Robert L. Hubbard Jr., *The Book of Ruth* [New International Commentary on the Old Testament; Grand Rapids: Eerdmans, 1988], 222). They might have been omers (in which case the amount would have been less than she brought home from her first day's gleaning), or simply undefined units of measure. Yet the emphasis of the text seems to be on the large amount; notice that Boaz helps her pick up the load (Ruth 3:15), whereas she was able to pick up an ephah unaided. She clearly expects her mother-in-law to be impressed by her haul, which also suggests that it is a larger load than the earlier one.

to your mother-in-law." ' She replied, 'Wait, my daughter, until you learn how the matter turns out, for the man will not rest but will settle the matter today' " (Ruth 3:16–18).

When Ruth arrived home, Naomi asked a question. It's not the question the ESV has, though: "How did you fare, my daughter?" Actually, she asked, "Who are you, my daughter?" That question has tended to puzzle translators and commentators alike. At first sight it doesn't seem to fit here. Doesn't Naomi know who Ruth is in the dark? But this question, exactly the same question that Boaz asked earlier in this chapter, is a question Naomi struggles with throughout the Book of Ruth. Who is this Moabitess? Is she a person of no significance, an outsider and outcast, as Naomi viewed her back in chapter 1. Or is she in fact rather more than Naomi had ever thought? Is she the one who ultimately will provide Naomi with an enduring place in the genealogies of Israel through the provision of a son?

The growing realization of Ruth's value is underlined by Boaz's generous gift. He sends her back with a large bundle of seed so that she will not go back to Naomi "empty" (Ruth 3:17), the same word that Naomi used to describe herself back in chapter 1. She came back to Bethlehem "empty," but the Lord is fulfilling all of her needs through Ruth and Boaz. She was no longer empty. The Lord had provided food for her hunger, and a place of rest for the weary. Would the Lord now withhold from her the one other thing she lacked, descendants? Certainly not! In the light of that, Boaz's earlier response ("There is a redeemer nearer than I") takes on a whole new significance (see Ruth 3:12). He was talking simply about Mr. So-and-So, the man whom we shall meet in chapter 4. But all through the story there has been a redeemer closer than Boaz, a redeemer for Naomi and Ruth who has hovered in the shadows of the narrative, behind all the human agents, reaching out to his beloved but wandering sheep and showing them grace upon grace.

RISKING REJECTION

Ruth 3 compels each of us to ask this question: "What am I willing to risk, and for what?" People willingly face all kinds of perils in life, both small and great. For the sake of having fun, or receiving a promotion, or having a family, people are willing to put up with all kinds of discomforts and potential costs. People climb mountains, cross seas, work long hours, and endure pain for all kinds of reasons. What are we willing to risk, though, for the sake of the gospel?

For most of us, the true answer is probably, "Not very much." We're not very willing to risk our lives or our health, our reputations or our comfort, our friends or our families for the sake of the gospel. The most obvious proof of our aversion to spiritual risk lies in our unwillingness to talk to others about God—what Francis Schaeffer called "our guilty silence." Never mind putting our reputations at risk at midnight during the barley harvest, we wouldn't even risk being thought odd by our friends over coffee because we talk to them about Jesus. We all have our excuses. Sharing our faith might cost us our friends, our reputation. People might think that we are weird. What have they done for us, to deserve our taking that kind of risk for them?

Yet what if Ruth had said the same thing? Her actions certainly could have cost her reputation or much worse. Did Naomi deserve to have Ruth go out on this limb for her? Certainly not. But Ruth had made a commitment to Naomi in spite of her earlier coldness and her lack of responsiveness. She would not let anything stand in the way of fulfilling her promises. Did Naomi deserve Boaz's willingness to accept the social and financial cost of welcoming outsiders into his home? Certainly not. If there was any self-interest that made the deal attractive to Boaz, it was the character of Ruth, not that of Naomi. Naomi was among the undeserving, but because Ruth and Boaz treated her with grace, she came to know the joy of God's salvation. Who are the people that we can reach for Christ, if only we will take a personal risk with the gospel?

The Real Love Story

The story of Boaz and Ruth is not really a love story at all, at least not in the modern sense. It's not a story about boy meets girl, in which both are physically attracted to one another and the rest is a history of passionate kisses and life viewed through a romantic haze. We know that Boaz was (relatively) old (see Ruth 3:10). We know that Ruth could work all day in the hot sun with hardly a break and then carry eighty pounds of grain home on her back. The two of them do not exactly sound like the typical Hollywood hero and heroine. In fact, it might be hard to find suitable actors to cast in the movie version of their story; it certainly wouldn't be the classic romantic leads! The Book of Ruth is a different kind of story than we are used to.

The commitment that Ruth and Boaz had to one another was built on their common character, which is always a much better foundation for a lasting relationship than mere physical attraction. Theirs was a character match, not a love match: they were both people of substance. This is exactly what King Lemuel's mother advised him to look for in a wife (see Prov. 31:1, 30). When Christian young (and not so young) people talk about what they are looking for in a spouse, their lists are not always replete with spiritual characteristics. In fact, it often emerges that a different list actually has priority in practice, a list in which beauty and outward charm turn out to be nonnegotiables. Boaz and Ruth seem to have had a far more biblical agenda in this area than most people do.

The real love story in this book is not about Boaz and Ruth, though. The real love story is behind the scenes. It is the love of God for his straying sheep. It is the love that prevented him from simply ending the world when Adam and Eve first sinned. It is the love that chose and called Abraham and then persisted in pursuing his rebellious offspring. It is the love that would not let them go, in spite of their centuries-long history of rebellion and idolatry. This love causes the sun to shine and the rain to fall. In the lives of God's children, this love feeds us our daily food and clothes us. In his providence, his love may bring us godly friends to encourage us and a godly spouse with whom to share our lives. For all these good gifts of God's love, we should be truly thankful.

This love took its fullest shape in the coming of Jesus Christ. His love for us took him much further than a grain pile at midnight. It caused him to leave the glories of heaven and come down and live as an ordinary worker. It led him to come as a baby to Bethlehem, where he found no refuge. Unlike Ruth, there was no place of rest for Jesus in Bethlehem, no godly Boaz to protect him. Instead, he had to make do with a temporary place in a stable, before he was driven out, having to flee for his life even when he was a baby. And this love caused Jesus to abandon his eternal glory and become a servant, someone who was of no reputation, despised and rejected by men.

This same love of God took Jesus all the way to the cross. There, in the midst of a darkness far deeper than any ordinary midnight, he offered himself up for the sins of his people. There he was abandoned by God the Father, who turned aside his face because he would not and could not look upon his own Son, disfigured as he was by bearing our sin. Jesus didn't just risk his life; he gave it. Why? Is it because we are such wonderful people and we thoroughly deserve it? Certainly not! It is because God was so committed to saving sinners like us, and this was the only way it could be done. It is because God loved the world so much that he gave his one and only Son, that whoever believes in him should not perish but have everlasting life (see John 3:16). It is because of God's covenant faithfulness to the undeserving.

Do you know this love of God? Have you responded by giving your heart to him? Disfigured by sin though it is, your heart is all you have to give. So give it to him. He will be your Redeemer and receive you into his family. He will cover you with his wings and be your refuge. He will spread the robe of Christ's righteousness to cover your nakedness. No matter how undeserving you are, no matter what you've done or where you've been, the invitation is open to come and be redeemed. God will welcome you for the sake of Christ; he loves you that much.

Christian, in that gift of love lies the reason why you should speak. There's a love story that needs to be told to the wandering sheep who are still out in the cold. There are people who do not yet know that God has loved them so much. So how can we keep quiet? How can we not speak of the glories of this God who has loved us so much, whatever the risk? We must look for and make opportunities to speak of this love of God. Having been loved so much, we must surely declare the praises of the Redeemer who saved us through his blood.

14

RUTH'S REWARD

Ruth 4:1–22

*So Boaz took Ruth, and she became his wife. And he went
in to her, and the LORD gave her conception, and she bore a son.
Then the women said to Naomi, "Blessed be the LORD, who
has not left you this day without a redeemer, and may
his name be renowned in Israel." (Ruth 4:13–14)*

All the best stories are filled with surprises. The plot twists and turns this way and that, and we are never quite sure where the author will take us next. In Ruth 3, in a twist worthy of a fine detective novel, Ruth discovered to her surprise that there was another kinsman redeemer closer in line than Boaz. In one sense, that meant that Ruth and Naomi's fundamental need for rest was already resolved. One way or another, Ruth and Naomi would be provided for, whether by means of Boaz or this other person. Yet in another sense, we are still in suspense about Ruth's future. Would Ruth end up with Boaz or with this mysterious stranger instead? Even though we have not yet met him, we instinctively feel that he couldn't possibly be the right man for her.

The choice of a husband is not the only issue that will be resolved in this final scene, however. The narrator also has another plot twist to spring on us at the very end of the book. With a wave of his hand, he reveals to us at the very end that the story has not just been about God providing a solution for the needs of certain individuals. No, in the process, God is also paving the way for the king that his people need. So this is not just a story of God's covenant faithfulness (*hesed*) to Naomi and Ruth. It is about God's covenant faithfulness (*hesed*) to Israel. The Israelites haven't even thought about asking for a king yet; they are still in the days of the judges (Ruth 1:1). However, in his sovereignty and faithful love, God was already preparing ahead of time the line of the one who will ultimately meet that need. Who would have guessed that surprise ending at the start of this story?

THE MAN WITH NO NAME

As the chapter opens, we see that Boaz wasted no time in seeking a resolution on Ruth's behalf: "Now Boaz had gone up to the gate and sat down there. And behold, the redeemer, of whom Boaz had spoken, came by. So Boaz said, 'Turn aside, friend; sit down here.' And he turned aside and sat down. And he took ten men of the elders of the city and said, 'Sit down here.' So they sat down" (Ruth 4:1–2). The town gate was the place where meetings were held and legal business was transacted. There Boaz soon encountered the mysterious stranger, the "man with no name." In fact, the story goes to some lengths not to give his name; when Boaz summons him over he literally says, "Come over here, *peloni 'almoni,*" a rhyming but meaningless phrase that is roughly equivalent to our "Mr. So-and-So" (4:1).[1]

Once Boaz had his quarry seated in front of a panel of witnesses, the elders of the people, he immediately broached the subject of their kinswoman Naomi and her future: "Then he said to the redeemer, 'Naomi, who has come back from the country of Moab, is selling the parcel of land that belonged to our relative Elimelech. So I thought I would tell you of it and say, "Buy it in the presence of those sitting here and in the presence of the elders of my people." If you will redeem it, redeem it. But if you will not, tell me, that I may know, for there is no one besides you to redeem it, and I come after you'" (Ruth 4:3–4). Boaz is really saying something like this: "Naomi has a field. She needs to sell[2] it to

---

1. As the New Jewish Publication Society translation renders it.
2. Strictly speaking, as a widow, Naomi had the right neither to buy nor to sell the land outright. However, she could potentially control the right to use the land until the next Jubilee year. This is technically what is on offer in this conversation. For an extensive analysis of the details see Frederic Bush, *Ruth, Esther* (Waco, TX: Word, 1996), 199–204, 211–15. It is doubtful, however, whether a detailed digression into ancient Near Eastern property rights would be helpful in a sermon. The simple concept of buying and selling land is probably close enough to be adequate for most people.

raise money to live on. If there were a kinsman redeemer, however, he could buy that field and keep it in the family. Of course, the buyer would ultimately get to add the property to his own inheritance, provided that there are no children involved. You are first in line ... are you interested?" This seemed like such a promising opportunity that the kinsman redeemer instantly agreed.

But then Boaz sprang the surprise on him: "The day you buy the field from the hand of Naomi, you also acquire Ruth the Moabite, the widow of the dead, in order to perpetuate the name of the dead in his inheritance" (Ruth 4:5). "Oh, by the way," Boaz was saying. "One more thing: When you acquire the field, along with it comes Ruth the Moabitess, the widow of the dead man whose field it was. You must marry her in order to raise up a child for the dead man, a child who will inherit the field when he grows up." All of a sudden, the kinsman redeemer changed his mind: "I cannot redeem it for myself, lest I impair my own inheritance. Take my right of redemption yourself, for I cannot redeem it" (Ruth 4:6). Mr. So-and-So backed away from the deal faster than a man faced with a coiled rattlesnake. What a moment before had seemed to be a "can't miss" real estate deal—taking care of an old lady in return for the long-term payoff of a field—had suddenly become an investment nightmare. If there were to be a child from the relationship with Ruth, the redeemer would lose the field and there would be no benefit to his own children and estate to compensate for the costs involved in taking care of Naomi and Ruth. In other words, Mr. So-and-So was interested in ministry to the poor only if there was a payoff for himself and his family. Costly ministry without any personal payoff? Forget it!

The irony is that by seeking to protect his future legacy in this way, Mr. So-and-So ended up leaving himself nameless, missing out on having a share in the biggest legacy of all: a place in God's plan of salvation. Boaz took a different and more sacrificial approach, embracing the opportunity to leave a legacy for someone else. This is clear from what he said when he made the transaction in the city gates:

> Now this was the custom in former times in Israel concerning redeeming and exchanging: to confirm a transaction, the one drew off his sandal and gave it to the other, and this was the manner of attesting in Israel. So when the redeemer said to Boaz, "Buy it for yourself," he drew off his sandal. Then Boaz said to the elders and all the people, "You are witnesses this day that I have

bought from the hand of Naomi all that belonged to Elimelech and all that belonged to Chilion and to Mahlon. Also Ruth the Moabite, the widow of Mahlon, I have bought to be my wife, to perpetuate the name of the dead in his inheritance, that the name of the dead may not be cut off from among his brothers and from the gate of his native place. You are witnesses this day." (Ruth 4:7–10)

Ruth 4 is all about preserving names. From the concern to preserve the names of Elimelech and Mahlon with their inheritance (4:10), to the wish in the blessing that Boaz's name would be remembered in Bethlehem (4:11), to the similar blessing at the birth of Obed (4:14), to the double naming of Obed (4:17), to the list of names with which the chapter concludes (4:18–22), throughout this chapter there is the common thread of the desire to keep one's name alive. Although neither Mr. So-and-So nor Boaz realized it at the time, a lasting name was what was at stake here. The one who married Ruth received not merely a woman of character with an impressive work ethic and the ability to lift and carry eighty pounds of grain, but he also received a place in God's plan. The line of Boaz and Ruth would stretch on to include Obed, then Jesse, then David, Bethlehem's most famous son, the king after God's own heart. By trying to protect his future, Mr. So-and-So would remain forever nameless.

God's New Math

We often evaluate our involvement in evangelism and ministries of mercy according to the same scale as Mr. So-and-So. We ask, "What is in it for me? Will it fulfill me? Will I enjoy it? What will it cost me?" In doing the arithmetic, we get the answers as completely wrong as he did, because we have left God entirely out of the equation. We calculate and protect ourselves and insist that two and two can only ever equal four . . . and we may never know the blessing that we have lost.

Indeed, part of the message of the Book of Ruth is that God's kingdom operates on a different kind of calculus, a "new math" in which the way to fullness runs through emptiness. Mr. So-and-So didn't do that kind of math, so the numbers didn't add up for him. He clung to what he had and in consequence lost something far greater, something he never even dreamed of.

By contrast, Naomi earlier lost all of the things she had been clinging on to, all of her earthly "fullness." Yet even this loss was part of God's gracious plan for her good. If she had not first lost everything, we would never have known about her, and she would never have come to appreciate Ruth's true worth, or to grow in her own understanding of the Lord. She had to lose her two sons to appreciate the one who was better than seven sons (Ruth 4:15). The crucible of suffering, painful though it was for her, was necessary for her spiritual growth and her place in God's plan.

Boaz, on the other hand, was an "A" student at the new math. He had an open heart for the poor. We saw that earlier, in his generous behavior to Ruth when she was just another unknown poor person gleaning in his field. There was nothing calculating about his generosity to her then—just the grace of a generous and cheerful giver. Likewise, Boaz was not marrying Ruth now for what he could get out of the deal. In terms of the financial and social equations, it was always likely to be a losing prospect for him to marry a Moabitess. Entering a relationship so that she could have a son to inherit the property he had just put out good money to buy could never make good fiscal sense. But then, the Lord's wisdom operates on a different kind of calculus from the wisdom of the world.

Part of that calculus is putting what the Lord thinks of us before what the world thinks of us. Boaz was more concerned with God's ability to give him a great name than he was about any attempts to preserve his own reputation. Boaz gladly took Ruth to himself, proudly giving her the same title from which Mr. So-and-So recoiled: "Ruth the Moabite" (Ruth 4:10). He made it clear that the transaction was not about him and his own interests but the interests of others—that is, meeting the needs of Ruth and Naomi and preserving the remembrance of their dead husbands. This was not normally the way to win a name for one's self, perhaps, but in God's sight Boaz knew he would always have a name. God's favor was more important to him than acquiring a name in the world.

Boaz's Reward

Nor are the rewards of the Lord's way always deferred. Even though Boaz was not motivated by the praise of others, he nonetheless received the respect and the blessing of the elders in the gate: "Then all the people who were at the gate and the elders said, 'We are witnesses. May the Lord make the woman, who is coming into your house, like Rachel and Leah, who together built up the house of Israel. May you act worthily in Ephrathah and be renowned in Bethlehem, and may your house be like the house of Perez, whom Tamar bore to Judah, because of the offspring that the Lord will give you by this young woman' " (Ruth 4:11–12).

The blessing the townspeople pronounced upon him in verse 12 may have been a conventional blessing on married couples in Bethlehem. However, the blessing had more than conventional significance in Boaz and Ruth's experience. Through Ruth, Boaz would indeed become famous and have his name remembered in Bethlehem. Although for ten years Ruth had been unable to bear a son for Mahlon, through the Lord's intervention she conceived and bore a son for Boaz: "So Boaz took Ruth, and she became his wife. And he went in to her, and the Lord gave her conception, and she bore a son" (Ruth 4:13). Notice what this Scripture says: "The Lord gave her conception." This is only the second time in the Book of Ruth that the Lord has been in the foreground of the action as the subject of a verb—the other time being the equally significant statement in 1:6 that the Lord visited his people and gave them food. Once again the Lord God has acted to bring redemption to his people.

Nor was this son simply for Boaz. He would be a comfort also for Naomi in her old age, her kinsman redeemer who would provide for her needs in her declining years. So the chorus of women said: "Blessed be the Lord, who has not left you this day without a redeemer, and may his name be renowned in Israel! He shall be to you a restorer of life and a nourisher of your old age, for your daughter-in-law who loves you, who is more to you than seven sons, has given birth to him" (Ruth 4:14–15).

The story closes with a touching domestic scene: "Then Naomi took the child and laid him on her lap and became his nurse. And the women of the neighborhood gave him a name, saying, 'A son has been born to Naomi.' They named him Obed. He was the father of Jesse, the father of David" (Ruth 4:16–17). The grandson on Naomi's lap was a clear sign that the emptiness she felt at the end of the opening chapter had now been replaced by fullness through God's grace. Though no one could bring back her husband or sons, now she had a daughter-in-law whom everyone recognized as "more ... than seven sons," an astonishing accolade in the ancient world. What is more, she had a descendant to carry on the family line.

THE BIGGER PICTURE

In the cartoon movie *Antz*, most of the action follows the small-scale life of a neurotic worker ant (Woody Allen) in his quest to win the love of a princess ant. But as the movie ends, the camera pans outward to show the audience that the narrower action has been taking place in Central Park in the heart of New York. Thus we are invited to consider the parallels between the lives of the ants in the movie and the lives of the real people around them.

The genealogy with which the Book of Ruth closes serves a similar narrative function. At the end of the book we discover that God has in all of this been pursuing bigger plans than bringing together two worthy individuals. What looked like a simple story of personal emptiness filled and personal needs met turns out to be God's way of meeting a far greater need. The story that opened with the statement "In the days when the judges ruled" (Ruth 1:1) closes with the genealogy of Israel's most famous king: "Now these are the generations of Perez: Perez fathered Hezron, Hezron fathered Ram, Ram fathered Amminadab, Amminadab fathered Nahshon, Nahshon fathered Salmon, Salmon fathered Boaz, Boaz fathered Obed, Obed fathered Jesse, and Jesse fathered David" (Ruth 4:18–22). This genealogy links the events of the story with the line that would build the house of Israel more than any family since the time of Jacob, the line of David. God used all of these events to bring about his own goals that were so much bigger than any of the characters involved in the story could possibly have imagined. The elders' blessing that sought lasting renown for Boaz was remarkably fulfilled long after his death, with the birth of King David.

The elders' blessing looked backward as well as forward, however. The themes of blessing, name, offspring, and the building of a house of Israel resonate with deep chords in the history of God's people. These themes go all the way back to God's promise to Abraham of a great name and a great nation that would come from his offspring, so that all peoples on earth would find a blessing for themselves in him (Gen. 12:1–3). Ruth herself, as an individual Gentile convert, is a fulfillment of that Abrahamic promise. At the same time, however, the genealogy shows us that she has a bigger part to play as an ancestor of King David. David is thus highlighted not simply as a great king and an answer for the anarchy of the days of the judges, but also as a fulfillment of the promise to Abraham in Genesis 12.

A WIFE FIT FOR A KING

We noted in our discussion of chapter 3 the striking observation that Proverbs 31, which in the Hebrew ordering of the Bible comes immediately before the Book of Ruth, describes a worthy woman whose deeds bring her praise at the city gate. According to Ruth 3:10, this is exactly what has happened in Ruth's case. But this is only one of several interesting parallels between the passages. Like the Proverbs 31 woman, Ruth is a hard worker, who certainly does not eat the bread of idleness (Prov. 31:27). Her efforts provide food not just for herself, but for her family (Naomi) also (Prov. 31:15). Beauty and charm are not listed among Ruth's attributes, but her husband, Boaz, is respected in the city gate (Prov. 31:23).

What makes this comparison particularly fascinating, though, is the fact that the woman described in Proverbs 31 is not merely a generically worthy woman, but a woman worthy to become the wife of a king (see Prov. 31:1)! The genealogy that makes Ruth the ancestress of David shows that her worthiness found its fitting reward!

RUTH AND TAMAR

Perhaps the most striking aspect of the blessing on Boaz and Ruth, however, is the analogy that is drawn between Ruth and Tamar (see Ruth 4:12). These two women are both like and unlike one another. Tamar's story is recorded in Genesis 38. Like Ruth, she too was an outsider to God's covenant people, who married into the family under doubtful circumstances. She too lost her husband and had no child. Both Ruth and Tamar dressed themselves up in pursuit of a child and a future. Here, though, the similarity ends. Ruth revealed her identity to Boaz and received a child legitimately through marriage, whereas Tamar concealed her identity and deceived Judah in order to receive a child outside of marriage. Tamar pretended to be a prostitute in order to trap her father-in-law Judah into sleeping with her, so that she might have a child. The end result of both unions, legitimate and illegitimate, was children who, in the providence of God, had an important part to play in God's plan.

Why does God do things this way? Why is he willing to be involved with such an array of dubious characters? Look at the women who appear in the genealogy of Jesus, as recorded by Matthew. Front and center there is Tamar, the Canaanite mother of Perez and Zerah (Matt. 1:3). Then there is Rahab, who didn't just dress up like a prostitute; she really was one! She too found a place in the ancestry of our Lord as she was rescued out of Jericho and brought into the covenant community (Matt. 1:5). Next there was Ruth who, for all her worthiness, was still the Moabitess, a despised foreigner. Finally, there was Bathsheba, the mother of Solomon and former wife of Uriah. That is quite a collection of family portraits!

Nor are the men in the family tree of Jesus any better. After all, it was Judah who slept with Tamar without any qualms, all the time thinking she was a prostitute. It was David who arranged for Bathsheba's seduction and Uriah's murder. In addition, in the list of Jesus' ancestors is Manasseh, the greatest idolater among the kings of Judah. Manasseh is the one whose sins were so great that from then on the exile of God's people was a foregone conclusion (see 2 Kings 21:10–15; 23:26–27). Together, these men and women make up a remarkable procession of the great unwashed. Why would the Lord Jesus, who could have chosen to be descended from anyone at all, choose to be descended from such a soiled line?

THE FRIEND OF SINNERS

Matthew explains Jesus' ancestry in the next section of his Gospel. The angel told Joseph, "You shall call his name Jesus, for he will save his people from their sins" (Matt. 1:21). As Jesus himself put it, "The Son of Man came to seek and to save the lost" (Luke 19:10). He came to rescue sinners, people like his own ancestors, people like us. When he came to seek and save that which was lost, he didn't come garbed in special protective clothing, like a scientist suited up to handle bubonic plague samples in a laboratory. At the beginning of his life, Jesus came into this world naked, unprotected, not separated from sinners but descended from a long line of them. During his lifetime, he was likewise surrounded by sinners. This was the way that people knew Jesus: as the friend of tax collectors and sinners (Matt. 11:19).

If he kept shocking company while he was alive, Jesus also kept scandalous company when he died. He was flanked by two thieves at his crucifixion (Matt. 27:38). Thus Jesus went out of this world the same way he had arrived, naked and unprotected.

Why would the Lord of the universe expose himself to such pain and humiliation? It is because that is how he would save sinners. He could not save them by staying at a safe distance from them, but only by coming alongside them and identifying with them. In order to save them, Jesus had to be their friend and ultimately perform the greatest act of friendship there is: laying down his life for them. Jesus gave up his life and went down into death, so that he might pay the price that their sins had earned. Our sins have paid our admission price into eternal separation from God; in one word, hell. Another way to think of it is that we, with the wages of our sin, have purchased a travel ticket to hell. What Jesus did on the cross was to take that ticket right out of our hands. Instead, he gave us the ticket that he had earned by his righteous life, a ticket that will admit the bearer into God's presence. He switched places with us, going where we deserved to go, while sending us to the destination he had merited.

The love of Jesus is thus far greater even than the love of Ruth for Naomi. He left his place in heaven, not just the greener fields of Moab. He left intimate fellowship with the Father for the pain of this fallen world. Jesus didn't merely risk his reputation for us; he bore being made of no reputation, despised and rejected by men. At the moment of his greatest pain and rejection on the cross, however, there was no nearer redeemer to rescue him. There was only the darkness closing around him on the cross, as he cried out in the agony of the pains of hell, "My God, my God, why have you forsaken me?" (Mark 15:34).

What awesome love Jesus demonstrated for us on the cross! Truly, it was amazing love because it was shown not to the lovely but to the very unlovely—to sinners. In Jesus, God's love came to people like us, those who have repeatedly said and thought and done things that we ought not to have said or thought or done. Some of our sins are large and some relatively small, but each and every one of them would be enough to condemn us for all eternity.

The result of Jesus' sacrifice is abundant seed, spiritual seed. Raised from the dead, he has been given the name above every name; history will never confuse him with the nameless Mr. So-and-So. Even the honorable name that Boaz earned for himself pales into insignificance when placed next to the glorious name of Jesus Christ. In addition, he has also been given a people for himself, a family of God's people that stretches across the continents and down through the centuries. Though he had no physical offspring of his own, the end result of his suffering and death was numerous spiritual offspring (Isa. 53:10). He is the King, not just of Israel, but of all nations, whose people come into his kingdom from north and south and east and west, redeemed by his blood, to the glory of God the Father.

Do you know that love of Jesus today? Do you know the love that still reaches out to outsiders? Then praise God for it! There are many around us who don't know that love yet. They are still trying to earn their own passage to heaven, still trying to switch the destination on their tickets through their own merits. They still think that somehow they can be good enough, or that God's standards will in the end prove to be flexible enough to let them in. It is a terrible delusion. Their very religious acts will testify against them, because they were done to justify themselves and build up their own image, not to glorify God. When such people are doing well in trying to live a good life, their efforts leave them secretly a little impressed at how wonderful they are. When they are struggling, their failing efforts leave them angry and despairing. Either way, though, their eyes are fixed on themselves as their only hope in life and death.

There is no room in Jesus' kingdom for people who are impressed with themselves, or whose eyes are fixed on their own efforts. People like Mr. So-and-So, who have the world all figured out and computed, with their little lives controlled and organized, find no place in God's plan, just as he has no place in their calculations. The door to God's kingdom is open only to those who know they have nothing to offer God. It is open only to outsiders like Ruth, to those desperate enough to try anything, like Tamar, to those who have utterly despaired of making any sense out of life, like Naomi. It is open to those like some in the early church in Corinth: former idolaters, swindlers, prostitutes, homosexuals, thieves, slanderers, and drunkards (1 Cor. 6:9–11). These are the people whom God welcomes through Christ, for he is the friend of sinners. Whoever you are, no matter what you have done, there is room for you to kneel at the foot of the cross.

God doesn't leave us as he found us, to be sure. Like Naomi, when we open our hearts to God, we will discover that he has already been at work in our lives, and he will continue to be at work in us until we are unrecognizably changed. The bitter Mara who returned to Bethlehem was transformed into a Naomi who could recognize God's hand of blessing at work. God's grace has enormous transforming power. Yet that grace works only in the lives of those whose eyes are opened to the desperateness of their need for salvation, who know that they can do nothing except cling to Christ.

BECOMING FRIENDS OF SINNERS

Ruth has come a long way in this book. She has gone from being an outcast and a stranger, the one whose existence Naomi herself would scarcely acknowledge, to becoming the wife of an upstanding citizen, the great-grandmother of Israel's future king, and the daughter-in-law who is recognized as being better than seven sons (Ruth 4:15). Yet she first found a welcome from Boaz and from God while she was still a complete outsider.

Can people like Ruth find a similar welcome in our churches and in our homes? Are they places where the last, the least, and the lost can come without feeling looked down upon? Are our churches safe places where people whose lifestyles are notorious in the community can come without being stared at and judged? Is there any danger of our fellowship being known as "that church where all those sinners go"? Or are we good only at welcoming those who are already somewhat religious, those who at least in some measure already speak the language of the church community and whose faces already fit? There is a serious challenge here for each of us to ponder, not just for pastors and church leaders. Each of us has a role to play in what people feel when they come through our church doors. Will we welcome them? Will anyone sit with them, or speak to them afterward? Will someone make them feel special, important, wanted, no matter how messy their lives are? Will *you* make them feel like a person of eternal worth and value?

That is what Ruth did for Naomi; at Naomi's lowest ebb, Ruth made it clear that she was bound to her forever, and nothing could tear her away. It is what Boaz did for Ruth; he demonstrated publicly that he found her a valuable human being, even though she was a Moabite widow. More fundamentally, though, this is what the Lord did for each of them. He is the Redeemer behind the human redeemer in Ruth and Naomi's story.

191

This is also what the Lord has done for each of us. He is the Redeemer behind each of our own personal salvation stories. He sought each of us while we were utterly lost. Not only did he make us *feel* valuable; in Christ, God actually made us valuable. It is not just Ruth's story that turned out to be part of a much bigger narrative than she ever imagined. Your story and my story are also woven into the bigger tapestry of what God is doing in Jesus Christ. He has seated us with him in the heavenly realms, exalted us along with him to the glories of heaven, made us coheirs with him and blessed us with every spiritual blessing. In him, we have been given a glorious genealogy: we are children of God! Though we in our sin wandered away empty, and became hardheartedly bitter toward him, he has brought us back full indeed. He has made sure and certain that in Christ each of our stories has a good and happy ending. As we come to him, he enables us to find rest for our souls in his house forever.

INDEX OF SCRIPTURE

195

INDEX OF SUBJECTS AND NAMES